CHRISTIANITY
AS MYSTICAL FACT

AND THE MYSTERIES OF ANTIQUITY

RUDOLF STEINER (1905)

CHRISTIANITY
AS MYSTICAL FACT

AND THE MYSTERIES OF ANTIQUITY

TRANSLATED BY ANDREW WELBURN

INTRODUCTION BY CHRISTOPHER BAMFORD

RUDOLF STEINER

SteinerBooks

CW 8

SteinerBooks
Anthroposophic Press

610 Main Street
Great Barrington, Massachusetts 01230
www.steinerbooks.org

Original translation from the German by Catherine E. Creeger

This book is volume 8 in the Collected Works (CW) of Rudolf Steiner, published by SteinerBooks, 2006. It is a translation of the German *Das Christentum als mystische Tatsache und die Mysterien des Altertums*, published by Rudolf Steiner Verlag, Dornach, Switzerland.

Library of Congress Cataloging-in-Publication Data is available

Printed in the United States

CONTENTS

* * * * *

INTRODUCTION

CHRISTOPHER BAMFORD

Two books (originally courses of lectures), which should be read back to back—*Mystics after Modernism* (1900–1901) and *Christianity as Mystical Fact and the Mysteries of Antiquity* (1901–1902)—inaugurate Rudolf Steiner's public activity as a spiritual teacher. As his first "theosophical" works—or, more precisely, "proto-theosophical" works, for it was only after these two lecture courses and books that Steiner officially became a Theosophist—they seem like a natural beginning of Anthroposophy for present-day readers who have the hindsight of the whole of Steiner's vast, endlessly creative anthroposophical work. At the time, however, and to those who knew Steiner as a radical, freethinking man of letters, a respected Goethe scholar, a defender of the individualism of Friedrich Nietzsche and Max Stirner, a proponent of the monism of the evolutionary biologist Ernst Haeckel, and a staunch upholder of the values of natural science, the two books came as a surprise and even an apparent reversal on many fronts.

What seemed most extraordinary, even inexplicable, to many who knew him—even more astonishing, perhaps, than his unconditional acceptance of the reality of the spirit or what seemed his unexpected embrace of Theosophy as a forum for his teaching—was the Christian, Christ-centered view that Steiner now clearly espoused. After all, here was someone, a near-anarchist freethinker, who had written frequently and passionately apparently *against* Christianity and who now claimed that the Christ event was central, the very pivot and ferment of evolution that revealed its very meaning. Some older friends turned from him in disbelief, feeling that he had betrayed them. Most could not follow him in his new endeavor, all of which undoubtedly must have been painful and disappointing to him—a fact that is also rarely taken into consideration. How alone Steiner must have felt! And yet he claimed, rightly, what he knew was true: that the course of the evolution of his thinking was continuous.

The question of whether Steiner's Christian "turn" constitutes a kind of reversal, or at the least a profound change, or whether his spiritual evolution was continuous and Anthroposophy, as he came to unfold it, represented a change of form or natural metamorphosis of his previous inner work is still a living issue, hovering over and clouding the question of Christianity in this evolution. In its briefest form, the question is this: Is Anthroposophy primarily simply a method or way of knowing (so that Christ and Christianity is secondary), or is Anthroposophy as such Christian or Christ-centered in essence? If the latter is the case, not only must there be continuity but also, finally, the method and true Christianity must be one. In the event, as with all such questions, the answer lies somewhere in-between the alternatives.

Steiner's own account of his inner growth, his *Autobiography*, clearly reveals by what paths his continuity was formed and won. Particularly fascinating are the early chapters, which lay out the various germinal parameters of influence and experience that came together in his destiny and give us the raw materials, as it were, out of which he wove what would become his way. It is often remarked how fortunate Steiner was to grow up placed by the railroad for which his father worked so precisely between nature (the "wonderful landscape" of the mountains and meadows of Lower Austria) and technology, represented not just by the railway but also by the continually expanding industrialization that accompanied it.

In the *Autobiography* glowing descriptions of the radiant landscapes of his childhood, along with mention of his clairvoyant capacity to perceive nature beings and his passion to understand the laws of nature and natural processes, alternate with stories of the mechanical puzzles posed by the new "communications" technology involved in the running of the railroad and his endless delight in unraveling the mechanics of practical things like the local textile factory. At the same time, besides technology and nature, both of which lead to the important discovery that reality has two sides, visible and invisible, Steiner also emphasizes and describes the growth of the power of his inner life, of the life of thinking, awakened above all through geometry, which seemed to give him access to a reality of a different order. As he says: "The ability to grasp something purely through the spirit brought me an inner joy. I realize I first knew happiness through geometry." Shortly after his discovery of geometry, he discovered the philosopher Kant; the reading and rereading of Kant's work strengthened and empowered his already growing experience of thinking as a cosmic reality.

Another reality likewise permeated his childhood. In addition to nature, science, and the sense-free individual life of thinking, something else, which is often overlooked, formed his embryonic spiritual life—namely, religion in the form of Christianity. It is astonishing how frequently Steiner speaks of religion, understood in the broadest sense, in the early chapters of the *Autobiography*. He begins the account of his life by mentioning that his father, later a freethinker (who returned in the end to the faith of his youth), spent his childhood in close contact with a Premonstratensian monastery. He adds, "He recalled this period of his life with great pleasure." Reading between the lines, then, we may assume that as Steiner warmly recalls his father, he also remembers the memories and anecdotes that he listened to attentively as a child and lived with ever since as part of his soul life. Next, he writes affectionately of the liberal, tolerant, genial parish priest of Pottschach. Then, when the family moved to Neudörfl, where (he emphasizes) they lived between the church and the cemetery, he tells us that one of his favorite places to be alone was a small, isolated chapel dedicated to the Sicilian hermit nun Saint Rosalie. Here, he tells us, he would meet on his walks the monks of the monastery of the Order of the Most Holy Redeemer. "I still remember how glad it would have made me if they had spoken to me, but they never did. As a result those meetings always left me with a somewhat vague but solemn impression that remained for some time.... I became convinced that very important matters were connected with the tasks of those monks, and that I had to learn what they were."

In Neudörfl, again the priest made an impression. Steiner writes that he was "by far the most significant personality I met before my tenth or eleventh year," introducing him to Copernican astronomy, another significant event. At this time, too, the young Steiner served as an altar boy, despite the fact that his relationship with the Church was not encouraged at home and was even a point of contention with his father (who was then still a freethinker):

> As schoolboys, we acted as servers and choir members at Mass, memorial services for the dead, and funerals. My youthful soul lived gladly in the ceremonious nature of the Latin language and the cultus. Until my tenth year I intensively took part in serving in the church, and this often enabled me to be in the company of the priest whom I revered so deeply....
>
> My most vivid memory of my childhood in Neudörfl is of the cultus and solemn liturgical music and how it caused the questions of existence to arise with moving power before my spirit. The priest's Bible instruction and the catechism had much less effect on my inner life than did his actions as celebrant of the ritual mediating between the sensory and the suprasensory worlds. From the very beginning, this was never a mere form to me, but was a profound inner experience. And this was even more so because it made me a stranger in my own home. Nevertheless, my home environment did not diminish the spiritual richness I received through the ritual.

Against this powerful background and with nature and technology still ever present as influences, Steiner continued to form his philosophical path of thinking. Kant's *Critique of Pure Reason* remained his favorite study. Famously, he hid its pages in his history textbook, so that he could wrestle his way through it during boring history lessons. This is well known. We often forget, however, that in his fourteenth year, as he wrestled with Kant and the meaning of thinking and sought to create his own philosophy, another influence was also present. As he tells us:

> During the holidays, I eagerly continued to study Kant. I read many pages twenty times before moving on. I worked to develop a judgment about the relationship between human thinking and the creation of natural phenomena. Two things influenced my feelings toward these efforts in thinking. First, I wanted to develop

my own thinking so that each thought would be completely clear and surveyable, unbiased by any arbitrary feeling. Second, I wanted to establish a harmony within myself between such thinking and religious teaching. This was also vitally important to me at that time. We had excellent textbooks in this particular field. From them, with tremendous devotion, I absorbed dogma and symbolism, and the description of the ritual and church history. I lived in these teachings with great intensity. But my relation to them was conditioned by the fact that, to me, the spiritual world was part of human ideation. These teachings deeply affected me because they proved to me how the human spirit finds a path into the suprasensory through knowledge.

What is striking here is Steiner's statement that his relationship to the teachings of the Church was determined by the fact that he took the spiritual world "as a content of human contemplation or intuition [*Anschauung*]"—in other words, as direct experience. Steiner was therefore already countering his other teacher of the time, Kant, for whom there were limits to knowledge and for whom a priori principles, like space and time, were simply assumed. For Steiner, from the beginning, there were no a priori dogmas but only (potentially) experiential contents available to our own intuitive capacities.

From this point in his development Steiner's path becomes above all a self-made initiatory path of cognition: of intense meditative-intuitive thinking and the moral transformation of being. The path would lead him through the inner effort to experience for himself the cognitive-spiritual experiences of the great "Romantic" philosophers Johann Fichte, Georg Hegel, and Friedrich Schelling and then ground them in Goethe's participatory non-dualism. *Nature's Open Secret: Introductions to Goethe's Scientific Writings, Truth and Science* (also known as *Truth and Knowledge*) and *The Philosophy of Freedom* (also available as *Intuitive Thinking as a Spiritual Path* and *The Philosophy of Spiritual Activity*) mark the milestones. As he describes this journey in his *Autobiography*, he makes only a few, but nevertheless significant, further references to Christianity or religion, until he recounts the great initiatory experience that occurred just before the turn of twentieth century when, as he says, "I stood spiritually before the Mystery of Golgotha in a deep and solemn celebration of knowledge."

However, on the basis of what he has told us of his childhood devotion (which had nothing particularly to do with the Church but rather with the spiritual reality that, however inadequately, it mediated), the reality of the "Mystery of Golgotha" must nevertheless surely have always been present at some level throughout the intervening period of intense, radical philosophical meditation as an experience awaiting realization. We may even say that the initiatory "soul awakening" to which Steiner refers as standing "spiritually before the Mystery of Golgotha" was the organic fulfillment to the inner work that led up to it.

Indeed, Steiner tells us enough for us to infer that theological and theosophical questions always remained in his soul as he sought to realize his chosen path of being-cognition. Reading the *Autobiography*, we have the sense that he always continued to pursue them on the side, as it were, though his main overt thrust remained philosophical and inevitably professional and Goethe-related. During his period in Vienna, when he was beginning his work on Goethe, we know from letters to his friend and initiate in ancient knowledge, Friedrich Eckstein, that they discussed alchemy, symbolism, Theosophy, Buddhism, and other esoteric matters. This is not surprising. Goethe, after all, was a Hermetic thinker. At the same time, we also know that he was studying the mystics; this is likewise not surprising, since Meister Eckhart and Jacob Boehme are acknowledged as the first German philosophers and, as such, were profoundly influential on Hegel and Schelling, respectively. We know, too, from other autobiographical statements that his meeting and friendship with the herb gatherer Felix Kogutzki led to the initiatory encounter with the "Master," perhaps Christian Rosenkreutz but certainly a Christian teacher, who confirmed and blessed his path.

As for Steiner's continuing interest specifically in Christianity, the *Autobiography* mentions as especially significant two meetings with Father Wilhelm Neumann, a learned Cistercian priest. The first concerned a conversation about the Christ:

I expressed my view that Jesus of Nazareth, through an extra-earthly influence, received the Christ into himself, and that the

Christ, as a spiritual being, lives within human evolution since the Mystery of Golgotha. This conversation remains deeply embedded in my memory. The conversation really took place between three individuals—Professor Neumann, me, and an invisible third, the personification of Catholic dogmatism, who appeared to the spiritual eye behind Neumann; it accompanied him, reprovingly tapping his shoulder whenever the scholar's logic led him to agree with me too much. It was remarkable how often the second half of what he said would be the opposite of the first half. I was face to face with Catholicism as expressed in one of its finest representatives; through him I learned to respect it, but also to thoroughly recognize it for what it is.

The second conversation was about reincarnation:

The professor listened and spoke of all kinds of literature that discussed the subject. He quietly shook his head several times, but he seemed to have no intention of going into details of what, to him, seemed a strange topic. Nevertheless, this topic also became important to me. Neumann's discomfort about not expressing his opinions about my statement has remained deeply inscribed in my memory.

Later in the chapter Steiner tells us that "through spiritual perception, [he] was just beginning to gain a definite understanding of repeated earthly lives." Given his stance on experience, we must assume the question of the incarnation and continuing working of the Christ was not just a theoretical issue but was equally based on experience. Such experience does not happen if it is not sought. Therefore, most likely, Christology, too, was always a subject of ongoing spiritual research, which could have been incited by the study of Hegel or Schelling (in both of whom the question is implicit) but more likely goes back to his earliest days and his desire to come to the realities of Christianity out of his own experience, irrespective of any teaching or dogma.

Still, to achieve such experiential understanding could never be his primary aim as such. Steiner's "aim"—as he worked through and made his own the philosophical struggles of Fichte, Hegel, Schelling, above all Goethe, and even, at the end, Nietzsche and Stirner—was always directed toward the expanding experience of freedom, the intuitive life of the "moral imagination" for which, in principle, limits to knowledge do not exist. In practical terms this meant, in the first place, the cultivation of pure thinking, which is sense free (that is, free of perceptual content) through the development of an empty receptive attention leading to the recognition of the I AM; this, of course, is none other than the Pauline "Christ in me." *The Philosophy of Freedom* marks a first watershed in the accomplishment of this goal.

Steiner was thirty when he left Vienna for Weimar, "still unfettered by any 'worldly profession,'" to be an independent collaborator on the edition of Goethe to be published by the Goethe Archives. Just before he left Vienna, he read a book called *The Seven Books of Platonism* by Heinrich von Stein, a professor of philosophy at Rostock University. (Steiner found the book and its author so sympathetic that he ended up submitting his doctoral dissertation, *Truth and Science*, to von Stein at Rostock.) The thesis of *The Seven Books of Platonism* is that Plato was the greatest among those who tried to create a philosophy resting upon its own foundations. He presents Plato's worldview in a marvelous, living way. Having done so, he then describes how the Christ revelation breaks into human evolution "at a higher level than the mere elaboration of a philosophy." Steiner comments:

> In Stein's view, the revelation of Christ gave philosophy its content from outside. I was unable to agree with him. I knew that the Christ revelation can become an inner experience once we have understood our own true being in spiritually awake consciousness; the Christ revelation can then become an inner, living reality in the human being through the conscious experience of ideas....
>
> In Stein I also missed the recognition that Plato's ideas do lead back to a spiritual, primordial revelation of the spiritual world. This (Pre-Christian) revelation ... does not enter Stein's consideration at all. He does not present Platonism as the last vestige of a primordial revelation in conceptual form—one that, through Christianity, regains its lost spiritual content in a higher form.

Rather, he presents Platonic ideas as though spun from themselves, a conceptual content that later attains life through Christ.

The inner experience of Christ in spiritually awake identity-consciousness is not easy or natural for our contemporary dualizing—and hence objectifying—observer mentality. Rudolf Steiner was enormously gifted, even graced, with spiritual capacities. From the beginning, his destiny was world historical, and yet even he too had to win for himself the transformation of being that would open up the spiritual world in such a way that he could become truly its servant in the highest sense.

In Weimar, the essential preparation for such an initiation was in place. With the work on Goethe finished and the path to the experience of cognitive freedom laid down, Steiner now stood before the holy of holies. It remained only to enter it. He was thirty-five. At about this time, he tells us, a profound and decisive change occurred within him, involving "a new attentiveness to sensory-physical phenomena." With the penetration of sensory observation, "a new door" opened. He discovered that when the sensory world "is approached objectively, free of all subjectivity, it reveals something about which spiritual insight has nothing to say." As a corollary, the purely spiritual also became accessible. Steiner thus became able to experience the mysterious relationship between the physical and spiritual: one, yet two. He understood, too, that "mysteries are not solved by thoughts," but must be lived. Lived, they revealed their own answer. "Human beings are themselves the solution," he writes, meaning that the struggle to unite sensory and spiritual must be *lived with the whole person*. Lived in this way, the human is revealed as the stage on which the world begins, in part, "to experience its own becoming and existence." In other words, in the simultaneously cognitive and ontological struggle to understand the relationship between sensory and spiritual, something new was happening. At the same time, as part of this general transformation, a change occurred in his meditative life. Meditation became a necessity:

I had led a meditative life before then, but that impulse was the result of an ideal knowledge of its value for a philosophy that acknowledges the spirit. But now something arose within me that demanded meditation as an absolute necessity for my soul life.

As he meditated, he observed that three kinds of knowledge seemed to be available to him: 1) conceptual knowledge gained through sensory observation; 2) conceptual knowledge based on spiritual reality experienced inwardly, independent of the senses in a continuous process of reciprocation with the spiritual world; and 3) purely spiritual, direct knowledge of the spirit, given through meditation to the "inner human spirit," the "I," and arising from "living intimate union" or identity with the spirit. Of the latter, he writes: "It led not only more deeply into the spiritual world but allowed a living intimate union with that world." Steiner now found himself uniting with the being or events of the spiritual world directly and continuously. Thus, he became increasingly aware of a "'spiritual human being" that can live, perceive, and move within the spirit realm entirely detached from the physical human organism." But even this last—the experience of the "I"—did not immediately lessen the struggle and the trials: the contrast between this world and that other one remained active.

In this mood—he calls it "standing before the portal of the spiritual world," but from his description of his "I"-experience we may perhaps call it "standing before the portal of the Christ"—Steiner was called to edit *The Review of Literature* in Berlin, where he became a busy man of letters, commenting on and participating in the weekly maelstrom of the literary and philosophical life of the cultural avant-garde. "At that time," he writes, referring to this entire period, "my experience of Christianity underwent a severe test. This lasted from the time of my departure from Weimar ... to the period when I wrote my book *Christianity as Mystical Fact*." He adds: "Tests of this kind are obstacles placed on one's path by destiny (karma); they have to be overcome in the course of spiritual development." What lay before him, which with hindsight we may now say was inevitable, was the necessity of discovering true Christianity—Christ—for himself.

To do so, he had to pass through and blow away like dust the chimaeras that passed for Christianity and with which he had wrestled for the previous twenty years. Consequently, he writes: "Some of what I said and wrote during that period seems to contradict the way I described Christianity later on. This is because I was referring to the teachings of a 'world beyond' … active in all Christian doctrines at that time." He continues:

> The whole meaning of religious experiences pointed to a world of spirit, one that was supposed to be unattainable by human intellect. Whatever religion might have to say and whatever precepts for moral life it might offer arise from what is revealed to human beings from outside. My own direct experience of spirit objected to this: it wanted to experience the worlds of both spirit and the physical in perceptions of the human being and nature. And my ethical individualism also objected to this. It rejected the external support of commandments for morality; such support came instead as a result of spiritual soul development within the human being, where divinity lives.

Just as when he was an adolescent, therefore, Steiner still sought to realize for himself the content of dogma as a human, spiritual experience. He knew that this was possible, that potentially nothing lay outside experience and that being was one—there was no beyond, no unknown, unknowable "other" world. However, until he had experienced the reality of Christian teaching for himself, he was passionately opposed to accepting all the error and falsity, politics and human fallibility that followed from blind belief outside experience. Statements like the following, then, taken from the conclusion to a report (1897) of a lecture course that he had given on "The Main Currents in German Literature from the Time of Revolution (1848) to the Present," should not surprise us:

> We move into the next century with essentially other feelings than those of our ancestors, who were brought up in Christianity. We have become truly "new" human beings, though we, who confess to this new worldview with our hearts, are a small group. Yet we wish to be fighters for our Gospel, so that in the coming century a new race might arise, one that knows how to live—

happy, cheerful, and proud—without Christianity, without any view of the hereafter.

In the *Autobiography*, Rudolf Steiner speaks most movingly of the trials through which he had to pass—trials in which the human remains trapped between two abstract and one-sided, even mechanical, experiences: one apparently outside nature as a world of idea-beings and the other apparently within it as the "laws" of natural science. Both had to be experienced and consciously turned away from. He says: "I had to rescue my spiritual worldview through the inner storms that took place behind the scenes of my everyday experience," adding, astonishingly, that he did so by turning to the deed of Christ. "I was able to make progress during that period of testing, only by contemplating through spiritual perception, the evolution of Christianity"—that is the ongoing living meaning for evolution of the Christ event itself.

In this context Steiner mentions again the conversation he had had earlier with the Cistercian Neumann, who, as if skeptically, had avoided the issue when confronted with the question of whether "Jesus of Nazareth, through an extra-earthly influence, received the Christ into himself, and that the Christ as a spiritual being lives within human evolution since the Mystery of Golgotha." But for Steiner the issue could not be avoided. "The Christianity that I had to find was not in any of the existing confessions." Then he adds: "After the severe inner struggles during that time of testing, I found it necessary to immerse myself in Christianity and, indeed, in the world where spirit speaks of it."

Thus, gradually, at about the turn of the twentieth century, as he approached his fortieth year, the "true content" of Christianity began to develop in a germinal way before his soul as a phenomenon of inner knowledge until finally he was able to stand spiritually before the Mystery of Golgotha in the most inward, most serious "celebration of knowledge."

Christianity as Mystical Fact is the first fruit of this "celebration" and indeed a watershed in Steiner's entire work. As such, it is the fulfillment of twenty-five years of intense inner and outer work. In that sense, it is not a sidebar between the earlier epistemological works and the later anthroposophical ones but something new—a truly evolutionary, creative transition; it is a flowering of what came before, containing the seeds of what is to come after. In it, what was achieved in earlier works epistemologically as a transformation of knowing is shown to be *ontological*, a question of the cosmic transformation of *being*—a new kind of transformation made possible by the transformative being of Being itself, the Christ, the Son of the Father, now available to all through the cosmic fact of the Incarnation.

Given the magnitude of what it seeks to communicate and the fact that for Steiner it was a hard-won experience, *Christianity as Mystical Fact* is a book that deserves very careful reading. As is the case with all of Steiner's written works, it is much more subtle and complex than it appears. At first glance, the thesis—or path—is simple enough and related through telling details and examples. What was available as an experience to a few, elite initiates into the pre-Christian Mysteries is now available to all through the Christian Mystery of Golgotha, in which the Word, the Logos, who was with God and was (a) God and who made all things and was life and light, became flesh and dwelt among us full of grace and truth. In the words of Augustine (quoted by Steiner), "What is now called the Christian religion existed already among the ancients and was not lacking at the very beginning of the human race. When Christ appeared in the flesh, the true religion already in existence received the name of Christian." The implications of this, of course, are staggering, for it means that the Logos or Christ, by whatever name he has been, is, and will be called, is the meaning of cosmic-human evolution, the active ferment of its unfolding from beginning to end, Alpha and Omega.

Much follows from this. The pre-Christian initiate, who attained Logos-Initiation experienced a state of spiritual vision and union that seemed to have no equivalent in the sense-perceptible world. The Mystery of Golgotha was, as it were, experienced only spiritually. According to Steiner's own experience, as they achieve this state, "Christian" initiates, on the other hand, behold the reality of the Mystery of Golgotha on the physical plane; they understand and are transformed by the reality that the sense-perceptible world now contains "the spiritual content that had been enacted supersensibly in the Mysteries." But there is more: Because the Word, the Logos, has been made flesh, all human capacities of thinking, feeling, and willing—however "darkened"—now have a quickened "logos-nature." That is to say that today, like Lazarus, the first Christian initiate (and first revealed in this book to be the author of St. John's Gospel), we can all die and be reborn in Christ. This is true, again, no matter what name we place upon the experience or whatever cultural-linguistic frame we use to understand and communicate it. Starting where we are, with our ordinary thinking, feeling, and willing, we can, through our own efforts, achieve Logos-consciousness (or Christ "I"-consciousness) here and now. In other words, the message of *Christianity as Mystical Fact* is as revolutionary today as it was more than a hundred years ago, when it was first published.

Written when Steiner was forty (traditionally the age when it becomes permissible to speak of esoteric matters), *Christianity as Mystical Fact* is perhaps not unsurprisingly also a personal work. Just as *The Philosophy of Freedom* was not written by Rudolf Steiner to convince anyone by its logic but rather to lay down for himself (and for the record) the path of knowledge that he had trod, so *Christianity as Mystical Fact* is not written as a biblical-critical or theological treatise but marks and bears witness to Steiner's own path to Christ. Read in this way it can serve as a path for others who, thinking along with it, are inspired to take it up meditatively and work through it individually, each in their own way.

TRANSLATOR'S PREFACE

ANDREW WELBURN

Christianity as Mystical Fact was a significant book in Rudolf Steiner's biography, being the first in which the well-known philosopher of freedom and Goethe scholar came forward with an interpretation of Christian beginnings and of the continuing relevance of Christianity to modern life—an interpretation he continued to develop and deepen over the next twenty-five years.[1] But it was even more significant for raising issues that have dominated the whole discussion of Christianity in the remainder of our century. It was among the first books to confront the crisis of the evidence about Christianity that had been uncovered by the biblical criticism of the last century, and even more the questioning of the uniqueness of Christianity which resulted from researches in "comparative religion," the rediscovery in the West of Buddhism, Hinduism, and so on. It is a great book, perhaps because it combines the personal authenticity of that moment when its author, as he put it in *Autobiography: Chapters in the Course of My Life*, "stood before the Mystery of Golgotha in a solemn festival of knowledge," and the awareness of those larger questions that are still dealt with, on the whole, so inadequately today, and to which Rudolf Steiner proposed some exciting and thorough-going answers.

Traditional Christians were already disconcerted by the growing evidence that the "historical" figure of Christ was in fact a complex creation, molded by biblical and extra-biblical ideas, expectations, and hopes. Scholarship had turned up parallels to the Redeemer's life and death in Eastern religions, and in the paganism contemporary with Christian origins. Was Christ perhaps just another dying-and-rising god such as Adonis or Attis, or the others surveyed in James Frazer's monumental study, *The Golden Bough*? Not at all, declared others, hastily dissociating Jesus from anything of the sort by turning him into "the simple man of Nazareth," an image equally inappropriate as an interpretation of the New Testament sources. Closer to our own day, these issues have been sharpened still further by the discovery of Essene and Gnostic texts from the early Christian time and milieu. In many of these, too, Christ (or the Messiah of the "Dead Sea Scrolls") seems often to be a "cosmic" figure rather than a historical individual. Despite all the interest in them, desperate special pleading has frequently been the response today also. This reflects a desire to keep treasured items of belief safe from the restless questioning of the modern world, even at the cost of a debilitating split between head and heart. If early Christian texts present Jesus in "cosmic" terms, relating stories that are less history than myths like those about the pagan savior-gods, or like the apocalyptic figures anticipated by the Essenes, these must be seen as unfortunate vestiges in the Christian message of former "superstitious" and unrealistic times. The response of Christian theologians must be to demythologize Christianity—a program relentlessly pursued by Bultmann and his many followers in particular, but tacitly followed by many more.[2] And what has the result been? Stripped bare of its cosmic imagery, of its relationship to the forces that early Christians imagined were going to bring about the imminent transformation of the world, Christianity has turned in upon itself, lost the initiative, lost its sense of direction.

Rudolf Steiner had the advantage of approaching the whole question from a profounder viewpoint. In other circles the rediscovery of myth, of cosmic symbolism and mystery, was taking a more positive course. Theologians and academics may have felt the threat to conventional ideas; Theosophists saw the need for a new synthesis that took seriously the insights both of Buddhism and the evolutionary science of the West, the evidence of recurring patterns in myth and research into the hidden structures of the mind. H.P. Blavatsky's idea of a unity behind it all touched a nerve of the age, and an attempt to explain the extraordinary and undeniable unity of religious phenomena has remained a central strand in twentieth-century thought, persisting far outside the theosophical circles where it was first nurtured.[3] But from the beginning Steiner followed his own critical line. It seemed as though the Theosophists wanted to manufacture a new synthetic religion that would replace the parochialism of local faiths. Steiner knew that any real spiritual life needed something more organic; that the universal patterns of religion had adapted themselves in subtle and complex ways through history to the changing needs of humanity, different cultures, different times. Above all Steiner was concerned that the attempt to deepen the impoverished spiritual life of the West was turning all too easily into a rivalry between West and East. Sometimes it appears that he takes sides in this struggle too, but his claim for the uniqueness of Christianity, it should be remembered, is a claim for the unique contribution of all religions in the evolution of the human spirit. Without any one of them our spiritual life would be incalculably the poorer. Christianity, however, is specifically adapted to deal with the sense of history, of individual responsibility, of individual consciousness, which had evolved in the West.

It was history with its relativism, not just the individual's questioning attitude that had brought the crisis to a head by the end of the nineteenth century. There no longer seemed to be a place for belief in a timeless truth we could all accept, and the questioning of everything led either to scientific reductionism or to a Nietzschean nihilism. But Steiner saw that the sort of inward migration to Eastern culture, one that had not experienced these problems, which was attractive to many, could never resolve the situation—though it might provide a temporary respite for some. By ignoring Christianity, the esotericists were bypassing the spiritual stream intimately connected with the problems facing modern civilization, which must either solve them or perish with them. Conversely, if Christianity were really sure of the truth it asserted it could lose nothing from the comparison with other religions. If its central symbols of a dying god and regeneration were held in common with other beliefs, that did not mean it must inevitably lose its identity in a mish-mash of faiths. On the contrary, such an encounter would bring it to understand itself more thoroughly. Steiner saw that what was needed was an evolutionary approach. Christianity did grow out of previously existing beliefs but developed them in a special way, a way that was linked with the emergence of the individual, and of historical, time-oriented understanding. That could not mean it should strive to leave behind all that bound it to the older Mysteries, which had given people the sense of belonging to a meaningful cosmic order, spiritual as well as physical. Indeed, to do so would simply be throwing one's lot in with the alienation and isolation that is the besetting disease of modern culture: the shadow side of our individualism and freedom to shape our future by detaching ourselves from the past. Rather, by understanding the spiritual pattern of regeneration in the Mysteries, in which people felt they shared in the death and return-to-life of a god, Christianity could also see how it had evolved—and still needed to evolve—in order to convey that experience to the individualistic and highly self-conscious humanity, which could never go back to the collective values and way of life of ancient humanity.

If Christianity were true to its conviction of God working in history, it could understand itself as part of the spiritual evolution of humanity and as a guide to human spiritual transformation still to come. Steiner therefore welcomed the comparative perspective that has seemed such a necessary yet bitter pill to Bultmann and the demythologizers of Christianity. His "esoteric Christianity" opened the way for deeper knowledge, not by detaching us from our history, and asking us to believe in a generalized and schematic "universal truth," but rather, by asking us to find our roots and to understand the need for similar roots in other cultures, other faiths.

The study of the setting of original Christianity pointed to the cosmic meaning of redemption, and it was through Rudolf Steiner that the cosmic Christ has been rediscovered in our century. (It was from Steiner's pupil Edouard Schuré, for example, that the concept reached Teilhard de Chardin, with whom it is most often associated.) But finding the cosmic vision once more was only one side of Steiner's attempt to give the new impetus Christianity needed for contemporary humanity. It needed to be matched by understanding for the real working of the Christian spirit in individuals—the "Christ-impulse," which has helped to make us what we are, and which can redeem and transform us if we consciously open ourselves to it. Awareness of Christ's presence in the world, the parousia, or so-called "second coming," would be realized according to Steiner in the awakening of individuals through the Christ within them. It would be the new consciousness he saw about to dawn, and not the literal return expected by many, even in the Theosophical Society, of a Messiah in the flesh.

Steiner unfolded his vision in kaleidoscopic richness through lectures and books in the decades that followed *Christianity As Mystical Fact*. I have attempted at least to hint at the place held by certain discussions in his developed views, or to refer to subsequent elaborations of a theme, by means of "forward references" and an occasional substantive footnote. All in all, it is remarkable how much is present in embryo in his first short treatment of this vast subject, but it is as well to be aware too of the larger context he himself subsequently established for many of its ideas. The early work certainly has its peculiarities. In parts the book is an odd mixture of sketchiness and profundity, while other sections like those on Heraclitus, Philo, or Augustine blossom into short monographs that could almost stand alone. Furthermore, much discussion elsewhere of Christianity and the Mysteries has focused on Paul, about whom Steiner chose to say virtually nothing in his book. It is worth realizing that this does not betoken any hostility toward Paul and his message, such as one occasionally and misguidedly finds in "spiritual" circles. Despite the "undeniable awkwardness" of the language, Steiner was later to comment:

> The Pauline letters are definitive statements of the whole direction taken by Christian evolution.... In them are announced the fundamental truths of Christianity: the resurrection, the "faith" that stands in opposition to the "Law," the working of grace, the living presence of Christ in the soul or in human consciousness, and much more. One finds increasingly that the presentation of Christianity has to take as its starting-point these letters of Paul.[4]

Or again, it might have been expected that an attempt to establish the evolutionary and cosmic purport of Christianity would have gravitated toward the brilliant and wide-ranging thought of an Origen,[5] rather than leading up to the highly personal yet Church-oriented Augustine. But here too Steiner has deeper purposes in view; for with the crumbling away of the ancient world and its learning, it is in Augustine that we see the individual struggle for faith that will set the tone for the future of Christianity. And it is in the working of that crisis of the individual through to the end, and not in turning back, that Steiner's understanding of the meaning of Christianity lies.

Christianity as Mystical Fact sets out to explore a pattern of spiritual life that Steiner regarded as crucial to the archaic religions and the Mysteries central to them. Before leaving the book to make its case, it is worth surveying briefly the state of the ongoing discussion to which Steiner can still, I suggest, decisively contribute. The argument has inevitably swung different ways. Early efforts to substantiate the direct derivation of Christianity from Mysteries of the East, such as *The Iranian Mystery of Redemption*—a book by the great comparative religionist Richard Reitzenstein—were later subjected to devastating criticism. (Certainly by comparison with Reitzenstein, it should be noted, Steiner's emphasis on an Iranian-Zoroastrian thread in the Mysteries and, indeed in Christianity, is more subtle and restrained.) But the arguments against showed, in turn, a failure to exorcise the specter that had been raised. Hugo Rahner's fascinating *Greek Myth and Christian Mystery* tried to limit the influence of the Mysteries to later phases, to the fourth century and after, when the Church took over the pagan establishment. Looking back on another classic study, Samuel Angus' *Mystery Religions and Christianity*, Theodore Gaster protested that many of the things claimed to have come from the Mysteries might really have been transmitted from Judaism. The situation has only really been clarified by the notable discoveries of new texts in 1945 and 1947. The Gnostic texts from Nag Hammadi showed that Christianity had been involved with Mysteries at a much earlier stage, leading to the complex situation of the second-century crisis. The "Dead Sea Scrolls" from Qumran showed that the Judaism of the type that influenced Christianity was itself "cosmic religion," centered on initiation into Mysteries like those of the Essenes. The discovery of other Gnostic texts from the semi-Jewish sect of the Mandaeans unleashed a further set of studies, of which the more valuable are perhaps those of A. Loisy, such as his *Birth of the Christian Religion*.[6]

Many of these studies suffered from the unfortunate but unavoidable lack of sources—and even more perhaps from the attempt to derive the inner significance of the process they described from the external evidence, which involved them in all sorts of excesses. Steiner's approach was just the opposite. He recognized a spiritual configuration, given manifold forms according to the needs of time and human development, existing in different religious settings. He knew that the connection must therefore have been there. "Historical research," he once said, "will one day vindicate completely the evidence drawn from purely spiritual sources, which forms the basis of my *Christianity as Mystical Fact*."[7] In the meantime he appealed to evidences where he found them—for instance, in the Mystery-oriented Judaism of Philo of Alexandria or, in the absence of documents relating to the Greek Mysteries, in the reflection of Mystery processes in the pre-Socratics and Plato. (Again I have tried in the footnotes to refer to discoveries that now prove his case.) Part of the roundaboutness of the book is thus explained; but he also clearly wanted to establish a larger perspective than the shortsighted historical approach. Later, especially in his lectures, he was to extend his treatment into the details of the Gospels and the Apocalypse, only touched on here. His "evolutionary" idea that in Christianity the processes of the Mysteries, hitherto experienced in vision and expressed in myth, had to become an individual life, already opens the way however for his intimate and deeply moving account of the founder's role. In obedience to his Father, the God of history, Christ had to be willing to translate that pattern of death and resurrection into personal destiny, thereby opening a new dimension of humanity's relationship to God. All those unfounded criticisms—that Steiner did not take seriously the Redeemer's suffering, even that he lacked any real relationship to the Christian tradition, or that he was simply giving out a novel revelation of his own—are thus shown for what they are. It is precisely the intimacy of this account that furnishes the assurance for Steiner's critical yet creative role within the Christian historical tradition that is so impressive and remarkable. Anyone who ignores it has failed to discern the man with whom they are dealing.

In rendering Steiner's book into English I have used a number of terms that may seem slightly technical. The special wisdom of the Mysteries, only understood by those who have been through their processes, is "mysteriosophy" (*Mysterienweisheit*), a term now in use among scholars and not at all alien to Steiner's usage. The one-to-be-initiated is an "initiand." One who has been through the process becomes a *mystes* (plural, *mystai*), the term retained by Steiner (*der Myste*), but not identical with the related and more familiar "mystic" (*der Mystiker*). The goal of the Mysteries is "divinization" (*Vergöttung*, equivalent to *apotheosis*, *theothenai*, or "becoming God").

Nineteenth-century conventions of long paragraphs and undivided chapters do not help modern readers to find their way through Steiner's many-sided approach. I have provided subtitles for the sections of each chapter, and tried to articulate the divisions of Steiner's thought rather than follow the stylistic habits of his day. Just occasionally I have reproduced an "aside" in Steiner's argument as a footnote, ascribed to (R.St.). Otherwise all numbered footnotes are mine. The translation is based on the original text of *Das Christentum als mystische Tatsache* of 1902, but including all the additions of 1910 (see Appendix). In preparing the translation and notes I have benefited from the edition and annotations of Caroline Wispler and Karl-Martin Dietz (Dornach 1976); from the previous version by A. Cotterell and its revision by Charles Davy and Adam Bittleston (London 1972); and from the version by Eva Frommer, Gabrielle Hess, and Peter Kändler (New York 1961), which remains valuable not least for its extensive indications of Steiner's further discussions of many themes.

Notes

1. Important landmarks in the development of his ideas are in particular his lectures on the Gospels: *The Gospel of St. John* (two cycles, 1908–1909), *The Gospel of St. Luke* (1909), *The Gospel of St. Matthew* (1910), and *The Gospel of St. Mark* (1910–1911); also *From Jesus to Christ* (1911), *Building Stones for an Understanding of the Mystery of Golgotha* (1917).

2. Rudolf Bultmann (1884–1976), a German theologian and professor who attempted to "demythologize" the New Testament by utilizing the modern terminology of existentialist philosophy; his theories became the starting point for most twentieth-century theological debate.

3. The idea of finding the unity behind religious phenomena all over the world has inspired such researchers as Mircea Eliade, Joseph Campbell, and

others into modern times. Eliade in particular has stressed the universality of initiation practices and the presence of their influence in all the great religions. H.P. Blavatsky's notion of a "secret doctrine" is a specific version of the idea that is actually less close to Steiner, and despite his early connection with the Theosophical Movement, there is no evidence that Steiner ever believed in it literally.

4. *The Bhagavad Gita and the Epistles of Paul*, Anthroposophic Press, Hudson, NY, 1971, pp. 60–61.

5. Origen, properly Adamantius Origenes (approximately 185–254).

6. R. Reitzenstein, *Das iranische Erlösungsmysterium*, Bonn, 1921; Hugo Rahner, *Greek Myth and Christian Mystery*, London, 1963; S. Angus, *The Mystery Religions and Christianity* (with a new foreword by T.H. Gaster), New York, 1966; A. Loisy, *The Birth of the Christian Religion*, London, 1948; for the relevance of Rudolf Steiner's ideas to the exciting situation since the "Dead Sea Scrolls" and the Nag Hammadi Library revealed something of the environment of early Christianity, see A. Welburn, *The Beginnings of Christianity*, Floris Books, Edinburgh, 1991. For Mandaean and other Mystery texts relevant to Christian origins, see A. Welburn, *Gnosis: The Mysteries and Christianity*, Floris Books, 1994.

7. *Building Stones for an Understanding of the Mystery of Golgotha*, p.19.

CHRISTIANITY
AS MYSTICAL FACT

AND THE MYSTERIES OF ANTIQUITY

Rudolf Steiner

1

THE MYSTERIES AND MYSTERIOSOPHY

The Mysteries and Initiation

IT IS AS THOUGH a veil of secrecy is drawn over the way in which, in the civilizations of the ancient world, those who sought a deeper religious life and knowledge than could be found in the popular religions were able to satisfy their spiritual needs. An inquiry into how those needs were met leads us immediately into the obscurity of the secret cults.[1] The individual seeker disappears there for the moment from our view. We see that the public forms of religion cannot give what the seeker's heart desires. He or she acknowledges the gods, but knows that the customary ideas about the gods do not resolve the great enigmas of life, and seeks a wisdom that is carefully guarded by a community of priestsages. The struggling soul seeks a refuge in their community. If the sages find one who is ready, they will lead that individual stage by stage, in a manner concealed from the outsider's gaze, to a higher insight. But the process is not disclosed to the uninitiated. Such a seeker seems to be entirely removed for a time from earthly life, transported to some hidden world.

Standing once more in the light of day, the seeker is utterly changed. We see one for whom no words can be sublime enough to express the meaning of what has been experienced. It seems that not just symbolically but in some existential sense he or she has passed through death and awakened to a new and higher life. And there is a conviction that no one who has not undergone a similar experience can understand what such a one has to say. Such was the case of those who, in the Mysteries, were initiated into the content of that secret wisdom which was withheld from the people, and which illuminated the profounder questions of life. Alongside the public religion, there existed a "secret religion" of the elect. Its historical beginnings are lost to sight in the obscurity of the beginnings of civilization. It is encountered everywhere among the peoples of antiquity so far discovered, and their sages spoke of the Mysteries with the greatest reverence.[2] What was it they concealed, and what were the secrets they laid bare to the initiated?

The enigma is intensified still further by what we know of the dangers which are repeatedly asserted by ancient sources to be characteristic of the Mysteries. The path conducting to the secret truths of life lay through a world of terrors. Woe to anyone unworthy to attain them! No transgression could be greater than the "betrayal" of the Mysteries to the uninitiated; the betrayer would be punished not just with the confiscation of property but with death. We know that the poet Aeschylus was accused of representing certain contents of the Mysteries on the stage. He escaped death only by taking refuge at the altar of Dionysus and legally proving that he was not an initiate.[3]

The ancient testimonies to the Mysteries are at once revealing yet full of ambiguity. The initiates were convinced that to tell what they knew would be sinful, and indeed that it would be sinful for the uninitiated to hear it. Plutarch mentions the terror of the initiand, and compares his position to a preparation for death.[4] A special mode of life was one of the requirements for a subsequent initiation. The senses were to be brought under the control of the spirit; fasting, isolation, ordeals, and certain meditative techniques were employed to that end. The stable realities of ordinary life were to lose all their value, and the whole orientation of perception and feeling to be completely altered. The implication of such exercises and ordeals cannot be in doubt; the wisdom to be presented to the initiate could work upon the psyche in the proper way only if one had already worked transformingly upon the world of the lower senses. The initiand was to be conducted into the life of the spirit, and behold a higher world order. Without the preparatory exercises and ordeals he or she would be able to form no connection with that world—and on that connection everything depended.

Real understanding here is possible only if we have an awareness of the subtle phenomena of living knowledge. It requires us to notice two quite different attitudes toward knowledge and its ultimate significance. In the first, "reality" is taken to mean our immediate environment. Processes there are registered by our senses of touch, hearing, and sight; and it is because we perceive them with our senses that we call them real. Our thinking about them uncovers them further and clarifies the relations between them. From this point of view, what rises up in answer from within the soul is not real in the same sense, being "only" thoughts and ideas. At best these are regarded as afterimages of perceptible reality; they have no validity of their own, since we can neither touch, see, nor hear them. But there is another way of relating to the world, incomprehensible though it must remain for those who cling to the "reality" we have just described. It comes to certain people at some moment in their lives, overturning their whole way of looking at the world. What they call "real" are the images that surface from the spiritual life of the psyche, and they ascribe a lesser degree of actuality to the sense-impressions of hearing, touching, and seeing. They are aware that their assertions cannot be proved. All they can do is to tell of their new experiences, knowing that they are then in the position of someone with eyesight addressing the blind. If they nevertheless try to communicate their inner experiences, it is in the conviction that around them may be others who, though their spiritual eyes are yet unopened, may be able to understand through the very power of what they have to convey. For they have a faith in humanity and wish to open the eyes of others. They can only offer the fruits that their own spirit has gathered. As to whether the visions of the spiritual eye are understood by others, that depends upon the degree of their understanding.

In the beginning there is resistance on the human side to seeing with the spiritual eye. Human beings have as yet nothing in their own nature that enables them to do so: the human being is at the outset a product of sense-experiences, and the mind is as yet nothing more than the interpreter and judge of the senses. The senses would be poor instruments if they did not insist upon their own truth and credibility; an eye would be a bad eye if it did not impress upon us the unconditional reality of what it sees. That is right for the eye. Nor is it deprived of its due by the spiritual eye. It is only that the spiritual eye permits us to see the things of sense in a higher light. Nothing perceived by the physical eye is thereby denied; and yet a new glory radiates from what is seen, showing that the former perception was only of a lower reality. What is seen remains exactly the same as before, but now it is merged into something higher—into the spirit.

The question then is how to realize and feel the truth of what is seen. Those who deny living response and feeling to everything except what the senses tell them will dismiss the higher vision as a *fata morgana*, mere fantasy. When such people try to grasp the spiritual images, they are left groping in the void, since they have feeling only for the outwardly perceptible. Spiritual images shrink from their touch. They remain "mere" ideas that pass through the mind; such a person is not vitally present in them. As images, they seem less real than restless dreams. Rising up like bubbles before the face of what one calls reality, they vanish before the massive structure of the solid truth of the senses. But things are quite different to one who has transformed his or her perceptions and attitudes toward reality, for whom the solid structure has lost its unconditional and unquestioned character. Not that one's senses and feelings are stunted, but their authority has become less absolute, so that room is left for something else. The world of the spirit begins to animate the space that is thus left open.

At this point a terrible possibility lies in wait. It may happen that someone loses that unreflecting confidence in perceptions and feelings, and yet no new world rises. Such a person is left suspended in the void as if dead. The previous values have deserted that individual, but no new ones have arisen. For such a one the universe and fellow human beings have ceased to exist. This is in fact not merely a possibility, but a stage that every seeker for higher knowledge must experience. One comes to a point in understanding where the spirit reveals all of life to be death. One is then no longer in the world, but under it, in the Underworld. One has descended into Hades.[5] It will be well for such a person not to go under, and if a new world comes into being either the seeker vanishes from sight, or emerges once more, transfigured, and looks out upon a new Sun and a new Earth. Out of the fire of the spirit the universe has been reborn.

Death and Rebirth

In testimony of what happened to them in the Mysteries we have the accounts of the initiates themselves. Menippus relates how he traveled to Babylon in order to be taken to Hades and brought back again by the followers of Zoroaster.[6] He says that in the course of his wanderings he crossed the great water, and that he passed through fire and ice. We hear that the *mystai* were struck with terror by a drawn sword, that blood was caused to flow. Such words are made intelligible by a knowledge of the stages leading from lower to higher cognition. It does indeed feel as though everything solidly material and perceptible has dissolved into water. The ground is taken from beneath us. Everything living has been put to death. The spirit has cut through the life of the senses like a sword through the living flesh; we have seen the blood of sensuality flow.

But life springs up anew. The initiate reascends from the Underworld. The ancient orator Aristides asserts:

> I thought I could touch the god, and feel his very presence. I was in a condition between sleeping and waking. My spirit was so light that no one except an initiate could comprehend or speak of it.[7]

This new existence is no longer subjected to the laws of lower life. It is untouched by growth and decay. Discussions about "the eternal" are endless, but unless the words draw their meaning from those who have actually descended into Hades, they are mere sound and fury, signifying nothing. For the initiates have a new perspective on life and death, which for the first time entitles them to speak of immortality. They know that all talk of it except on the basis of the initiates' knowledge is uncomprehending, and will ascribe immortality to something that is still bound up with coming-to-be and passing-away. It is not just the conviction that life at its core is eternal that the *mystai* seek. Such a conviction would be quite valueless from the standpoint of the Mysteries. From the Mystery-standpoint the eternal has no living presence in one who is not a *mystes*, so when speaking of the eternal such a person would speak of precisely nothing. Rather it is the "eternal" itself that the *mystai* seek to possess; they have first to awaken the eternal to existence within them, and then they can speak of it. Plato's hard saying is absolutely true for them, that the uninitiated sink into the mire, and only those who have passed through the Mysteries enter into eternity.[8] That is the meaning too of Sophocles' fragment:

> Thrice blessed when they come to the realm of shades who have seen these rites! They alone have life, for the rest there is only pain and toil.[9]

That is why to speak of the Mysteries is at the same time to tell of dangers. For is not to lead someone to the door of the Underworld to rob that person of happiness, of the very meaning of life? A terrible responsibility is incurred by such an act. And yet the initiates had to consider whether they could shirk that responsibility. For they considered that their knowledge was related to the ordinary soul life of the people as light to darkness. An innocent happiness is contained in that darkness, with which the mystai would not wantonly interfere. For indeed what could be the result if the *mystai* betrayed their secret? Their words would have been just that—empty words. The experiences and emotions needed to evoke the shock of the spirit out of the words would have been lacking without the preparation, the exercises, and ordeals, the total transformation of perceptual life. Lacking this, anyone who heard would be thrown into emptiness, nothingness, deprived of happiness but receiving nothing in return. In reality, of course, nothing could be taken away. After all, empty words have no power to alter our experience of life. Actual experience would still be limited to feeling, mediated by the senses. Nothing could come to such a person except a terrifying, paralyzing uncertainty—which it would be criminal to impart. This is no longer completely valid for the attainment of spirit knowledge today. Such knowledge can be conceptually understood because modern human beings have a conceptual ability that ancient humanity lacked. Today one can find human beings who have knowledge of the spiritual world through their own experience; and others they meet can understand conceptually what they have experienced. Earlier humanity lacked this conceptual ability.

The mysteriosophy of the ancient world resembles a hothouse plant, which requires seclusion in which to grow and flourish. Bring it into the atmosphere of mundane ideas and it cannot thrive; before the sharp judgment of modern scientific logic it evaporates utterly. It is necessary therefore to put aside for a time our scientific education based on the microscope and telescope, purify our hands that have grown clumsy with all the business of dissection and the search for proof. Then, free of all presuppositions, we may enter the pure temple of the Mysteries.

Of primary importance is the frame of mind in which the *mystai* approach what they consider to be the highest truth, the answer to all the riddles of life. Our own age is one that trusts only to hard physical facts as the source of "knowledge," and finds it difficult that in the most exalted concerns we should be dependent upon a mood. That makes of knowledge something personal and intimate. For the *mystes* it is such. Go and give someone the answer to the enigma of the world! Present the conclusion ready-made! The *mystes* would find that utterly hollow; a person must reach the answer in the right way, otherwise it will be nothing. Without the feeling which kindles the essential fire, it will mean little.[10] A god comes to meet you—either it is everything, or nothing; nothing, if you make the encounter in the spirit of the humdrum tasks of life; everything if you are duly prepared and attuned to the experience. As to what it may be in itself, that does not concern you—what matters is whether it leaves you as it found you or changes you. And that depends entirely on you. A training and development both intimate and intensive must have prepared the personality in order that the encounter with the god may kindle and release the powers within. What you receive in the encounter depends upon what you bring to meet it.

Plutarch has described the intensive preparation, and recounted the "greeting" addressed by the *mystes* to the god when he approaches him:

> The god, as it were, addresses each of us as he enters with his "Know Thyself," which is at least as good as "Hail." We answer the god in return with "*EI*" (Thou Art), rendering him that designation which is true and has no lie in it, and alone belongs to him and to no other, that of Being.
>
> For we really have no part in real being; all mortal nature is in a middle state between becoming and passing-away, and presents but an appearance, a faint unstable image, of itself. If you strain the intellect and wish to grasp this, it is as with water—compress it too

much and force it violently into one space as it tries to flow through, and you destroy the enveloping substance. Even so when the reason tries to follow too closely the clear truth about each particular thing in the world of phase and change, it is foiled and rests either on the becoming of that thing or on its passing-away. It cannot apprehend anything that abides or really is.

"It is impossible to go into the same river twice," said Heraclitus. No more can you hold mortal being twice, so as to grasp it; so sharp and swift is change, it scatters and brings together again—nay, not again, nor afterward: even while it is being formed it fails, it approaches, and is gone. So becoming never ends in being, for the process never leaves off, or is stayed. From seed it produces, in its constant changes, an embryo, then an infant, then a child; in due order a boy, a young man; then a man, an elderly man, and an old man; it undoes former becomings and that age which has been to make those which come after.

Yet we fear (how absurdly!) a single death—we who have died so many deaths, and yet are dying. For it is not only that, as Heraclitus would say, "Death of fire is the birth of air," and "Death of air is the birth of water." The thing is much clearer in our own selves. The man in his strength is destroyed when the old man comes into being, the young man was destroyed for the man in his strength to be, so the boy for the young man, the babe for the boy. He of yesterday has died into him of today; he of today is dying into him of tomorrow. No one abides, no one is. We who come into being are many, while matter is driven around, and then glides away about some one appearance and a common mold. Else how is it, if we remain the same, that the things in which we find pleasure now are different from those of a former time; that we love, hate, admire, and censure different things?

How is it that our look, our bodily form, our intellect are not the same as then? If a man does not change, these various conditions are unnatural; if he does change, he is not the same man.

But if he is not the same man, he is not at all. His so-called being is simply change and new birth of man out of man. In our ignorance of what being is, sense falsely tells us that what appears is.[11]

Plutarch repeatedly characterizes himself as an initiate and what he describes here is an absolute requirement for the life of the *mystes:* the attainment of a wisdom in which the spirit sees through the delusions of the senses. In the flux of becoming lies everything which the senses take for real being—and that applies not only to the things round about, but to oneself. Before the spiritual gaze one's own being dissolves into unreality, one's inner unity is dissipated, and one becomes a play of transient appearances. Birth and death lose their distinctive meanings, and refer to moments of becoming and passing-away that are like all the other events in nature. The highest cannot be found, however, in becoming and passing away, but only in the truly enduring that looks both back to the past and forward into the future.

To gaze at once into the past and future is a stage of higher knowledge. It is the discovery of the spirit. The spirit lies behind the manifestations of the senses, but has nothing to do with becoming and passing away, which characterizes all appearances to the senses. Everyone who lives only in the world of the senses bears this spirit occultly, deep within. Everyone who has pierced through the illusion of the sense-world bears the spirit within as a manifest truth.

To attain insight is to unfold a new organ, an event comparable to a plant unfolding the color of its blossom out of its former green and leafy state. The ability to produce flowers was always there in the plant, but it was hidden, and became manifest only with the blooming of the flower. Even so, the divine spiritual forces lie hidden within sense-dominated human beings, and become manifest truth for the first time in the *mystes*. That is the nature of the Mystery "transformation."

Through inner development, the *mystai* bring to the world, as it formerly existed, something radically new. The world order known to the senses had formed them as natural human beings, and then abandoned them. Nature's role is then fulfilled, and her deployment of creative forces in humanity comes to an end. But the forces in humanity are not themselves exhausted. They lie as though spellbound in the natural human being and await their release. Unable to release themselves, they ebb away unless human beings take hold of them and transform them —unless they awaken to real existence their hidden potentiality. Nature brings forms from the rudimentary to the completed state, in a long series of stages from the inanimate, the variety of living forms, to physical humanity. Looking around them, human beings perceive themselves to be subject to change. But they detect also within their own being the powers that brought the natural human being into existence. These powers are not subject to the law of change. Rather they are the source from which everything changeable has sprung. They are a sign that the human being is greater than can be known by means of the senses.

These powers constitute as yet a nothing, a sheer possibility. Yet people are illuminated from within by the power that fashioned all things, including themselves. They also feel something urging them on to higher creative life. There lies within them something that pre-existed their natural being and will outlive it. It brought them into existence; nevertheless they can seize hold of it and share in its creative force. Such feelings pervaded the life of the ancient *mystai* as a result of their initiation.

It was the felt presence of the eternal, the divine. Human action became an integral part of divine creativity. A higher Self had been discovered, a Self extending beyond the bounds of perceptual process, prior to physical birth and existing after death. It is an eternally creative Self, spanning time past and time to come. The empirical personality is a product of the Self; but that is henceforth only a subordinate part of its creative life within. Now is created something higher than the senses can grasp, something for which the personality is a mere instrument of its creative power, something in humanity that is divine. This is the "divinization" experienced in the Mysteries.[12]

The Hidden God

For the *mystai* that power which illuminated them from within was what they called their true spirit, the spirit of which they themselves were the product. It was as though a new being had penetrated them and taken possession of their faculties. Such a being stood between them, in their ordinary identities, and the supreme cosmic power or Godhead. It was the true Self or *daimon* that the *mystai* were seeking.[13] They had come into existence in the great realm of nature, but nature's work was incomplete, and its fulfillment had to be undertaken by human beings themselves. To accomplish that within the gross conditions of nature, however, which included even the empirical personality, was impossible. For in that realm the limit of development had already been reached. One therefore had to leave nature behind, and thus to construct further within the condition of the spirits (*daimons*) at the point where nature left off.

An atmosphere had to be created that did not exist anywhere in the outer world. That atmosphere in which the *mystai* could breathe was to be found in the temples of the Mysteries. There took place the awakening of the slumbering powers within, and metamorphosis into a higher, creative and spiritual being. The transformation of the *mystai* was a delicate process, unfitted to the harsh light of common day. But if they stood the test, they became a rock founded on the eternal, defying all life's storms. They had simply to accept, however, that they could not communicate directly to others what they had been through on the way.

According to Plutarch, it was in the Mysteries that he found "the truest information and explanation about the nature of the *daimons*."[14] Cicero also adds that the Mysteries,

> when they are explained and traced back to their original meaning, are concerned more with the nature of things than with the nature of the gods.[15]

Their evidence shows that the *mystai* acquired a higher knowledge about the nature of things than that obtainable in the public cults of the gods. Indeed the *daimons* or spiritual existences, and even the gods, were felt to need explaining. And so we come to still higher beings than the *daimons* and the gods: this belonged to the essential content of mysteriosophy.

The ordinary people pictured the gods and spirits in forms whose content was borrowed from the sense-world. But to one who had looked upon eternity, how dubious must these "immortal gods" now appear! Can Zeus as he was publicly represented be an eternal god, bearing as he does all the features of perishable existence? It was clear to the *mystai* that a person's idea of the gods did not come in the manner of other ideas, like those of things around one, which constrain one to represent them in a particular way. By contrast, people's ideas of divinity are unconstrained, even willful. Attention reveals an absence of control from the outer world on the idea of the gods. This brings us to a logical quandary. There is a suggestion that human beings create their own gods. Then the question arises of how ideas can be in a position to transcend physical reality at all. The *mystai* grappled seriously with these issues, and quite legitimately adopted a skeptical position. They scrutinized the public representations of the gods, and noted that in fact they resemble things encountered in the sense-world. Is it not the case that they are made by someone who selects and brings together features from the natural world? The primitive hunter makes a heaven where the gods engage in marvelous hunting. The Greeks populated their Olympus with divine personalities, but the originals belong to the real world of Greek cultural life.

The early Greek philosopher Xenophanes (575– 480 B.C.) exposed this situation with rude logic. The early philosophers were entirely dependent upon mysteriosophy. (We shall presently demonstrate this in detail, beginning with Heraclitus.) We may assume therefore that the views of Xenophanes are equally those of the *mystai*:

> But men believe that the gods must be born, and in shape
>   must be human,
> Wearing their clothes and their shape, like them in mind
>   and in voice.[16]
> But if the oxen and lions had hands and themselves were
>   like mankind
> Able to fashion a work of their hands, and a representation
> To show how the beasts would conceive of the gods they
>   believe in and worship,
> Then would the horses make gods assuming the visage of horses,
> The oxen would fashion an ox, and each separate species
> Would give them the form and the shape that each derived
>   from himself.[17]

Such insights might lead to total skepticism in face of the divine. The epic accounts of the gods would then be rejected. A person might acknowledge as real and compelling only the results of sense-perception.

But the *mystai* did not give in to mere doubt. The skeptics, they realized, resembled a plant rejecting its own colorful flower because it felt complete with its green leaves, and therefore regarding anything more as "illusory appearance!" Yet it was no longer possible for them to rest content with the fabricated gods of the public cults. A plant that could really think would realize that the same force that made its green leaves grow is destined to produce its colorful blossom. And it would not rest until it had understood that force and grasped it directly. Thus did the *mystai* look upon the public divinities, not denying them, not declaring them redundant, but understanding nonetheless that they were the product of human beings.

It is the forces of nature—the gods working in nature that are at the same time the creative forces in the mystes. And it is these, working internally, that engender the images of the gods. The *mystes'* aim is to grasp the god-making power,[18] which is something higher than the public divinities, and on a different plane. Xenophanes alludes to it as follows:

One God is greater than all, whether gods, whether Earth-
    dwelling mortals;
Unlike whatever can die is his form, and unlike theirs his
    thinking.[19]

And this was also the God of the Mysteries. He might be called a "hidden god."

For nowhere, the teaching asserted, could this God be found by one who trusted the senses alone. One's gaze could be turned toward the wide world, but find there nothing divine; exert one's intelligence to grasp the laws of coming-to-be and passing-away, and yet find no proof of the divine; intoxicate one's imagination with religious fervor to make images taken to be gods, only to undermine them once more with the realization that they are manufactured by human beings from the material of the sense-perceptible world. To comprehend merely the things of the world around, leads only to a denial of God. On the evidence of the senses, God does not exist any more than he does for the intellect that interprets sensory experience. God lies spellbound in the world. To find God requires a power from God himself. That power must actually be awakened in the candidate for initiation, it was stated in the ancient teaching.

So began the great cosmic drama in which the initiand's life was engulfed. The drama consisted of nothing less than the deliverance of the spellbound God.

Where is God? Such was the root-question of the soul of the *mystes*. God is not existence; but nature exists. In nature he must be discovered, where he lies in his enchanted grave. The *mystai* understood that "God is love" in a special higher sense. For God has gone to the utmost lengths of love. He has sacrificed himself in infinite love, poured himself out, dismembered himself into the manifold things of nature. They live, but he is not alive in them; he slumbers in them, but comes alive in human beings who are able to experience the life of God within themselves. But if human beings are to attain this *gnosis*, they must creatively release it within themselves. Looking into their own being, they find the divine as a hidden creative power, not yet released into existence. Within the soul lies the place where the spellbound God may return to life.

The soul is the mother who can receive the divine seed from nature. If the soul allows herself to be impregnated by nature she will give birth to the divine. Out of the marriage of the soul with nature the divine is born, no longer a "hidden God" but something manifest, alive—palpably alive and moving among humankind. In human beings the spirit has been released from enchantment; yet it is the offspring of the spellbound God. He is not the great God who was, and is, and shall be, yet he may in a certain sense be taken as a revelation of him. The Father remains at rest in the unseen. The Son is born to human beings out of their own souls.

Initiatory knowledge is thus an actual event in the cosmic process. It is the birth of a divine child—a process just as real as any natural process. The great secret of the *mystai* was precisely this, that they creatively release the divine child in themselves. First of all, however, they must be prepared so as to recognize it. The uninitiated know nothing of the Father of this divine child. The Father slumbers under a spell. The child seems to be born of a virgin, the soul giving birth to him without impregnation. Whereas all her other offspring are begotten by the world of the senses, and have a father who can be seen and touched in perceptible existence, the Son of God is uniquely begotten of the eternal, hidden Father himself.

2

THE MYSTERIES AND PRE-SOCRATIC PHILOSOPHY

Heraclitus of Ephesus

A WHOLE RANGE of considerations leads us to the conclusion that the
ideas of the Greek philosophers depended upon the same way of thinking as the knowledge of the *mystai*.[20] The great philosophers only
become comprehensible when we approach them with feelings gained
in the study of the Mysteries. With what veneration does Plato speak of
the "secret teachings" in the *Phaedo*:

> Perhaps these people who direct the religious initiations are close
> to the mark, and all the time there has been an allegorical mean-
> ing beneath their doctrine that he who enters the next world
> uninitiated and unenlightened shall lie in the mire, but he who
> arrives there purified and enlightened shall dwell among the gods.
> You know how the initiation practitioners say, "There are many
> who bear the sacred wands, but the Bacchoi are few." Well, in my
> opinion these latter are simply those who have lived the philo-
> sophic life in the right way; I myself have done my best in every
> way to join that company, leaving nothing undone which I could
> do to attain this end.[21]

One who speaks about initiation in this way must indeed have dedicated his search for wisdom to the way of thinking that was begotten by

the Mysteries. And there is no doubt that a brilliant light is shed on the words of eminent Greek philosophers when that illumination comes from the Mysteries.

The relationship of Heraclitus of Ephesus (c. 535–475 B.C.) to the Mysteries is immediately clear from a saying that is handed down about him, to the effect that his thoughts were "an impassable road." Anyone who was not an initiate would find in them nothing but "obscurity and darkness," but they were "brighter than the Sun" to those who approached them in the company of the *mystai*. It is said that he deposited his book in the temple of Artemis—indicating that he could be understood only by the initiated.[22] Heraclitus was called "the Obscure," because the key of the Mysteries alone cast light on his views.

In Heraclitus we witness a figure of the utmost earnestness in his approach to life. It is evident, when we reconstruct his thought in its essentials, that for him knowledge bore an inner meaning that words could gesture toward rather than directly express. It was out of some such realization that there arose his celebrated utterance "Everything is in flux." Plutarch explains its meaning as follows:

Heraclitus holds it impossible to go into the same river twice; no more can you grasp mortal being twice so as to hold it. So sharp and swift is change; it scatters and brings together again, not again, no nor afterward; even while it is being formed it fails, it approaches, and it is gone.[23]

Heraclitus' thought sees through the nature of transitory things, and he is constrained to lay bare the essence of transitoriness in the sharpest terms conceivable. Such a characterization can only have come about because he was contrasting the transitory with the eternal.

Nor could the characterization have been extended to include human beings unless Heraclitus had seen into their inner nature. Yet he does include humanity under this characterization:

Life and death, waking and sleeping, youth and age are the same. This changes into that, and that into this.[24]

The saying connotes full cognition of the illusory nature of the lower personality. Still more radical is his saying:

> Both life and death are to be found in our living, and in our dying.[25]

What does this signify if not that a preference for life over death shows that we are only judging from the standpoint of the transitory? Death is a passing away in order to make way for new life. The Eternal lives in the new life, however, just as it did in the old. Whether in the passing life or in death it is the same eternal reality. The knowledge of this enables people to face death or life with the same emotion. It is only when they have not been able to awaken the Eternal within them that they attribute to life any special significance.

The saying "All is in flux" can be repeated a thousand times, but it is vacuous unless it evokes this content of feeling. The acknowledgment of eternal becoming is worthless if it does not lift us above our attachment to transitoriness. Heraclitus indicates a renunciation of the sensual urge toward transitory enjoyments when he says:

> How can we claim that in ordinary life "we are?" We know that from the vantage point of the Eternal "we are, yet we are not."

Or according to another fragment:

> Hades and Dionysus are one.[26]

Dionysus, god of the joy of life, of sprouting and growing, celebrated in the Dionysiac festivals, is for Herclitus the same as Hades, god of death and destruction. The right perspective on the deficiencies and excellences of existence is granted only to those who see death in life and life in death, and in both the Eternal that transcends both life and death. The deficiencies then become justified, since in them too the Eternal is present. What they are from the standpoint of the limited, lower life turns out to be mere illusion:

What people want is not always what is best for them. It is illness that makes health sweet and good; hunger that makes food satisfying; toil that brings rest.[27]

The sea is the purest and impurest water. For fish it is drinkable and salutary, but for men it is undrinkable and harmful.[28]

The primary thrust of Heraclitus' thought here is not the perishability of earthly things, but rather the splendor and sublimity of the Eternal.

Heraclitus denounces Homer, Hesiod, and the learned men of his time. His aim was to demonstrate the dependence of their thought on transitory things. He wanted nothing to do with gods whose qualities derived from the perishable world; nor could he exalt a form of knowledge that sought for laws in the flux of becoming and passing away. For him, there is something eternal that announces itself from the midst of the perishable.

For this eternal he has a profound metaphor:

The connectedness of things is a tension between opposites, just as in a bow or a lyre.[29]

How much lies concealed in this metaphor! Tension in one direction is exactly balanced by that in the other, resulting in a unity and harmonization of forces. There are high and low notes; yet their contradictions are resolved in the musical scale. Heraclitus' thought extends the analogy to the spiritual world:

Immortals are mortal, mortals immortal; living the ones' death, dying the others' life.[30]

The primal fault of human beings was to fix their thought on changeable things, and so become estranged from the Eternal. Life became a danger to human beings, for all that happens to them comes from life. The sting of this danger is removed, however, once people cease to set an uncritical value on life. They regain their innocence. It is as though they abandon their serious attitude toward life and regain their childhood. The child plays with many things taken seriously by the adult. The Heraclitean thinker resembles the child. "Serious" issues lose their value when viewed from the eternal standpoint; life seems like play. "Eternity," says Heraclitus, "is a child at play. It is the reign of a child."[31] The beginning of error lies in taking too seriously a great deal that does not deserve it.

God has poured himself out into the world of things. To treat things seriously, apart from God, is to make them into "tombs of the divine." To disport ourselves with them like a child is to turn our serious intent toward rediscovering the underlying divinity, the God who sleeps spellbound in things.

There is a "burning" process, a consuming fire, in the vision of the Eternal when it acts upon our customary notions about the world. The spirit dissolves thoughts that derive from the senses, evaporates them, as a destructive fire. It is in this higher sense that Heraclitus considers fire to be the first principle of all things. Of course, it is primarily a straightforward explanation of physical phenomena. But it is easy to misunderstand Heraclitus if we debate his concept of fire, asking whether he meant by it sense-perceptible fire or whether it was not rather a metaphor for that eternal spirit which dissolves and reconstitutes all things. For that is to misconstrue his thought. He meant both, yet neither of these things.[32] For him, the spirit was vitally active in ordinary fire. The energy of physical fire works in a higher mode in the human soul, and in its crucible melts sense-perceptions down to draw forth from them the vision of the Eternal.

It is all too easy to misunderstand Heraclitus, for example when he makes war the father of things—but only of things, not of the Eternal. If there were not contradictions in the world, if there were not the most diverse conflicting tendencies, there would indeed be no becoming, no transitory things. Yet diffused through this contradictoriness and revealing itself there is not war, but connectedness. For though there is war in all things, for that very reason the mind of the wise should flame up over things and bring them into connectedness.

Here we come upon one of Heraclitus' great insights. It is from such a viewpoint that he develops his answer to the question of individual identity. For the human being is composed of the warring elements, into which the Divinity is poured out. In that divided state human beings find themselves. In addition, they become aware of the spirit, the *Logos*, which stems from the Eternal. For such people, however, the spirit comes to birth out of the clash of the elements. Indeed it is the spirit that brings the elements into equilibrium. Thus, in human beings nature transcends herself: all things are one, and it is the same power that made conflict and opposition that now, in its wisdom, reconciles them once again. Humanity lives in an eternal duality, in the contradiction between the flux of time and eternity. Through the eternal *Logos* human beings attain to individual existence, and must henceforward fashion their higher being. They live in a state of dependence, but also independence. They behold the *Logos*, but they can only participate in it according to the proportion of the mixture that the eternal *Logos* brought about in their case. Hence human beings derive their unique calling: to fashion the eternal out of the temporal.

It is the spirit, the *Logos*, that works in human beings. But it does so in a special way: out of the temporal. The uniqueness of the human soul consists in this: a temporal being is active and powerful in the same way as an eternal being, and can be likened both to a god and to a worm. Human beings are placed between god and animal. The active, powerful component of them is their *daimonic* part. It is what reaches out beyond their own self. As Heraclitus strikingly puts it, "A man's *daimon* is his destiny."[33]

Thus for Heraclitus something far more extensive than personality is to be found in humanity; personality is the vehicle of the "daimonic" self, which is not limited by the bounds of individual existence, for which personal dying and being-born have no significance.

What has the "daimonic" self to do with the transient form of the personality? The personality is no more than a mode of appearance for the *daimon*. The one who attains this insight is able to look forward and backward, beyond the individual self. The presence of the daimon within is a sign of one's own eternal self, and this one can no longer be limited to the role of informing one's own particular personality; the personality as such is simply one mode of appearance for the *daimon*, which cannot in principle be confined to a single personal manifestation. It has the power to inhabit many personalities and may shift from personality to personality. The important idea of reincarnation arises self-evidently from the premises of Heraclitus' thought. Or rather, not just the idea but the experience of reincarnation. The idea merely goes before the experience; for when one becomes aware of the "daimonic" self within, one does not find something guiltless and simple. The *daimon* possesses particular characteristics. Where do they originate? Why do I possess such predispositions?

It is because my *daimon* has been shaped by other personalities. And unless I am to assume that the task I have to accomplish in the *daimon* is fulfilled with my own personality, I am preparing another, future personality. Thus there is something that intervenes between myself and the cosmic "One-and-All," something that reaches out beyond myself, but which is not yet the Godhead as such; it is my *daimon* that occupies this intermediary position. Today is simply the outcome of yesterday, and likewise this life is the outcome of a previous one—and the foundation for the next. Earthly humanity looks back over numerous yesterdays and forward to many tomorrows, and the wise soul upon many former lives and lives to come. The ideas and abilities I developed in the past, I make use of now—and does not life show us that people rise over the horizon of existence already with the most varied capacities? Surely this diversity of gifts does not come from nowhere.

Natural science currently congratulates itself on expelling from the domain of biology any notion of the miraculous. David Friedrich Strauss mentions it as one of the great achievements of the modern age that a whole living being is no longer regarded as springing into being out of nothing by an act of creation. Its wholeness and completeness is understood as a result of evolution from more primitive forms. The developed form of an ape no longer seems miraculous when we realize that it has arisen through the gradual modification of ancestral forms, going back originally to primeval fishes. Is it not reasonable to assume the same conditions of evolution for the spirit as we know to prevail in nature? Does a more highly developed spirit emerge from the same conditions as a primitive one—say, Goethe and a Hottentot? It is no more possible for a fish to develop from the ancestors of an ape than for Goethe's spirit to issue from the same spiritual conditions as a savage; the spiritual ancestry is simply quite different. Spirit as well as a body

are in a process of evolving. Goethe's spirit has more stages of development behind it than that of the savage. If we understand the idea of
reincarnation in this evolutionary sense it need no longer be pronounced unscientific.[34]

It is a matter of knowing how to interpret the content of the soul and
of not leaping to the idea of the miraculous. I am able to write because
I learned how to do so; no one is able to sit down, having never held a
pen, and write. What then of those with the spark of "genius?" In some
cases, talent seems to border on the miraculous. Even here, the spark of
"genius" is something that has emerged, that has been learned. When it
shows itself in a personality, we may call it something "spiritual," with
the proviso that we understand that this "spiritual" was also originally
something learned, something acquired through former lives before it
appears as a spontaneous ability in a later one.

It was in this form alone that the concept of everlasting life hovered
before the inner eye of Heraclitus and the early Greek philosophers: they
never spoke of the survival of the empirical personality. Take, for example, the poem of Empedocles where he speaks of those who appeal to a
"miraculous" creation:

> Childish and ignorant they—they do not reach far with their
>   thinking
> Who suppose that what has not existed can ever come into
>   being,
> Or that something may die away and wholly vanish forever![35]

> It never can happen that being should arise from what never
>   existed,
> Impossible also that being should ever fade into nothing.
> For wherever being is shifted, it still will continue to be.[36]

> Never will any believe who are wise and interpret their thinking
> That only as long as they live what is called by the name here of
>   living
> Do men continue existing, receiving their joys and their
>   sorrows,

Or that before they were born or when they are dead they are
nothing.[37]

In the case of Empedocles, no question concerning the existence of an
eternal part in human nature is raised, but only the question concerning
its nature and how it can be cherished and cultivated. It is assumed from
the outset that humanity occupies a mediating position between the
earthly and the divine.

Empedocles' thought knows nothing of a God outside and transcending the world. Divinity lives in human beings—though in a human way.
It is the force in them which makes them strive to become more and
more divine. Thinking in this way, one can say with Empedocles:

When, set free from the body, released you rise to the ether,
You become divine, an immortal, escaped from the power of
    death.[38]

Looking at human life from this perspective, the prospect of initiation
into the magic circle of the Eternal becomes a real possibility. Forces that
would not unfold under purely natural conditions of life must certainly
be present in human beings, and if they remain untapped their life will
pass away unfructified. It was the role of the Mysteries, as it was the task
set for themselves by the Greek philosophers, to release those forces and
thereby to make humanity akin to the divine.

Thus we can understand Plato's assertion that those who enter the
next world uninitiated and unenlightened shall lie in the mire, but those
who arrive there purified and enlightened shall dwell among the gods.
There is a concept of immortality here whose meaning lies *within* the
cosmic order; everything whereby one strives to rouse the Eternal to life
within oneself is done to increase the existential value of the world—and
emphatically not to turn oneself into an inessential onlooker at things,
one who merely images in cognitive life an objective order that is wholly
independent of the mind. One's power of knowledge is a higher creative
force in nature. What flashes like spiritual lightning within one is a
divinity, hitherto subdued by magic spells; without one's act of cognition, the god would lie fallow and have to await another deliverer. Hence

human personality has a living meaning not just for itself and in itself, but for the world. From the Mystery point of view, life far transcends the limits of individual existence, making intelligible that glimpse of the Eternal conveyed by the verses of Pindar:

> Blessed is he who has seen these things, and then is laid in the hollow Earth. He knows life's end; he knows the beginning ordained by Zeus.[39]

We understand too those characteristic proud gestures of the philosophers such as Heraclitus, who could justly say that much had been revealed to them, since they attributed their knowledge not to the transitory self but to the immortal *daimon* within them.

It was a pride necessarily impressed also with the seal of humility and modesty. That is shown by the words: All knowledge of transitory things is as changeable as those things themselves. For Heraclitus, Eternity is a game. It could be called the most serious matter, were it not that the word "serious" has been worn out by its application to mundane experiences. "Eternal play" gives us a freedom from anxieties in life, which human beings could not have if they took transitory conditions "seriously."

Pythagoras of Samos

On the ground of the Mysteries there also came into being an understanding of the world that was nevertheless different from that of Heraclitus. It sprang up in the communities founded in southern Italy by Pythagoras (sixth century B.C.).[40] The Pythagoreans regarded numbers and geometrical forms, understood mathematically, as the foundation of reality. Aristotle says of the Pythagoreans:

> The so-called Pythagoreans led the field in mathematics and their studies convinced them that the principles of that science were of universal application. Numbers, of course, are by their very nature (i.e., as the simplest of mathematical objects) the first of those

principles; and the Pythagoreans thought they saw in numbers, rather than in fire or earth or water, many resemblances to things that exist or that come into being. Thus they identified with certain properties of number justice, soul or mind, opportunity, and indeed, almost everything. They also realized that the properties and ratios of musical scales depend on numbers. In a word, they saw that other things, in respect of the whole of their nature, resemble numbers, and that numbers are the primary elements of the whole of nature.[41]

The study of natural phenomena by means of the mathematical sciences must always lead to a kind of Pythagoreanism.

If a string of a specific length is struck, it generates a particular note (a pitch). Shorten the string in accordance with certain numerical ratios, and other notes will be produced. Thus pitch can be expressed in terms of numerical proportions. Physics likewise expresses relationships of color in numerical terms. And when two substances combine in a compound, it happens always in certain specific quantities that can be numerically expressed that the two substances come together. The Pythagoreans paid special attention to such instances of measure and proportion in nature. Geometrical figures play a similar role in nature, for instance in astronomy, in the application of mathematics to the heavenly bodies.

Central to the way of thinking developed by the Pythagoreans is the fact that one discovers numerical and geometrical laws purely through autonomous mental activity. And when one's gaze is turned toward the natural world, things obey the same laws that have been ascertained in one's own soul. If one grasps the idea of an ellipse, one knows the laws of the ellipse. The heavenly bodies are found to move according to such laws, which have been so ascertained.[42] A direct corollary of this is that the operations of the human soul are not an activity set apart from the rest of the world. What is expressed in those operations is the pervasive cosmic order. In the Pythagorean view, the senses reveal sense-perceptible phenomena, but not the harmonious ordering principles that regulate them. These harmonizing and ordering principles must rather be discovered in the human mind, if one wishes to see them at work in outer nature. The deeper meaning of the world, which is expressed as an eternal law of necessity, appears in the human soul and first achieves immediacy and actuality there.

The meaning of the cosmos is revealed in the soul. That meaning is not to be found in what we perceive by sight, hearing or touch; it must be brought up from the hidden depths of the soul, for it is there that the eternal laws lie hidden. To find the Eternal, one must go down into the psychic depths. In those depths is God—the eternal harmony of the cosmos.

Thus, the human psyche is not limited to the confines of the body, enclosed within the skin; for what come to birth in the human soul are the laws which govern the stars in their courses. The soul is not confined by our personal consciousness. In fact the personality is no more than the instrument through which the cosmic order manifests itself. The spirit of Pythagoras is caught by one of the Church Fathers, Gregory of Nyssa, who declared:

> We are told that human nature is a paltry thing, confined and small, whereas God is infinitely great. How then can what is paltry embrace the infinite? Yet who says this? Was the infinite God shut up within the flesh as in a vessel? Even in our own life, our own spiritual part is not shut in by the boundaries of the flesh. The physical substance of the body is subject to limitation in space, but the soul reaches out in thought to move freely through the whole creation.[43]

The soul does not coincide with the personality; its home is with infinity. From the Pythagorean point of view, it could only be foolishness to suppose that the power of the soul is exhausted in its personal expression. For the Pythagoreans as for Heraclitus, the point was the awakening within the personality of the Eternal.

Knowledge to them meant an encounter with the Eternal. They valued people exactly to the degree that they brought the Eternal to manifestation. Life in a Pythagorean community consisted of fostering in people that sense of an encounter with the Eternal, and their education was designed to bring the members to such an experience. Their education was thus a philosophical initiation; the Pythagoreans could well say that in their mode of life they were striving for a goal similar to that of the Mystery cults.

3

PLATONIC MYSTERIES

The Mysteries of Immortality

T HE SIGNIFICANCE of the Mysteries for the intellectual life of the ancient Greeks can be appreciated when we examine the case of Plato's idea of the world. There is in fact only one way of making Plato fully intelligible, and that is to place him in the light that streams from the Mysteries. According to his later followers, the Neoplatonists, he taught an esoteric doctrine to those he admitted as worthy to receive it, and placed them under a "seal of secrecy." His teaching was regarded as secret in the same way that mysteriosophy was secret.[44]

For our purposes it matters little whether or not the Seventh Letter attributed to Plato is genuine; it has been disputed—he, or someone else, expressed in the Letter the essentials of Plato's attitude to the world. Take the following passage from the Letter:

> But this much at any rate I can affirm about any present or future writers who pretend to knowledge of the matters with which I concern myself, whether they claim to have been taught by me or by a third party or to have discovered the truth for themselves; in my judgment it is impossible that they should have any understanding of the subject. No treatise by me concerning it exists or ever will exist. It is not something that can be put into words like other branches of learning; only after long partnership in a common life

devoted to this very thing does truth flash upon the soul like a flame kindled by a leaping spark, and once it is born there it nourishes itself thereafter.[45]

The words might be taken to signify merely the inadequacy of verbal expression, a personal failing on the part of the writer, if we did not detect in them a Mystery-sense. Something that cannot and never will be put into words by Plato must refer to a matter about which all writing would be futile. It must mean a feeling, a sense of experience that cannot readily be communicated, but can be gained only by "long partnership in a common life." This indicates a special process of education given by Plato to the elect, who caught the fire that flashed from his words, whereas others received only ideas.

Interpreting Plato's dialogues depends very much on the manner of approach we adopt. Everyone, according to his or her spiritual condition, will find in them either more or less significance. What took place between Plato and his pupils was much more than the imparting of the words in their literal meaning. Studying with him meant living in the atmosphere of a Mystery. The words possessed overtones and resonances that could only be heard, however, in the atmosphere of the Mystery; outside it, they died away unheard.

The personality who stands at the center of the world we encounter in Plato's dialogues is Socrates. We need not concern ourselves here with the actual, historical Socrates, only with the figure as he is presented by Plato. Through his death, as a martyr to truth, Socrates assumes a kind of saintliness. He died in the unique manner of an initiate, for whom death is simply another phase of life. He encountered death just as he would any other circumstance, and such was his bearing that even among his friends the usual feelings connected with death were not stirred up. In the dialogue on the immortality of the soul, Phaedo says:

My own feelings at the time were quite extraordinary. It never occurred to me to feel sorry for him, as you might have expected me to feel at the deathbed of a very dear friend. The Master seemed quite happy, Echecrates, both in his manner and in what he said; he met his death so fearlessly and nobly. I could not help feeling that even on his way to the other world he would be under the providence of God, and that when he arrived there all would be well with him, if it ever has been so with anybody. So I felt no sorrow at all, as you might have expected on such a solemn occasion. At the same time I felt no pleasure at being occupied in our usual philosophical discussions—that was the form our conversation took; I felt an absolutely incomprehensible emotion, a sort of curious blend of pleasure and pain combined, as my mind took it in that in a little while my friend was going to die.[46]

The dying Socrates discourses to his pupils on the theme of immortality. As one who has realized the worthlessness of life, he furnishes a kind of proof utterly distinct from any logical, rational arguments. It seems as if it were not a man speaking—the man who is passing away— but eternal truth itself which had taken up its abode in a transitory personality. The atmosphere where truth can resound seems to be found where temporal reality dissolves into nothingness.

We hear nothing in the way of logical proofs of immortality. The entire discourse is designed to conduct his friends to a vision of the eternal. At that point they will require no proofs. What would be the point of proving that a rose is red to someone who can see it? What would be the point of proving the eternity of spirit to one whose eyes are open to the spirit?

Socrates directs our attention to concrete events, actual experiences— above all to the experience of wisdom, and the fundamental quality of the struggle for wisdom: the struggle to free oneself from the superficial impressions of the senses, and to find the spirit within the world of the senses. Is that not in fact something equivalent to a kind of death? So at any rate thinks Socrates:

Those who really apply themselves in the right way to philosophy are directly and of their own accord preparing themselves for dying and death, even if ordinary people seem not to realize it. If this is true, and they have actually been looking forward to death all their lives, it would of course be absurd to be troubled when the thing comes for which they have so long been preparing and looking forward.[47]

And he reinforces this by asking one of his friends:

Do you think that it is right for a philosopher to concern himself with the so-called pleasures connected with food and drink?... What about sexual pleasures?... And what about the other attentions that we pay to our bodies? Do you think that a philosopher attaches any importance to them? I mean things like providing himself with smart clothes and shoes and other bodily ornaments; do you think that he values them or despises them — insofar as there is no real necessity for him to go in for that sort of thing?... Is it not your opinion in general that a man of this kind is not concerned with the body, but keeps his attention directed as much as he can away from it and toward the soul?... In this, then—in despising the body and avoiding it, and endeavoring to become independent—the philosopher's soul is ahead of all the rest.[48]

In conclusion, says Socrates, the pursuit of wisdom has this much in common with dying, that it leads a person away from the body.

But to what does it lead? To the spiritual. Socrates takes up the theme:

Now take the acquisition of knowledge; is the body a hindrance or not, if one takes it into partnership to share an investigation? What I mean is this: is there any certainty in human sight and hearing, or is it true, as the poets are always dinning into our ears, that we neither hear nor see anything accurately?... Then when is it that the soul attains to truth? When it tries to investigate anything with the help of the body, it is obviously led astray.[49]

Everything we perceive with the help of bodily organs is subject to generation and decay: that is the very reason we are deluded. It is only the deeper insight into things furnished by reason that enables us to participate in their timeless truth. Hence the senses do not show the eternal to us in its real Form, and if we trust them uncritically they become delusive. They cease to be so when we confront them with the evidences of rational insight, and put their results to the test of insight derived from thought.

Now, how would it be possible for reason to pass judgment on the things of sense if there were not within it something that transcended sense perception? If that is so, then, our faculty of distinguishing true things from false must be set in opposition to our bodily senses and is not subject to the conditions that bind them. In particular it cannot be subject to the law of coming-to-be and passing-away, for it contains in it the True, which has no yesterday or today, and unlike the things of sense cannot fluctuate from one day to another. The True must itself be eternal. And insofar as the philosopher turns away from the perishable objects of sense and turns toward the True, he or she enters the domain of the eternal. And if we immerse ourselves totally in the spirit, we are living totally in the True. The sense-world is simply no longer there for us in its merely sensible form. Socrates says:

> Don't you think that the person who is likely to succeed in this attempt most perfectly is the one who approaches each object, as far as possible, with the unaided intellect, without taking account of any sense of sight in his thinking, or dragging any other sense into his reckoning—the man who pursues truth by applying his pure and unadulterated thought to the pure and unadulterated object, cutting himself off as much as possible from his eyes and ears and virtually all the rest of his body, as an impediment which by its presence prevents the soul from attaining to truth and clear thinking?[50]

And a little later:

> Is not what we call death a freeing and separation of soul from body?... And the desire to free the soul is found chiefly, or rather only, in the true philosopher; in fact the philosopher's occupation consists precisely in the freeing and separation of soul from body.... Well then, as I said at the beginning, if a man has trained himself throughout his life to life in a state as close as possible to death, would it not be ridiculous for him to be distressed when death comes to him?... Then it is a fact, Simmias, that true philosophers make dying their profession, and that to them of all men, death is least alarming.[51]

All higher moral action springs also, according to Socrates, from the liberation of the soul from the body. Anyone who just follows the promptings of the body is not behaving morally. Socrates asks:

> Who is that we call valiant? The man who, rather than following the body, follows the dictates of the spirit, even when these imperil the body. And who shows self-control? Is it not called self-control when we see someone not being carried away by the desires, but preserving a decent indifference toward them; is not this appropriate only to those who regard the body with the greatest indifference and spend their lives in philosophy?[52]

And Socrates treats all the other virtues in like manner.

He then goes on to characterize intellectual insight itself. What is it that we call "knowing" as such? Without doubt, knowing is attained by the forming of judgments: I form a judgment about some object before me, for example, that the thing in front of me is a tree. Now, how do I reach that assertion? Only by knowing already what a tree is, and recollecting my idea of a tree. A tree is a perceptible thing; thus when I recollect a tree, I am recalling at the same time a perceptible object, and in saying that something is a tree I am likening it to other things that have formerly been objects of my perception and that I know are trees. In this sense knowledge is dependent on the power of recollection.

Recollection permits me to compare with one another the multiplicity of perceptible things; but this does not explain the sum total of my knowledge. Suppose I see two things that are alike, and form the judgment "These things are alike." But in actuality no two things are exactly alike, only alike in certain particular ways. The idea of likeness therefore cannot arise from perceived actuality, but is independent of it. It comes to my aid in forming a judgment, just as recollection helps toward judgment, toward knowledge when, in the case of a tree, I recall other trees. In the case of two things related in particular ways, I recollect the idea of likeness. Ideas thus come before me in the same way as recollections but without being dependent on perceived actuality. All kinds of knowledge that are not derived from sense-perception rely on such ideas. The field of mathematics consists entirely of such ideas. It would be a poor geometrician who could only deal mathematically with things one can see or touch! In this way we have thoughts that are not derived from transitory outer nature but arise purely in a spiritual way. And it is these very ideas that show all the marks of timeless truth. The content of mathematics will be eternally valid, even if the universe were to go to pieces tomorrow and a completely new world arise. The conditions of a new world order might be such as to render current mathematical ideas inapplicable; but they would remain intrinsically valid in themselves.

When the soul withdraws into itself, only then is it able to bring forth such eternal ideas.[53] Therefore the soul is akin to the True, the Eternal, not to the transitoriness and appearance of the sense-world. Hence Socrates asserts:

> But when the soul investigates by itself, it passes into the realm of the pure and everlasting and immortal and changeless; and being of a kindred nature, when it is once independent and free from interference, consorts with it always and strays no longer, but remains, in that realm of the absolute, constant and invariable, through contact with beings of the same nature. And this condition of the soul we call Wisdom.... Now, see whether this is our conclusion from all that we have said. The soul is most like that which is divine, immortal, intelligible, uniform, indissoluble, and ever self-consistent and invariable; whereas body is most like that which is human, mortal, multiform, unintelligible, dissoluble, and never self-consistent.... Very well, if this is the soul's condition, then it departs at death to that place which is, like itself, invisible, divine, immortal, and wise; where, on its arrival, happiness awaits it, and release from uncertainty and folly, from fears and uncontrolled desires, and all other human evils; and where (as they say of the initiates in the Mysteries) it really spends the rest of time with God.[54]

It is not the aim here to summarize all the ways in which Socrates leads his friends to the Eternal. For the spirit of all of them is the same: all point to the difference between the path of the changeable impressions of the senses and that of the mind alone with itself. It is to the inherent character of the spiritual that Socrates points his hearers. If they can find this out, they will see for themselves with the inner eye that it is eternal.

The dying Socrates does not give a proof of immortality. He simply lays bare the nature of the soul. And then it transpires that coming-to-be and passing-away, birth and death, have nothing to do with the essential soul. This has its being in the True; and the True cannot come into existence nor pass away. The soul and becoming can have no more to do with one another than an odd number with an even number. But death belongs to the process of becoming. Hence the soul can have nothing to do with death. How can we do other than admit that the immortal can as little participate in mortality as the even in the odd? And, continues Socrates:

> If what is immortal is also imperishable, it is impossible that at the approach of death soul should cease to be. It follows from what we have already said that it cannot admit death, or be dead; just as we said that three cannot be even, or any odd number.[55]

Surveying the whole course of the dialogue conducted by Socrates, which leads to a perception of the Eternal in human individual existence, his hearers take up his ideas; they search within themselves for something that will answer in the affirmative to those ideas from their own experience; they make objections as these occur to them. But what has happened by the end of the dialogue? They have discovered something within themselves that they did not formerly possess. They have not just acquired abstract knowledge, but have gone through a process, and something has stirred to life in them that was not previously there. Is that not comparable to an initiation? Is that not the reason why Plato chooses to set forth his philosophy in dialogue form? It is a literary Mystery, exactly analogous to the processes that took place at the centers of initiation.

There are many places in his writings where Plato testifies to this in his own words. Plato's aim as a teacher of philosophy was to be a hierophant, insofar as this was possible in the philosophical medium. Clearly Plato realized the agreement of his methods with those of the Mysteries, and regards them as successful precisely when they lead to the goals that the *mystai* too would reach. Thus he says in the *Timaeus*:

Of course everyone with the least sense always calls on God at the beginning of any undertaking, small or great. So surely, if we are not quite crazy, as we embark on our account of how the universe began, or perhaps had no beginning, we must pray to all the gods and goddesses that what we say will be pleasing to them first, and then to ourselves.[56]

Plato promises those who follow such a course that "some protecting deity will see us safely through a strange and unusual argument and bring us to a likely conclusion."[57]

The Mystery of Creation

It is in the *Timaeus* above all that the Platonic worldview stands revealed in its character of a Mystery. From the very beginning of the dialogue the conversation concerns an "initiation"; Solon is "initiated" into the Mysteries of creation and into the mythological traditions which use pictures to symbolize eternal truth by an Egyptian priest. "There have been, and will be many different calamities to destroy mankind," the priest tells Solon:

The greatest of them by fire and water, lesser ones by countless other means. Your own story of how Phaethon, child of the Sun, harnessed his father's chariot, but was unable to guide it along his father's course, and so burnt up things on the Earth, and was himself destroyed by a thunderbolt, is a mythical version of the truth that there is at long intervals a variation in the course of the heavenly bodies and a consequent widespread destruction by fire of things on the Earth.[58]

This passage in the *Timaeus* demonstrates the attitude of the initiates toward the well-known myths. They see through to the truth that is veiled behind their imagery.

As the cosmogonic drama unfolds in the *Timaeus*, we are led by following the traces that point back to the origin of the world to an intimation of the primordial power, out of which everything came into existence:

For to discover the maker and Father of this universe is indeed a hard task, and having found him it would be impossible to tell everyone about him.[59]

The *mystai* understand the force of that word "impossible." It points toward the inner drama of the Godhead. For them, God is not revealed in the materially comprehensible world where he is manifest only as nature, in which he lies under a spell. He can be apprehended, as was taught in the Mysteries, only by one who awakens the divine within. That is why he cannot be made intelligible to everyone.

But even to one who draws near to him, he does not appear in his own nature. This too is explained in the *Timaeus*.

The Father made the universe out of the world-body and world-soul. He mixed the elements, in harmony and perfect proportion—elements that he himself brought into being by pouring himself out, giving up his separate existence. Thus he produced the world-body. And stretched out upon it, in the form of a cross, is the world-soul, the divine presence in the world. It suffers death on this cross so that the world can exist. And Plato therefore calls nature the "tomb" of the divine—not however a tomb in which lies something dead, but the tomb where lies the Eternal, for which death is nothing but the opportunity to demonstrate the omnipotence of life! Hence the right way to look upon nature is for humanity to undertake the rescue of the crucified world-soul, which should rise, released from death, released from the spell that binds it. And where can this happen except in the soul of an initiate? Thus wisdom takes on its proper meaning in a cosmic setting: knowledge is the resurrection, the liberation of God.

In the *Timaeus* the world is presented developing out of the imperfect into the perfect. The concept is one of progressive process, of beings developing; and in this process God reveals himself. Coming-into-being is the resurrection of God from the "tomb." And within this development the human being appears. Plato demonstrates that with the appearance of the human being something unique enters in. Now of course for Plato the whole world is itself a divine being, and humanity is not more divine than other beings. But in other beings God is present only in a hidden manner, in humanity God is manifest. The *Timaeus* concludes with the words:

> We can now claim that our account of the universe is complete. For our world has now received its full complement of living creatures, mortal and immortal; it is a visible living creature; it contains all creatures that are visible and is itself an image of the intelligible; and it has thus become a visible god, supreme in greatness and excellence, beauty, and perfection, a single, uniquely created heaven.[60]

But this single and uniquely created world would not be perfect if it did not contain among its images the image of its Creator himself. And that image can arise only from the human soul; it is not the Father himself, but the Son, the living child of God in the soul who is of like nature with the Father, to whom humanity can give birth.

The expression "Son of God" is used in this context by Philo of Alexandria, who was called a Plato *redivivus*. It designates the Wisdom that lives in the soul and is born of human beings, having as its content the reason immanent in the world; while this world-reason, *Logos*, figures as the book in which "every permanent characteristic of the world is recorded and inscribed."[61] Or elsewhere it is the "Son of God":

> Following the ways of the Father, he fashions material objects after his contemplation of their eternal Forms.[62]

Philo anticipates the language applied to Christ when he speaks of this *Logos* from a platonizing viewpoint:

> As God is the first and only king of the universe, the way to him is rightly called the "royal road." Consider this road as philosophy... the road taken by the ancient company of ascetics, who turned away from the entangling fascination of pleasure and devoted themselves to a noble and earnest cultivation of the beautiful. The Law names this royal road, which we call true philosophy, the Word and Spirit of God.[63]

To travel this road is for Philo equivalent to an initiation in the Mysteries. On it he will encounter the *Logos*, which is for him the "Son of God":

> I do not shrink from relating what has happened to me innumerable times. Often when I wished to put my philosophical thoughts in writing in my accustomed way, and saw quite clearly what was to be set down, I found my mind barren and rigid, so that I was obliged to give up without having accomplished anything, and seemed to be beset with idle fancies. At the same time I marveled at the power of the reality of thought, with which it rests to open and close the womb of the human soul. At other times, however, I would begin empty and arrive, without any trouble, at fullness. Thoughts came flying like snow-flakes or grains of corn invisibly from above, and it was as though divine power took hold of me and inspired me, so that I did not know where I was, who was with me, who I was, or what I was saying or writing; for then a flow of ideas was given me, a delightful clearness, keen insight, and lucid mastery of material, as if the inner eye were now able to see everything with the greatest clarity.[64]

Anyone can see from the mode of presentation of this "road" that it leads to the consciousness, when the *Logos* is vitally active within, of flowing in one current with the divine. That is clear too in the following passage:

> When the spirit, moved by love, takes its flight into the holy of holies, soaring joyfully on divine wings, it forgets everything else and itself. It holds to and is filled only with the Power of which it is the follower and servant, and to this it offers the incense of the most sacred and chaste virtue.[65]

For Philo there are only two alternatives—to follow the way of the senses (perception and intellect), in which case one is confined in the limits of oneself and draws back from the cosmos; or to become aware of the universal Power and so, within one's own self, experience the Eternal:

He who wishes to escape from God falls into his own hands. For there are two things to be considered: the universal spirit, which is God, and one's own spirit. The latter flees to and takes refuge in the universal spirit, for one who goes out beyond his own spirit says to himself that it is nothing, and relates everything to God; but one who turns away from God discards him as First Cause, and makes himself the cause of everything that happens.[66]

In the Platonic worldview, knowledge possesses an intrinsically religious character. It serves to bring the act of knowing into connection with the highest aspirations of human feeling—and only when it fulfills human desire completely does it rank, for Plato, as certain knowledge. It is then no longer representational or picture-making knowledge: it is an achieved reality of life.

Knowledge according to Plato is a higher humanity within the external human form, the essence, of whom the personal self is nothing more than a secondary image. Within human beings themselves is born the transcendent, "macrocosmic Man." And this brings us once more into the terrain of the Mystery-cults and their secret teachings, given a new form of expression in the Platonic philosophy. We know of this secret doctrine from the report of Hippolytus, one of the Church Fathers. "This is the great and ineffable Mystery of the Samothracians," he says, referring to the guardians of a particular Mystery-cult:

> Only the initiates are permitted to know it. For in their Mysteries the Samothracians have the explicit tradition of a primordial, macrocosmic Man (Adam).[67]

The Mystery of Love

It is also as an "initiation" that we have to interpret the *Symposium*—the platonic "Dialogue on Love."

Love figures here as the herald of wisdom. We have seen that wisdom is the eternal *Logos*, the "Son" of the eternal world-Father. To this *Logos* love stands in the position of a Mother. Before even so much as a spark of the light of wisdom can be struck in the human soul, there must be present in it an obscure urge or longing for the divine. Unconsciously it must draw one in the direction of what will subsequently, when it is raised into consciousness, constitute one's highest bliss. Heraclitus apprehended the *daimon* in human beings; in Plato this is connected with the idea of love.

The *Symposium* comprises speeches on love from men of the most diverse social standing and attitudes to life: ordinary people, politicians, and intellectuals are represented, from the comic poet Aristophanes to the tragic poet Agathon. In keeping with their different places in life, they all have different experiences and views of love. And from the way they express themselves, the level at which their *daimon* stands is made manifest. The role of love is to draw one being to another. The diversity of "the many" into which the unified Godhead has poured itself out strives through love to return to unity and connectedness. Thus love is tinged with divinity. To understand it, one must also participate in the divine.

After people of several stages of maturity have expounded their notions of love, Socrates takes up the thread of the discourse and treats of love from the viewpoint of the knower. Love he denies to be a god, though it is something that leads humanity toward God. But love—*eros*—is not a divinity; for God is perfection, and contains the idea of the Beautiful and the Good, whereas *eros* is only a longing for the Beautiful and the Good. It occupies an intermediate position between humanity and God. It is a *daimon*, a being whose nature stands between the earthly and the heavenly.

It is a significant point that Socrates does not purport to give his own ideas on the subject of love, but only claims to recount what he received as a revelation from a woman; it is from the mantic art (divination) that he derives his conception of love. The priestess Diotima woke within Socrates the daimonic power that would lead him to the world of the divine. It was she who "initiated" him, as we are told in a highly revealing passage of the *Symposium*. And now the question cannot be avoided: Who is this "wise woman" who woke the *daimon* in Socrates? She must certainly be more than a poetic fiction. No actual "wise woman" on the perceptible plane could have woken the *daimon* in his soul, however, since the power of awakening lies in the soul itself. It is in Socrates' own soul in fact that we must look for this "wise woman." At the same time there must be some reason why the one who raises the *daimon* in the soul into full reality should take on external, actual existence. It is because this power does not work as do the forces that are inherent in and native to the life of the soul itself. Evidently it is the soul-force that precedes the coming of wisdom that Socrates represents with the figure of a "wise woman": the Mother-principle, which gives birth to Wisdom, the "Son of God," the *Logos*.

The "Woman" stands for the power that is active unconsciously in the soul, that brings about the raising into consciousness of the divine element in humanity. The soul, which has not yet found wisdom, is the "mother" of that experience of divinization. Here we come to one of the central conceptions of Mystery-teaching, which acknowledges the human soul as the mother of the god, leading human beings unconsciously and with the inevitability of a natural force to their union with the divine.[68]

All this casts light on the Mystery-interpretation of Greek myths. According to this, as we have seen, the world of the gods is something generated in the human soul, and the gods we behold are images we have ourselves created. But then we must win through to a further understanding. We must be able to take the divine creative power that is present in ourselves—from which the images of the gods are derived—and form that power itself into divine images, so that behind the world of the gods we shape an image of the divine Mother. This is none other than the archetypal power of the human soul.

Thus mythology places the goddesses alongside the male gods. Our interpretation of this may be exemplified in a study of the myths about Dionysus.

Dionysus is the son of Zeus and a mortal mother, Semele. But the mother is killed by lightning. Zeus, however, snatches the still unformed child and allows it to grow within his own thigh where it lies concealed. Hera, the mother of the gods, stirs up the enmity of the Titans against Dionysus, and they tear the child limb from limb. But Pallas Athene rescues the still-beating heart and brings it to Zeus. Out of it he engenders his son for a second time.[69]

The myth can be seen as representing a psychological process of an extremely inward character. Let us interpret it after the fashion of the Egyptian priest who instructed Solon in the nature of myths.

It is related that Dionysus was born as the son of God and a mortal mother, was dismembered and then reborn. This has a fantastic ring to it, but the truth contained in the story is the birth of the divine and its subsequent destiny in individual human souls. The divine is united with the soul, which is still subject to time and earthly conditions; and as soon as the god, the Dionysiac spirit, stirs within the soul, it experiences a longing for its real spiritual form. However, consciousness—again imaged as a female deity, Hera—appears and becomes jealous of the offspring from a qualitatively higher consciousness. She rouses the lower aspects of human nature—the Titans—and the unformed divine child is dismembered. The divine knowledge exists in humanity, but "dismembered" by the understanding that is bound to the senses. If on the other hand there is within the individual sufficient higher wisdom, this latter nurses and cherishes the unformed child until it is born again as a second son of God—Dionysus. And thus sense-derived understanding, the dismembered divine force in human beings, is reborn as the undivided wisdom that is identical with the *Logos*. It is the son of God and a mortal mother, who is the transitory human soul aspiring unconsciously after the divine.

We are still far removed from the spiritual reality that is played out in the myth if we recognize in it only psychological processes, and pictures of psychological events, at that. This spiritual reality is not something that the soul experiences as confined to itself. It is rather released from itself to take part in a cosmic event. The reality of the myths is enacted not within but outside the soul.

Platonic philosophy is closely related to Greek myth, just as mysteriosophy is close to myth. Once begotten, the gods were the objects of external religious devotion. The story of their genesis was kept as a secret belonging to the Mysteries. We can hardly be surprised that it was considered dangerous to betray the Mysteries, for it meant betraying the way the public divinities came into being. To those who understand it rightly this is salutary knowledge, but destructive to those who do not.

4

MYTH AND MYSTERIOSOPHY

The Structures of Myth

THE POWERS AND BEINGS that the initiates in the ancient Mysteries sought to find within themselves remain unknown to anyone whose horizon is bounded by received ideas. For the *mystai* did not hold back from the great question. They inquired into their own spiritual nature and into powers and laws beyond those of lower, natural existence.

In our ordinary life of thought based on the senses and what may be inferred from them, we worship gods of our own making, or—when we find this out, are driven to disclaim them. The *mystai*, however are aware of their god-making, and they understand the reasons why they do so. They have won through, as we should say, to the underlying laws that govern the process of making gods.[70] It is rather as if a plant were suddenly to become aware of the laws that determine its own growth and development. Up to now it has developed in serene unconsciousness, but once it knows the laws of its own being, it necessarily changes fundamentally its whole relationship to itself. The poet's celebration of the plant-world, the scientist's investigation of botanical principles would now come before it as a conscious ideal. Such is the case of the *mystai* in their own sphere with regard to the laws and the forces active within them. They have attained a *gnosis*, and consciously create something divine, something beyond themselves.

The initiates looked upon the well-known gods and myths, created by the people in an activity transcending the given world of nature, in the same way. They aspired to understand the laws governing the world of gods and myths. Where they found the figure of some divinity worshipped by the people, or a myth being told, they looked for a higher truth.[71] Let us take an example.

The Athenians had been forced by King Minos of Crete to deliver up to him every eight years seven boys and seven maidens. These were thrown to the Minotaur, a horrible monster, to be devoured. When it came to the third time for the mournful tribute to be paid, Theseus, the King's son, went to Crete as part of the tribute. On his arrival in Crete, King Minos' daughter Ariadne came to his aid. The Minotaur was kept in the Labyrinth, a maze from which no one who entered it could ever find the way out. Now Theseus wished to deliver his native city from such a shameful tribute, and so had to be cast into the Labyrinth, as if to become the monster's prey, and then kill the Minotaur. This task he undertook, overcame the formidable enemy, and then regained the open air; for Ariadne had given him a ball of thread to help him.

The *mystai* wanted to understand how the creative human mind came to invent such a story. They studied the creative spirit in order to understand it, rather as a botanist studies plants. They were looking for a truth, an implicit wisdom, in what the myth expressed in popular form. Sallust adopts the standpoint of the Mysteries when he characterizes "myth" in such terms:

> The universe itself can be called a myth, since bodies and material objects are apparent in it, while souls and intellects are concealed. Furthermore, to wish to teach all men the truth about the gods causes the foolish to despise—because they cannot learn—and the good to be slothful; whereas to conceal the truth by myths prevents the former from despising philosophy and compels the latter to study it.[72]

The *mystai* were aware of adding something to the myth that did not exist in the consciousness of the ordinary people when they sought for its "implicit truth." They placed themselves in the position of a scientist studying a plant. They were putting into words something totally foreign to the mythological consciousness, yet they looked upon it as the deeper truth, expressed in symbols through the myth; thus we confront our own sensual nature as though it were a fierce monster. The fruits of our personal development fall as sacrifices to it, and it continues to devour us until the hero, the conqueror (Theseus) awakens in us. And it is through knowledge that we are able to slay the enemy—spinning the thread by means of which we find the way out of the labyrinth of our sensual nature. Human knowledge itself is the mystery expressed in this story of the conquering of sensuality. This is the "secret" known to the *mystai*.

The Mystery-interpretation points to a psychological power in us. It is not a power of which we are normally aware; nevertheless it is active within us, generating the myth. And the myth has the same structure as the truth of the Mysteries. It is in this way that the truth finds its symbol in the myth.

What, then, do we find in myths? They are the expression of a creative spirit, of the unconscious activity of the soul. The soul's creative work is determined by specific laws; it must be active in a particular way if it is to create something with a meaning beyond itself. On the mythological level it works with images. But the way these images are structured follows psychological laws. Hence one could add that when the soul develops beyond the mythological stage of consciousness to deeper forms of truth, these nevertheless bear the imprint of the same power that generated the myths.[73]

The relationship between mythical imagery as a form of representation and higher, philosophical knowledge is thus stated by Plotinus from the standpoint of the Neoplatonic school, in connection with the guardians of priestly wisdom in Egypt:

Whether as a result of rigorous investigations, or instinctively, in imparting their wisdom, the wise men of the Egyptians do not expound their teaching and precepts by means of written signs, which are imitations of voice and speech. Instead they draw pictures; and in their temple engravings they illustrate the thought that goes with each particular thing, so that every picture is an object which embodies knowledge and wisdom as a totality, without any analysis or discussion. Only afterwards is the content of the picture elicited verbally, and it is explained why it is so and not otherwise.[74]

The best place to examine the relation of mythical narratives to the nature of the Mysteries is in the outlook of those thinkers who acknowledge a harmony between their way of representing the world and the Mystery-process. That harmony is most fully documented in the case of Plato.

From Myth to Philosophy

Plato's interpretation of myths, and use of them in his teaching, may be regarded as a model case. Thus in the *Phaedrus*, or dialogue on the nature of the soul, we are introduced to the myth of Boreas. This is the god whose presence was felt in the blustering north wind. He caught sight one day of the beautiful Oreithyia, who was the daughter of Erechtheus, king of Attica, as she was out plucking flowers with her playmates. He was seized with love for her, carried her off, and brought her to his cave. Through his mouthpiece in the dialogue, Socrates, Plato rejects the purely rationalistic interpretation of the myth, according to which the story is a poetic expression of purely natural, physical happenings—the stormwind caught the princess and blew her over the edge of the cliff. Socrates comments:

> Such explanations are too ingenious and labored, it seems to me, and I don't altogether envy the man who devotes himself to this sort of work, if only because when he has finished with Oreithyia, he must go on to put into proper shape ... all the other such monsters of mythology.... A skeptic who proposes to force each one of them into a plausible shape with the aid of a sort of rough ingenuity will need a great deal of leisure.... So I let these things alone and acquiesce in the popular attitude toward them; as I've already said, I make myself, rather than them, the object of my investigations, and I try to discover whether I am a more complicated and puffed-up sort of creature than Typhon, or whether I am a more gentle and simpler creature, endowed by heaven with a nature altogether less typhonic.[75]

Thus we see that Plato is no enthusiast for the intellectual and rationalistic interpretation of myth, and this must be taken into account when we examine his own use of myths to express his own views.

Plato has recourse to myth when he comes to speak of the life of the soul. At that juncture, where he leaves the transitory world to seek after the eternal core of the soul, concepts deriving from the senses and from the thinking based upon them no longer apply. The *Phaedrus* is devoted to the theme of the eternal in the soul, and the soul is described as a chariot with two horses, each many-winged, and a charioteer. One of the horses is docile and intelligent, the other headstrong and wild. When the chariot meets with an obstacle on its path, the head-strong beast seizes the chance of impeding the reliable one and defying the charioteer. And when the chariot reaches the point of ascending in the wake of the gods up the celestial steep, the intractable horse throws it into confusion. Whether the chariot can surmount these difficulties and attain to the realm of the supersensible depends on their relative strengths and so whether the good horse can gain the mastery. But the soul can never raise itself to the divine without some sort of a struggle. Some souls rise higher in their pursuit of the eternal vision, others less high.

Those souls that have attained the transcendent vision are kept safe until the next cycle, while those who have seen nothing but were thwarted by the unruly horse must enter upon a new cycle and try again. The cycles here designate the several incarnations of the soul—one cycle standing for its life as a particular personality. The unruly horse and the intelligent horse stand for the lower and the higher aspects of human nature; the charioteer for the soul, which aspires to "divinization" as in the Mysteries. Plato appeals to the power of myth when he wants to describe the course of the eternal soul through its manifold transformations. And elsewhere in the Platonic canon myth is used to render intelligible through symbolic stories the non-sensory, inner reality of human existence.[76]

In the light of this principle it is worth considering the Egyptian Mystery of Osiris.

In Osiris we have a figure who gradually became one of the most important gods of the country. A significant cycle of myths grew up concerning Osiris and his consort Isis. According to the story, Osiris was the son of the Sun-god; he had a brother, Typhon (Set), and a sister, Isis. Osiris married his sister and with her reigned over Egypt. But his wicked brother Typhon plotted to overthrow Osiris and prepared a chest that was exactly the length of Osiris' body. The chest was presented as a gift at a banquet to whatever person it fitted exactly; this turned out to be none other than Osiris, who lay down in the chest. Immediately Typhon and his confederates seized upon Osiris, closed the chest, and threw it into the river. When Isis heard the terrible news, she wandered in despair searching for her husband's body. But when she found it, Typhon again managed to take possession of it; he tore it into fourteen pieces, which were dispersed in different locations; several "tombs of Osiris" were shown in Egypt. The limbs of the god were thus to be found scattered here and there in widely separated places. Osiris himself, however, came forth from the netherworld and vanquished Typhon. A ray from him fell upon Isis, who in conse-quence bore his son, Harpocrates (Horus).[77]

And now compare with the myth the worldview presented by the fifth century B.C. Greek philosopher Empedocles. He asserted that an original unity was torn apart into the four elements (fire, water, earth, and air) or into the multiplicity of existent beings. He posited two opposing powers, which bring about within the world of existing things the processes of becoming and passing-away, namely Love and Strife. Empedocles says of the elements:

> They remain forever the same, yet mingling each with the
>   others
> Become transformed into men and numberless creatures
>   besides them.
> Now they are joined into one, Love binding the many together,
> Now they are scattered once more, dispersed through hatred
>   and Strife.[78]

From the Empedoclean standpoint, everything in the universe is simply the elements in different combinations. Things could only come into existence because the primal unity was torn apart into four natures, dispersed into the elements of the cosmos. Hence if we encounter something, it is a constituent part of the scattered divinity. But the divinity is hidden in things as we see them; it had to perish in order for things to come into existence. For what are things but combinations of the members of God, organized into wholes by Love and Strife? In the words of Empedocles:

> See, for a clear demonstration, how the limbs of a man are
>   constructed,
> All that the body possesses, in beauty and pride of existence,
> Brought together by Love, the elements forming a union.
> Then come hatred and Strife, and fatally tear them asunder,
> Once more they wander alone, on the desolate confines of life.
> So is it with the bushes and trees and the water-inhabiting
>   fishes,
> Animals roaming the mountains, sea-birds borne by their
>   wings.[79]

Empedocles clearly implies that the philosopher is one who rediscovers the divine original unity in things, hidden under a spell, whirled about by Love and Strife. But if we find the divinity who is hidden there, we must ourselves be divine beings. For Empedocles adheres to the view that "like can only be known by like."[80]

These ideas about the nature of humanity and the cosmos transcend considerations of sense experience. They are ideas that the *mystai* found in their myth of Osiris: the god, the creative power is poured out into the world. This appears in Empedocles' four elements. God—Osiris—is slain. Human beings, with their knowledge (which is divine in nature) will restore him to life. We are to rediscover him in the form of Horus (Son of God, *Logos*, wisdom) in the opposition between Strife (Typhon) and Love (Isis). In a Greek way, Empedocles expresses his basic ideas in terms that still have a mythical ring; his Love is the goddess Aphrodite, his Strife is Neikos, divine beings who bind and loose the elements.

Myths of Initiation

The style in which the content of myth has been described here should not be equated with a "symbolic" or "allegorical" approach to myth. Nothing of that kind is intended. The images that form the content of the myth are not invented symbols for abstract truths. They are actual experiences in the soul of the initiates.

The initiates in the Mysteries experienced these images with spiritual organs of perception, as ordinary people experienced the impressions of their eyes and ears. Just as such impressions are nothing in themselves but must be evoked in perception through contact with an external object, so are the mythological images nothing unless they are activated by spiritual facts; the difference is only that in sense-perception a person is outside the objects, whereas the mythological images can only be a real experience when a person stands within the spiritual processes to which they correspond. And that means, as the ancient *mystai* knew, going through an initiation.

The spiritual happenings that the initiate perceives are then given pictorial form by the images of the myth. It is impossible to understand the workings of myth unless we realize that it clothed in pictures actual spiritual experiences. The spiritual processes themselves are supersensible. The images, whose content is a reminiscence of the sense-perceptible world, are not themselves spiritual but only clothe the spiritual in pictures. To live merely in the images would be to dream. The spiritual experience is only accessible to those who are able to sense the reality behind the images, just as we sense the real rose through the impressions of our senses.

This is the reason [also] why mythological images are never unambiguous. Their character as pictorial illustrations means that the same myths may give expression to a variety of spiritual events. Hence it is not a contradiction when interpreters of myth relate a particular story now to one and now to another spiritual fact.

From this point of view we can follow a thread through the multiplicity of the Greek myths. To begin with we may consider the saga of Heracles. A new light is thrown upon the "twelve labors" imposed on the hero, deepening their significance, when we notice that before the culminating, most difficult labor he has himself initiated in the Mysteries of Eleusis. In the service of Eurystheus, king of Mycenae, he has to descend into the underworld and bring back with him the hellhound Cerberus. To enable him to descend into hell, Heracles has to be initiated; the role of the Mysteries was to lead a person through the death of the perishable nature, that is, into the under-world. And through initiation, his eternal part was redeemed from the power of death. Thus it was that the *mystes* overcame death, and it is as an initiate that Heracles overcomes the dangers of the underworld.[81]

The voyage of the Argonauts can be similarly interpreted. Phrixus and his sister Helle, children of a Boeotian king, suffered badly at the hands of their stepmother. The gods sent them a ram with a golden fleece, which carried them away through the air. As they flew over the strait between Europe and Asia, Helle fell in and was drowned—which gives the strait its name, Hellespont. Phrixus however reached the king of Colchis on the eastern shore of the Black Sea, where he sacrificed the ram to the gods and gave its fleece to King Aeetes. He caused it to be hung up in a grove and guarded by a terrible dragon. It was the Greek hero Jason, in company with the other heroes Heracles, Theseus, Orpheus, and so on, who undertook to fetch the fleece from Colchis. Aeetes laid upon Jason severe conditions for the attainment of the fleece; but Medea, the King's daughter, was skilled in magic and came to his aid. He harnessed two fire-breathing bulls and ploughed a field, sowing it with dragon's teeth. When these sprang up into armed men, on Medea's advice he threw a stone amongst them, whereupon they turned and killed one another. It is by Medea's magic that Jason lulls the dragon to sleep and so wins the fleece. He then returns with it to Greece, taking Medea as his wife. The king pursues the fugitives, and in order to delay him, Medea kills her little brother Apsyrtus and scatters his limbs in the sea. Aeetes pauses to collect them and so the pair reach Jason's homeland with the fleece.

Every detail of the story requires elucidation in depth. The fleece is something pertaining to humanity that is infinitely precious, something lost since the time of the beginning, and which can be recovered only by the overcoming of terrible powers; such is the situation with regard to the eternal in the human soul. The eternal belongs to human beings, yet we find ourselves divided from it by our own lower nature, and we can attain to it only when we conquer and lull to sleep our lower self. That is made possible when the magic power of our own consciousness (Medea) comes to our aid. Medea becomes for Jason what Diotima was for Socrates when she instructed him in the Mysteries of love. Humanity's own wisdom possesses the magic power of conquering the transitory and attaining to divinity. From our lower nature, on the other hand, only a debased humanity—the armed men—can spring; this is overcome by spiritual and intellectual means, the advice of Medea. But even when the hero has found the eternal—the fleece—he is not yet safe. A part of his consciousness—Apsyrtus—must be offered up as a sacrifice. This is demanded by the nature of the sense-perceptible world, which is only to be comprehended by us as a manifold, "dismembered" domain. We might go still further into the spiritual processes underlying these images, but the intention here is only to indicate the principle underlying the formation of myths.

Special interest attaches from this point of view to the saga of Prometheus. Prometheus and Epimetheus are sons of the Titan Iapetus. The Titans are the children of the oldest generation of the gods, Uranus (Heaven) and Gaia (Earth). Kronos, the youngest of the Titans, usurped his father's throne and seized the rulership of the world. He was overthrown in his turn by his son, Zeus, along with the other Titans; Zeus then became the supreme among the gods. In the Titanomachy, Prometheus sided with Zeus, and it was on his advice that Zeus banished the Titans to the underworld. Nevertheless the Titan disposition still lived on in Prometheus—he was only half a friend to Zeus. When Zeus was about to destroy humankind on account of their *hubris*, Prometheus took up their cause and taught them numbers, writing, and that other prerequisite of culture, the use of fire.[82] This provoked Zeus' rage against Prometheus. Hephaestus, a son of Zeus, was commissioned to make a female form of great beauty, which all the gods adorned with every possible gift. She was named Pandora ("all-gifted"). The messenger of the gods, Hermes, brought her to Prometheus' brother, Epimetheus, to whom she gave a casket as a gift from the gods. Epimetheus accepted the gift, despite the fact that Prometheus had warned him on no account to accept a gift from the gods. When the casket was opened, out flew every possible human affliction. Only Hope remained inside, because Pandora quickly shut the lid, and Hope exists still as a dubious gift from heaven. As for Prometheus, on account of his relationship to humanity he was chained at Zeus' command to a crag in the Caucasus mountains. An eagle continually gnaws his liver, which perpetually grows again. He is to pass his days in agonizing loneliness, until one of the gods freely sacrifices himself, that is, dedicates himself to death. Prometheus meanwhile bears his suffering with unflinching patience, for he knows that Zeus will be dethroned by the son of a mortal woman unless he himself becomes her husband. It was important for Zeus to know this mystery; he sent the messenger-god Hermes to Prometheus to inquire about it, but Prometheus refused to say anything. At this point the sagas of Heracles and of Prometheus are connected: in the course of his wanderings, Heracles reaches the Caucasus. He slays the eagle that gnawed at Prometheus' liver. And the centaur Chiron, who cannot die, though he suffers from an incurable wound, sacrifices himself for Prometheus. The Titan is thereupon reconciled with the gods.

The Titans here are the force of will, a force of nature (Kronos) originating from the primal spirit of things (Uranus). They are not an abstraction personified as "forces of will," but actual beings of will. Prometheus is one of them, which indicates his nature, but he is not wholly a Titan; he belongs in some ways on the side of Zeus, that is, the spiritual power that assumed cosmic rule when the unbridled force—Kronos—had been quelled.

Prometheus is a representative of those worlds from which humanity draws its forward-striving will, which is half nature-force, and half spiritual force. The will inclines toward both good and evil. Indeed its destiny is fixed by its tendency either toward the spiritual or toward the perishable; and this destiny is the destiny of human beings themselves: chained to the perishable, gnawed by the eagle, we must suffer. Our ultimate goal can be reached only when we withdraw into solitude to seek our destiny. But we have a secret. It consists in this: the divine power—Zeus—must be married to a mortal, that is, a consciousness bound to a physical human body, so as to beget a son—human wisdom, the *Logos*, who will set free the god.

In this way consciousness achieves immortality. But the secret must not be betrayed until the coming of a *mystes*—Heracles—who overcomes the power that threatens him constantly with death. The centaur, a creature that is half animal, half human, has to sacrifice itself to redeem him: this is human nature itself, half animal and half spirit, which must die in order that the purely spiritual human being may be released.

The gifts spurned by Prometheus, the human will, are taken up by Epimetheus—cleverness or shrewdness. But he gains nothing from them except troubles and sorrows. The rational mind clings to the inessential and perishable. Only one thing remains behind: the hope that even from the perishable the eternal may one day be born.

The thread that runs through the sagas of the Argonauts, Heracles, and Prometheus can also be traced through Homer's *Odyssey*. The use of such a method of interpretation may seem forced, but on closer consideration of all that has been said, even the strongest doubts must be dispelled.

In the first place, it is a surprise to hear it said of Odysseus that he made a "descent into the underworld" (*nekyia*, Book XI). Whatever theories we may hold about the author of the *Odyssey*, it is impossible to accept that he portrayed the descent of a mortal into the underworld without thereby relating him to the meaning of the descent in Greek thought—namely the conquest of transitoriness and the awakening of the eternal in the soul. Odysseus' feat must be presumed to achieve this, and his experiences thus take on a profounder significance, just as did those of Heracles; they become a description of something that does not belong to the world of sense perception, but rather to the inner development of the soul. That is why the narrative course of the *Odyssey* is not adapted to external events, but the hero voyages in enchanted ships, and geographical distances are handled in the most arbitrary fashion; the real and perceptible are not the point. It is easy to understand why, if the outward events are narrated in order to clothe in pictures a spiritual process. The poet himself says in the opening invocation that his poem treats of the search for the soul.

> Sing in me Muse! sing the tale of the man, the resourceful hero, destroyer of Troy's holy towers, sing all that he suffered, the cities he saw, the men and the ways that he learned there, buffeted long on the sea, enduring it all in his heart, seeking to save his own soul, and win his companions their homeland.

This is a man seeking for the soul—the divine in humanity—and it is his wanderings on that quest that the poet will relate.

He comes to the land of the Cyclopes, uncouth giants with one eye in their forehead. Polyphemus, the most horrifying of them, devours several of the travelers, but Odysseus saves himself by blinding the Cyclops. This refers to the first stage of life's pilgrimage: physical strength, the lower nature, has to be broken, for if its power is not broken, if it is not blinded, it will devour you.

Then Odysseus reaches the island of the enchantress Circe, who transforms some of his companions into grunting swine, but he manages to subdue her. She is a spiritual power, but of a lower kind, still directed toward the transitory world. Spiritual power misused can have the effect of degrading human beings still deeper into animality. Odysseus has to master it. He is then able to descend into the underworld, becoming a *mystes*. The dangers to which he is subsequently exposed are those that beset initiates in their progress from the lower to the higher stages; he passes the Sirens, who lure travelers to their death by means of the magic sweetness of their songs; they are images of the lower imagination, the first objects of pursuit by those who have freed themselves from the limits of the senses. Odysseus grasps the spirit in its free creative activity, but he is not yet an initiate—he is still chasing illusions, from whose power he must break loose. Odysseus has to accomplish the passage between Scylla and Charybdis—the novice vacillates between spirit and sense, not yet able to realize the full value of the spiritual, though the sense-world has lost its former meaning. A shipwreck ends the lives of all Odysseus' companions; he alone escapes, being befriended by the nymph Calypso who cares for him for seven years. Eventually, at the behest of Zeus, she permits him to return to his homeland. Here the *mystai* attain to a level where all their fellow aspirants fall short, and only one, Odysseus, is found worthy. The one who is worthy enjoys for a time—seven years in accordance with the number-symbolism of the Mysteries—the tranquility of a gradual initiation-process.

Before reaching home, however, Odysseus is brought to the island of Phaeacia where he is an honored guest. The King's daughter takes his part, King Alcinous himself entertains and fêtes him. Odysseus reenters the world, meeting once again its delights, and the spirit of attachment to the world once more awakes in him! But he finds the way home, the way to the divine. At home, on the other hand, nothing good awaits him. His wife Penelope is besieged by a crowd of suitors, and has promised them that she will choose a husband when she has completed a garment she is weaving. She evades keeping her promise by unraveling every night what she has woven during the day. Before he can rest, united again with his wife, Odysseus therefore has to overcome the suitors. The goddess Athene changes him into a beggar, so that he can enter unrecognized, and in this way the suitors are conquered.

What Odysseus is seeking is his own deeper consciousness, the divine powers in the soul. It is with these that he wishes to be united. But before the *mystai* can discover them, they must conquer everything that comes as a suitor for the favor of their consciousness—that is, the world of mundane reality, transient nature, from which the horde of suitors stems. The logic that pertains to them is a weaving that unravels itself when it has been spun. Wisdom—the goddess Athene—is a sure guide to the deepest powers that the soul possesses. She turns one into a beggar, meaning that she divests one of all that is transitory in origin.

The Myth and Mysteries of Eleusis

The spirit of mysteriosophy is all-pervasive in the festivals celebrated at Eleusis in Greece in honor of Demeter and Dionysus. A "sacred way" stretched to Eleusis from Athens, lined with mysterious signs intended to bring the soul into an exalted mood. At Eleusis itself there were mysterious temple-complexes,[83] under the direction of a priestly dynasty. The wisdom which qualified them for this task was handed down from generation to generation in the priestly families; it was the wisdom which enabled them to perform their ritual service at Eleusis, the wisdom of the Greek Mysteries, mysteriosophy.[84]

The festivals were celebrated twice in the course of each year, and dramatized the cosmic events governing the fate of the divine in the world and of the human soul. The Lesser Mysteries took place in February, the Greater Mysteries in September. Initiation into the Mysteries took place in connection with these festivals. The climax of the initiatory proceedings was a symbolic enactment of the human and cosmic drama on the site.

The temples at Eleusis were dedicated to the goddess Demeter. She is a daughter of Kronos, and before his marriage to Hera, Zeus had by her a daughter, Persephone. Once while Persephone was out playing, Pluto, the god of the underworld, carried her off. Demeter went wandering through the world lamenting and seeking for her. At Eleusis she sat down on a stone, and there she was found by the daughters of Celeus, a governor of Eleusis. In the form of an old woman, she was taken into the service of the family of Celeus, as nurse to the Queen's son. She wished to endow the son with immortality, and to this end she hid him every night in the fire. But when his mother learned of it she cried and wailed, after which the bestowal of immortality was no longer possible, and Demeter left the house. It was then that Celeus built the temple. The grief of Demeter for Persephone was boundless, and spread sterility over the Earth. To avert total disaster, the gods had to find a way of appeasing her, so Zeus induced Pluto to let Persephone return to the upper world. However, before he let her go he gave her a pomegranate to eat, and because of this she was compelled to return to the under-world ever after at regular intervals; for a third of the year she dwelled in the underworld, and for two thirds in the upper world. Comforted, Demeter returned to Olympus. But at Eleusis, where she had undergone her grief, Demeter founded the cult-festivals in which her fate was ever afterward commemorated.

The mythology of Demeter and Persephone is not hard to interpret. It is the soul that lives alternately in the underworld and in the upper regions; the myth clothes in a picture the eternal nature of the soul that persists throughout its endless transformations, its births and deaths. The soul has an immortal mother—Demeter—but is carried away into the realms of transitoriness, and even induced to share in the destiny of the perishable world. It has eaten the fruit of the underworld—that is to say, the human soul has found satisfaction in perishable things, and therefore cannot live always in the heights where the gods abide. It has to return ever and again to the kingdom of transience.

Demeter stands for the essential source out of which human con-sciousness arises. Thus we must conceive of consciousness as arising from the spiritual forces of the Earth—for Demeter is the archetype of the Earth. And the fact that through her the Earth is endowed with the regenerative power of the crops, points to still deeper aspects of her nature. It is she who wishes to grant immortality to human beings— Demeter places her charge secretly in the fire every night. Human beings, however, cannot bear the pure energy of fire (or spirit) and Demeter has to cease her attempt. All she can do is to institute the temple cult. Through this, so far as they are able, human beings can participate in the divine nature.

The festivals at Eleusis were an eloquent confession of the belief in the immortality of the human soul. The conviction was expressed in the imagery of the myth about Persephone. But alongside Demeter and Persephone at Eleusis, the god Dionysus was honored. If Demeter stood for the divine origin of the eternal within humanity, Dionysus was worshipped as the divine presence in the world, which assumes an endless variety of forms. He is the god poured out into cosmic existence, torn apart in order to be reborn spiritually. He rightly takes his place beside Demeter in the festivals.[85]

5

THE EGYPTIAN AND
OTHER EASTERN MYSTERIES

The Egyptian Mysteries: Becoming Osiris

THE SO-CALLED "Egyptian Book of the Dead,"[86] now restored to us by the diligence of nineteenth-century scholarship, demonstrates the existence among the ancient Egyptians of ideas concerning humanity's eternal existence and communion with the divine, which might be summed up in the words attributed to Empedocles:

> When, set free from the body, released you rise to the ether,
> You become divine, an immortal, escaped from the power of death.

It contains, in fact, all kinds of teachings and invocations, which were put into the grave along with the deceased in order to furnish guidance when they were released from the mortal state. By means of this literary work we can explore the most intimate ideas of the Egyptians concerning the eternal world and cosmogony.

The ideas of the gods that we find there remind us constantly of those familiar from the Greek Mysteries. Osiris is a god who gradually came to be popular and was universally worshipped in Egypt, eclipsing the other local divinities and subsuming the attributes of the other gods into himself. But whatever the ordinary people of Egypt thought about the nature of Osiris, in the Book of the Dead we have evidence of a priestly doctrine, according to which Osiris was to be found within the human soul. That emerges from everything said there about death and about the dead.

When the body is given over to the Earth, preserved under earthly conditions, humanity's eternal part enters into the eternal condition that was in the beginning. It appears before Osiris. It stands before him for judgment, surrounded by the forty-two Judges of the Dead. The destiny of one's eternal being depends upon their verdict. If the soul has confessed its sins, it is deemed to be reconciled with the eternal Justice. Invisible powers then draw near and speak to it:

> Osiris N. has been purified in the pool which lies south of the Field of Hotep and north of the Field of Locusts, where the gods of verdure purify themselves at the fourth hour of the night and the eighth hour of the day, with the image of the heart of the gods, coming forth from the night into day.[87]

This shows that in the world of eternal order, one's eternal nature becomes Osiris; after the name Osiris stands the personal name of the deceased. Moreover, the one being united with eternity designates himself Osiris:

> I am the Osiris N. Growing under the blossoms of the fig tree is the name of Osiris N.[88]

He has "become an Osiris."

Yet being an Osiris is nothing but the final, perfected stage of human life and development. It is clear in this context that even Osiris in his cosmic role as a judge is no more than a man who has attained to the stage of perfected existence. The difference between human existence and divine existence is one of degree—and also of number. Behind this mystery of the "one and the many" lies the framework of ideas that belongs to the Mysteries.

Osiris in his cosmic form is a unitary being; hence he exists undivided in each human soul. Everyone is an Osiris; yet the unitary Osiris has to be represented as a separate entity. Humanity is looked upon as a being still in process of development, and at the end of the process comes existence as a God. We should speak of a divinized condition of being, rather than of the independent existence of a Godhead, in the framework of Egyptian thought. Now it can hardly be doubted that in that framework of ideas no one could be considered to attain Osirian existence after crossing the threshold of eternity, unless they had already evolved to that level of being. Thus we must conclude that the highest mode of life that someone can lead is the transforming of oneself into an Osiris. To be truly human, one must already live the most perfect life of an Osiris that is possible under transitory conditions. Human perfection means living like an Osiris—it means undergoing all that Osiris underwent.[89]

It is in this way that the Osiris myth takes on its deeper dimensions of meaning, becoming the paradigm of life for someone who wants to awaken eternal being within him- or herself. Osiris is torn to pieces by Typhon; he is killed. The members of his body are cherished and cared for by his consort Isis. After his death, he caused a ray of light to fall upon her and she bore his son Horus, who then takes over the earthly tasks of Osiris; he is the second, still immature Osiris, but he is in the process of becoming an Osiris in the full sense. This true Osiris is to be found in the human soul. For although the soul is to begin with connected to the transitory realm, it is destined to give birth to the eternal. Humanity may therefore be termed the tomb of Osiris; it is our lower nature—Typhon, or Set—that has killed him. The love that is present in his soul—Isis—must cherish and care for the members of his corpse, and then the higher nature or eternal soul—Horus—can be born, and in due course rise to the state of "being an Osiris."

This then is the "initiation" practiced in Egypt. It taught that whoever aspires to the highest stage of being must recapitulate, inwardly microcosmically, the universal and macrocosmic events connected with Osiris. Plato has described such a cosmic process: the Creator had stretched out the World-Soul on the World-Body in the form of a cross, and the subsequent organization of the cosmos constitutes a redemption of the crucified World-Soul.[90] If someone is to "become an Osiris" the same process must take place in miniature. The initiand must allow the inner experience of "becoming an Osiris" to unfold and fuse with the events of the cosmic Osirian myth.

If we were able to look inside the temples where the initiatory "transformation into Osiris" took place, we would see that the events enacted there on the human scale were a representation of the cosmogony. Humanity originates from the "Father" and is to bear within it the Son; the actual presence within human beings of the divinity, held captive by a spell, is to be brought to manifestation. The god within is held down by the power of earthly nature; that lower nature must become a grave, from which the higher nature can rise to new life. The information we possess about the scenarios of initiation makes sense when we understand this. People were subjected to procedures whose character was mysterious, but which were intended to "kill" the earthly and awaken something higher. Further detail is not needed here, for we comprehend the intention behind these procedures.

The intention was that everyone who had undergone initiation would be able to make a "confession." All the initiates could declare that they had seen hovering before them the prospect of infinity, reaching up to the divine, that they had felt within them also the power of the divine, and had laid to rest in the tomb all that held down that power. The initiate had died to earthly things, and was indeed dead, having died as a lower being and having been in the underworld among the dead—that is, with those who are already united with eternity. After a sojourn in the other world, the initiate had risen again from the dead, but as another, no longer as one belonging to transitory nature. All that is transitory was absorbed into the all-permeating *Logos*, and the initiate belonged henceforth among those who live forever at the right hand of Osiris. Such a person will become a true Osiris, united with eternal order, and the power of judgment over life and death will be put in his hand. The initiand had to undergo whatever experience was necessary in order to be able to make such a "confession"—an experience of a most exalted kind.

If these experiences came to the attention of the uninitiated, however, it is easy to see that they would comprehend nothing of what actually took place in the soul of the neophyte. They would take the latter's death, burial, and resurrection as a physical occurrence, and the spiritual realities of a higher existential plane would take on the appearance of an event contradicting the whole natural order of things: a miracle. And in that sense, a miracle is what initiation was.

The Life of an Initiate: Buddha and Christ

Those who wished to comprehend what initiation meant had to awaken in themselves the powers enabling them to adopt a higher stance, on a new existential plane. It required a premeditated course of life, leading to such a higher experience. And though in each individual case these experiences might come about in various ways, it always happens that we can point to specific, typical forms. The life of an initiate has a typical character, which can be described without reference to the particular personality concerned.

To put it another way: an individual could be described as treading the path to divinization only after having undergone the particular typical experiences of an initiate. One example is the Buddha as seen by his disciples, and as such a one did Jesus first appear in his own society. We know today of the parallelism between the biographies of the Buddha and Jesus. One has only to observe the detailed correspondences between them to realize that any attempt at denial would be vain.[91]

There is an annunciation of Buddha's birth to Queen Maya by a white elephant, which overshadows her and tells her that she is to bring forth a "divine man." "And he will attune all beings to love and friendship, and will unite them in a bond of religious fervor." Compare with this the passage from the Gospel of Luke where an angel is sent:

> to a virgin pledged to be married to a man named Joseph, a descendant of David. The virgin's name was Mary. The angel went to her and said, "Greetings, you who are highly favored!... You will be with child and give birth to a son, and you are to give him the name Jesus. He will be great and will be called the Son of the Most High.

The Brahmans (Indian priests) understand the meaning of the birth of a Buddha. They interpret Maya's dream according to a totally schematic concept of what a Buddha is: the individual's life must correspond to this concept exactly. Similarly we find in the Gospel of Matthew that Herod:

called together all the people's chief priests and teachers of the law, and asked them where the Christ was to be born.

One of the Brahmans, Asita, says of the Buddha:

This child is the one who will become a Buddha, the savior, the leader to immortality, freedom, and the light.

Compare with this what happens in the Gospel of Luke:

Now there was a man in Jerusalem called Simeon, who was righteous and devout. He was waiting for the consolation of Israel, and the Holy Spirit was upon him.... When the parents brought in the child Jesus to do for him what the custom of the Law required, Simeon took him in his arms and praised God, saying: Lord, as you have promised you now dismiss your servant in peace. For my eyes have seen your salvation, which you have prepared in the sight of all people, a light for revelation to the Gentiles, and for glory to your people Israel.

Tradition reports of the Buddha that when he was a child of twelve he went missing, and was found again under a tree, surrounded by the poets and sages of the time. Correspondingly we find in the Gospel of Luke:

Every year his parents went up to Jerusalem for the Feast of the Passover. When he was twelve years old, they went up to the Feast, according to the custom. After the Feast was over, while his parents were returning home, the boy Jesus stayed behind in Jerusalem, but they were unaware of it. Thinking he was in their company, they traveled on for a day. Then they began looking for him among their relatives and friends. When they did not find him, they went back to Jerusalem to look for him. After three days they found him in the Temple, sitting among the teachers, listening to them and asking them questions. Everyone who heard him was amazed at his understanding and his answers.

The Buddha withdrew into solitude, and when he returned a virgin greeted him with words of benediction: "Blessed are the mother, the father, and the wife to whom you belong." But he answered: "Only those are blessed who have reached *nirvana*." The reference is to those who have entered the world of the eternal order of things. Compare in the Gospel of Luke:

As Jesus was saying these things, a woman in the crowd called out: "Blessed is the mother who gave you birth and the breasts that fed you!" He replied, "Blessed rather are those who hear the word of God and obey it."

At one point in his life, the Tempter (Mara) comes to the Buddha and promises him all the kingdoms of the Earth. The Buddha rejects it all with the words: "I know well that I am destined to have a kingdom, but I do not desire an earthly one; I will achieve enlightenment and make all the world rejoice." Mara has to admit, "My power is at an end." Jesus responds to the same temptation, saying:

Away from me, Satan! For it is written: "Worship the Lord your God, and serve him only."
Then the devil left him....

The parallels could be documented at considerably greater length, all pointing in the same direction.

The Buddha's life comes to a sublime ending. While on a journey, he fell ill. He came to the river Hiranya, near Kusinagara, and there he lay down on a rug spread for him by his beloved disciple Ananda. His body began to shine from within. He died transfigured, as a body of light, saying "Nothing is permanent." This death of the Buddha corresponds to the Transfiguration of Jesus:

About eight days after Jesus said this, he took Peter, John, and James with him and went up onto a mountain to pray. As he was praying, the appearance of his face changed, and his clothes became as bright as a flash of lightning.

The Buddha's earthly life ends at this juncture. But in the life of Jesus this is just the beginning of the most important part—his suffering, death, and resurrection. The difference between the Buddha and Christ is shown in the necessity for the life of Christ Jesus to continue beyond the furthest point of the Buddha's life.[92] Buddha and Christ cannot be comprehended simply by lumping everything together.

The correspondence between these two redemptive lives leads unambiguously to the conclusion, already indicated by the narratives themselves, that when the priests or sages hear what kind of birth has occurred they know already what is involved. They have to do with a "divine man," and they know what course of life the personality must adopt so that it shall correspond to what they know of such a "divine man." Mysteriosophy contains the eternal prototype for such a course of life, which only he must and can fulfill. It is like a law of nature, and as the properties of a chemical are exactly determined, a Buddha or Christ must live a precisely determined life. Their lives are not narrated to reveal the accidents of biography, but rather to show the typical features, defined by mysteriosophy for all ages to come.

The legend of the Buddha is no more a biography in the ordinary sense than the Gospels are supposed to be such a biography of Christ Jesus. Neither is concerned with contingent events, but rather with the prototypical life of a world-redeemer. The model for both accounts is not external, physical happenings but the traditional teachings of the Mysteries. For those who recognize their divine nature, the Buddha and Jesus are essentially "initiates";[93] their lives are raised above everything transitory, and what is known about the nature of the initiated must be applicable to them. The contingencies of their lives are not narrated, but one says of them "In the beginning was the Word, and the Word was with God, and the Word was a God.... And the Word became flesh and dwelt among us."

Yet the life of Jesus transcends the life of the Buddha. The Buddha's life ends with his transfiguration, whereas the most significant part of Jesus' life begins after the Transfiguration. Translated into the terms of initiation, the Buddha reached the point at which the divine light begins to shine in human nature, standing on the verge of earthly life and becoming one with the light of the world. Jesus goes further: he does not physically die at the moment when the light of the world shines through him. At that moment he is a Buddha; but at that moment he enters upon a higher stage of initiation, that of suffering and death. And when his earthly part is lost to view, the spiritual light, the light of the world, does not go out but leads on to his resurrection. To his followers he is revealed to be the Christ.

As soon as he achieves his "transfiguration," the Buddha is lost in the all-pervading blissful life of the spirit. Christ Jesus, however, rekindles the all-pervading spirit once more to life in the form of present human existence. Something like this had been achieved by the initiates in the higher stages of the Mysteries. But there it had a mythical image-character. The initiates of Osiris experienced a "resurrection" on the level of image-consciousness. In the life of Christ, initiation in the "Great Mysteries" was added to the stage of Buddha-initiation, not however on the plane of mythological images but as a real event. The life of the Buddha demonstrated that the human being is in essence the divine *Logos* (Word); when our earthly part perishes, we return to the *Logos*, to the light. But in Jesus, the *Logos* takes on existence as an actual man, the Word becomes flesh.

The ritual pattern enacted by the Mystery-cults of the ancient world in the secrecy of their temple precincts was grasped by Christianity in an event of world history. Christ Jesus appeared in his own time as an initiate—but one initiated in a uniquely great way. He was a proof of the divine presence in the world. Henceforth for the Christian community, mysteriosophy would be indissolubly bound up with the personality of Christ Jesus. The fact that he had lived, and that those who acknowledge him are "his own" now constituted a belief that was able to take the place of the Mysteries and their practices. From then on, part of what had formerly been attainable only through the techniques of the Mysteries was accessible to the Christian communities through their conviction that God had shown himself in the presence of the Word among them.

The long preparation required for each individual was no longer the sole way to the spirit. To it had to be added the witness to the deeds and words of Jesus that had been handed down:

> That which was from the beginning, which we have heard, which we have seen with our eyes, which we have looked on and our hands have touched—this we proclaim concerning the Word of life.... We proclaim to you what we have seen and heard, so that you also may have fellowship with us.[94]

That sense of immediate presence is to be a bond of living union for all generations and all peoples, embracing them all mystically in a universal Church. Hence we understand the declaration of Augustine:

> I would not believe the message of the Gospel, if I were not urged to do so by the authority of the Catholic Church.[95]

The Gospels do not carry weight as statements of truth in themselves. They are to be believed because they are grounded in the personal presence of Jesus, and because the Church in a mysterious way draws from that personal presence its power to make the truth manifest.

The Mysteries handed down the techniques of coming to the truth. The Christian *ecclesia* propagates this truth in itself. The Mysteries had fostered a trust in the spiritual powers that were awakened inwardly through initiation. To this was added the trust in the Founder, the Initiator as such. The Mysteries had been a process of divinization, an actual experience of being made God. Jesus attained oneness with God; therefore one must cling to him, so as to share in his divinization as part of the community that he founded. That is the Christian claim.

The divinization of Jesus has a universal significance, in which the community of his faithful can share: "See, I am with you always, to the very end of the world."[96]

So the birth in Bethlehem bears the stamp of an eternal reality. Hence when the birth of Jesus is mentioned in the Christmas antiphon, it is said to happen every Christmas:

> *Hodie Christus natus est, hodie Salvator apparuit,*
> *Hodie in Terra canunt Angeli, Laetantur Archangeli, etc.*
> (Today Christ is born, today the Savior has appeared, today the angels sing on earth, the archangels rejoice....)

The Christ-experience, then, was a specific stage of initiation. In pre-Christian times the *mystai* attained to this stage of Christ-initiation, but they were then in a state of spiritual vision in the higher worlds, to which there was nothing equivalent among the facts of the sense-world. The inner meaning of the Mystery of Golgotha was experienced spiritually. When the Christian initiates achieve this stage of initiation, however, they behold at that very moment the historical event on Golgotha. And they know that in the event that took place in the sense-perceptible world is contained the spiritual content, which had been enacted super-sensibly in the Mysteries.

In the Mystery-places the spirit had been poured out upon the *mystai* of old. Through the "Mystery of Golgotha" it was poured out upon the whole Christian community. There was still a place for initiation. For whereas faith allows a person to participate unconsciously in the content of the Mystery of Golgotha, initiation leads to a fully conscious connection with the power that streams invisibly from the events depicted in the New Testament, and which ever since then has pervaded spiritually the life of humanity.

6

THE EVIDENCE OF THE GOSPELS

THE MATERIALS we have for a historical investigation into "the life of Jesus" are furnished by the Gospels. From other sources we have in total no more than "would easily be written on a single page (quarto)"; these are the words of Adolf Harnack, the greatest historical authority on the subject.

But the question is, what sort of documents are the Gospels?

The fourth, or Gospel of John, is so utterly different from the others that those who feel themselves committed to strictly historical research conclude:

> If John possesses the authentic tradition of the life of Jesus, that of the Synoptics (the first three Gospels) is untenable. Or, if the Synoptics are right, the writer of the fourth Gospel must be dismissed as an historical authority.[97]

Such is the historian's point of view.

From our standpoint, which is concerned with the Mystery-content of the Gospels, this approach need neither be accepted nor denied, though we may note the conclusion of a Christian theologian:

> Measured by the criteria of consistency, inspiration, and completeness, these writings leave much to be desired. Even by ordinary human standards they suffer from manifold imperfections.[98]

But if our perspective is the Mystery-origin of the Gospels, much of the disagreement between the Gospels falls readily into place, and we can even find a harmony between the fourth Gospel and the first three. For none of these writings asks to be taken as a straightforward account of mere historical events.

Parables and Signs

The Gospels are not put forward as historical biography. What they advance had always existed as the typical life of a "son of God" in the traditions of the Mysteries. They were not created out of historical events but out of Mystery-traditions.

Now it is naturally the case that among the several distinct cults of the Mysteries the traditions would not be in complete verbal agreement. (Nevertheless there was such close agreement that the Buddhists relate the life of their "divine man" in almost identical terms to those of the evangelists when they relate the life of Christ.)[99] There would naturally be discrepancies. It is clear that we must assume the Gospel writers based themselves upon four different Mystery-traditions.

It is a sign of the personal greatness of Jesus that he could awaken among the writers who stemmed from four different traditions the belief that he was the one who so perfectly fulfilled their ideal of an initiate, that they could accept him as the one who lived the archetypal life ascribed in their Mystery-teachings to such a personality. When they described his life, it was in terms of their own particular Mystery-traditions. If the Synoptics describe it in similar ways, that proves nothing except that they were working out of similar traditions from the Mysteries. The writer of the fourth Gospel steeps his narrative with ideas that recall the thought of the philosopher of religion, Philo of Alexandria; again, that proves nothing except the proximity of the tradition out of which he wrote to that of Philo.[100]

In the Gospels we meet with several sorts of material. There are in the first place reports of events, which apparently lay claim to historicity. Secondly, there are the parables, where the story only serves to present a deeper truth in imaginative terms. And thirdly, there are teachings, intended to form the content of a Christian view of life.

In the Gospel of John there is no parable as such; it came from a Mystery school in which the use of parables was not considered necessary.

Much light is shed on the role of actual historical events and imaginative parable in the Synoptic Gospels by the narrative of the cursing of the fig tree. This appears in Mark where we read:

> Jesus entered Jerusalem and went to the Temple. He looked around at everything, but since it was already late, he went out to Bethany with the Twelve. The next day as they were leaving Bethany, Jesus was hungry. Seeing in the distance a fig tree in leaf, he went to find out if it had any fruit. When he reached it, he found nothing but leaves, because it was not the season for figs. Then he said to the tree, "May no one ever eat fruit from you again." (11:11ff.)

Luke gives this same episode in the form of a parable:

> Then he told this parable: A man had a fig tree, planted in his vineyard, and he went to look for fruit on it, but did not find any. So he said to the man who took care of the vineyard, "For three years now I've been coming to look for fruit on this fig tree and haven't found any. Cut it down! Why should it encumber the ground?" (13:6f.)

The parable indicates symbolically the uselessness of the old teachings, under the image of the barren fig tree. The same meaning is conveyed by Mark, who narrates it as if it had taken place as a fact of history.

The conclusion to be drawn from this is that the Gospels should not be read primarily as historical accounts, based upon occurrences in the perceptible world. They have a Mystery-meaning; they relate experiences perceptible to the spiritual faculties alone, drawing upon several Mystery-traditions. Hence there is no real difference between the Gospel of John and the Synoptics. Historicity is not the issue. One may also date this Gospel or that a decade earlier or later. From the standpoint of research into their Mystery-signification their historical value is equal—the Gospel of John not excepted.

Coming now to the "signs" (miracles): their elucidation poses no problems for a Mystery-interpretation. They are supposed to overturn the laws of nature; but they only do so for as long as we consider them happenings in the physical, perishable world, which could have been apprehended by our unaided sense perception. However, they are really experiences that can only be grasped by perception of a higher, spiritual type. Their character makes it clear that they cannot be understood in terms of the natural, physical order.

It is imperative, then, that we read the Gospels in the right way. We shall then understand what they have to tell us about the Founder of Christianity. The style of the Gospels is that used to communicate a Mystery, and they speak in the way the *mystai* spoke of an initiated one. The only difference is that they ascribe the initiation to a unique personality, a single being. And they make the salvation of humanity depend upon a connection with this uniquely initiated being.

For the initiates this was the coming of "the Kingdom of God."[101] The unique one had brought this Kingdom to all people who made a connection with him. The separate concern of each individual gave way to a shared concern of all those who were prepared to acknowledge Jesus as their Lord.

To understand how this could be so, we need to see how mysteriosophy had found its way into the national religion of Israel. For it was out of Judaism that Christianity arose.

The Mysteries and the Jews

It need cause no astonishment that with Christianity we should find grafted onto the stock of Judaism those ideas from the Mysteries that, as we have seen, were the common heritage of Greek and of Egyptian spiritual life. In the religions of the several peoples, conceptions of the spiritual assumed various forms. But at the heart of them all, when we go back to the more profound priestly wisdom, there is overriding agreement. Plato knew of his agreement with the Egyptian priestly authorities when he put the core of Greek wisdom into the form of a philosophical world-picture. It was said of Pythagoras that he had traveled to Egypt and India and was instructed by the wise men there. At the period of Christian origins we know of people who found so much agreement between Platonic doctrines and the deeper meaning of the books of Moses, that they called Plato "a Moses speaking the language of Athens."[102]

Mysteriosophy was a universal phenomenon. What it drew from Judaism was a form which it had to take in order to become an actual world religion. Judaism expected the coming of a Messiah. No wonder that the figure of the uniquely initiated one could only be identified by the Jews with their Messiah. And this connection helps explain the shift from concern with individual initiation in the Mysteries to a concern for the whole people.

Judaism had been from the beginning a national religion, through which the Jewish people defined its identity. Its Yahweh was the people's God. The birth of his Son must mean the redemption of the whole people. There was no question of an individual initiate being saved; salvation must be brought to the entire people. It belongs to the basic idea of Jewish religion that one dies on behalf of all.

The existence of Mysteries within Judaism, which could be brought out of the obscurity of secret rites into the religion of the people, is also certain. A fully developed mysticism existed in Pharisaism, alongside the priestly wisdom that had there become outer formalism. A Mystery-wisdom is described here, just as it is elsewhere.[103]

It is said that an initiate discoursed on wisdom, and his hearers realized the hidden sense of his words. They cried:

> Old man, what have you done? Would that you had been silent! You think that you can sail the boundless ocean without sail or mast. What are you attempting? To ascend upward? You cannot. To descend into the depths? An immeasurable abyss opens before you![104]

This comes from the Kabbala (mystical "tradition"). We also hear of the four rabbis who sought the way to the divine realm (Paradise). The first died, the second went mad, the third caused great destruction; only the fourth, Rabbi Akiba, entered in peace and returned.[105]

Jesus and the Preaching of the Kingdom

Thus we see that within Judaism there was a foundation for the emergence of a uniquely initiated figure. It was only necessary for such a one to say that salvation should not be limited to a few elect individuals, that all the people should share in the redemption. Someone had then to spread through the world what had formerly been the experience of the chosen ones in the temples of the Mysteries. That would mean being willing to take upon himself the spiritual role, as a personality, that had been formerly played in the community by the Mystery cult.

Now it is true that the community was not able to enter into the actual experiences of the Mysteries without more ado; nor could that be his intention. But he did wish to impart the conviction of the truth contained in the visions of the Mysteries. By a further step forward in the spiritual development of humanity, the life of the Mysteries would flow out into the world. He would bring people to a higher existential plane: "Blessed are those who believe, and have not seen."[106] The conviction that there is a divine reality would be rooted in human hearts in the form of faith.

One who "stands outside," yet has this faith, will certainly go further than one who does not have it. The thought that many were standing outside, uncertain of the way, must have weighed upon the mind of Jesus with nightmare heaviness. He had to close the gulf that separated the initiates from the ordinary people.

Christianity presents itself as the means by which everyone can find the way. Even those who are not inwardly ripe do not need to forgo the possibility of participating, albeit unconsciously, in the current of the Mysteries.

The Son of Man has come to seek out and save that which was lost.[107]

The fruits of spiritual development could be enjoyed henceforward also by those who had not been able to attain initiation in the Mysteries. The Kingdom of God would no longer depend upon externals at all:

The Kingdom of God does not come visibly, nor will people say "Here it is" or "There it is," because the Kingdom of God is within you.[108]

Hence it was of little consequence whether such and such a person was further advanced in the spiritual Kingdom; what mattered was the shared conviction of belonging to a spiritual Kingdom that includes everybody.

That spirits are subjected to you is not a cause for you to rejoice; rejoice rather because your names are written in heaven![109]

In other words, have faith in the divine and the time will come when you will find it.

7

The "Miracle" of Lazarus

Among the "miracles" attributed to Jesus, special place must without doubt be accorded to the raising of Lazarus, which took place at Bethany. Everything conspires to give it a unique importance within the New Testament. In fact, it is given only in the account of one evangelist, namely John. The Gospel of John opens with such profound introductory words that we must take everything it communicates as charged with special meaning. It begins:

> In the beginning was the Word, and the Word was with God, and the Word was a God.... And the Word became flesh and dwelt among us, and we saw his glory as of an only Son of the Father, full of grace and truth.[110]

To begin a work in this way is quite obviously to claim that it has to be interpreted in a specially deep sense. Anyone who wants to explain it away intellectually, or to approach it superficially, is left in the position of someone investigating the "murder" of Desdemona by Othello on the stage.

What, then, is the meaning of the opening words of John?

He speaks explicitly of the Eternal, of what was "in the beginning." He also narrates factual events. Yet they are plainly not events simply known through sight or hearing, or understood by the thinking mind. Behind the events is the Word (*Logos*), an aspect of the cosmic Spirit.

For him these events are actually the manifestation of some higher meaning.

It is safe to suppose that in the instance of a man being raised from the dead—a case that poses the greatest challenge to the eye and ear and to the reasoning mind — the very deepest meaning lies concealed. Moreover, as Renan has pointed out in his *Life of Jesus*, the raising of Lazarus was undoubtedly an event of decisive significance influencing the end of the life of Jesus. At the same time, Renan's own standpoint seems untenable. For why should the idea that Jesus had raised someone from the dead, when it circulated among the populace, have appeared so dangerous to his opponents as to threaten the very existence of Judaism? It is all very well for Renan to assert:

> The other miracles of Jesus were passing events, repeated in good faith and exaggerated by popular report, and they were thought of no more after they had happened. But this one was a real event, publicly known, and by means of which it was sought to silence the Pharisees. All the enemies of Jesus were exasperated by the sensation it caused. It is related that they sought to kill Lazarus.

But this renders incomprehensible Renan's own view that what happened at Bethany was merely the staging of a piece of mummery, designed to strengthen belief in Jesus:

> Perhaps Lazarus, still pale from his illness, had himself wrapped in a shroud and laid in the family grave. These tombs were large rooms hewn out of the rock, entered by a square opening closed by an immense stone slab. Martha and Mary hastened to meet Jesus, and brought him to the grave before he had entered Bethany. The painful emotion felt by Jesus at the grave of the friend he believed to be dead (John 11:33–38) might be taken by those present for the agitation and tremors which were wont to accompany miracles. According to popular belief, divine power in a man was like an epileptic, convulsive force. To continue our hypothesis, Jesus wished to see once more the man he had loved, and when the slab had been moved away, Lazarus came forth in his grave-clothes, his

head bound with a napkin. This apparition was naturally looked upon by everyone as a resurrection. Faith accepts whatever is true for it, and knows no other law.

Renan's exegesis seems excessively naive; but he joins to it an additional comment:

Everything seems to suggest that the miracle of Bethany contributed essentially to hasten the death of Jesus.[111]

Renan's perception here is undoubtedly acute. But with the means at his disposal he is not able to explain or justify his opinion.

Certainly Jesus must have performed something of significance at Bethany, as we gather from passages such as this:

Then the chief priests and the Pharisees summoned a meeting of the Sanhedrin. "What are we to do?" they asked. "This man is performing many miraculous signs...."[112]

Renan too grasps intuitively that something out of the ordinary had occurred. "It must be acknowledged," he says,

that John's narrative is of an essentially different kind from the accounts of miracles of which the Synoptics are full, and which are the outcome of popular imagination. Let us add that John is the only evangelist with accurate knowledge of the relations of Jesus with the family at Bethany, and that it would be incomprehensible how a creation of the popular mind could have been inserted in the frame of such personal reminiscences. It is probable, therefore, that the miracle in question was not among the wholly legendary ones, for which no individual was responsible. In other words, I think that something took place at Bethany which was looked upon as a resurrection.

This amounts to an admission from Renan that something took place in Bethany that he is not in a position to explain. He is clearly on the defensive when he says:

At this distance of time, and with only one text bearing obvious traces of subsequent additions, it is impossible to decide whether, in the present case, all is fiction, or whether a real event which took place at Bethany served as the basis of the report that was spread abroad.[113]

Maybe what is really needed in this case is to read the text in the right way. We might then no longer wish to speak of "fiction."

It is as well to admit that much in this whole Johannine narrative is shrouded in mystery. To take only one point: if the narrative is to be understood literally, what are we to make of Jesus' words, "This sickness does not lead to death but to the glory of God, to the glorification of the Son of God?"[114] Such is the usual rendering of the words, though we come closer to the content of the Greek if we understand it to mean revelation, manifestation of God, so that the Son of God may be revealed by means of it. And then what of the other words Jesus speaks?

I am the resurrection and the life. The one who believes in me will live even though he dies.[115]

It would be trivial to take Jesus to mean that Lazarus' sickness gives him the opportunity to show off his skill; still more so to assume that Jesus claimed that faith in him would literally revive the dead. Where would be the point in bringing someone back from the dead if after his resurrection he were just as he was before? It is inconceivable that such a life could be meant by the words, "I am the resurrection and the life."

It is only when we understand them in reference to a real spiritual event that Jesus' words take on living significance. They can resume even the literal sense they have in the text.

Jesus asserts that he is the resurrection that has occurred in the case of Lazarus; he is the life that Lazarus is now living. Let us take literally what Jesus is. According to the Gospel of John he is "the Word made flesh." He is the eternal, that "which was in the beginning." Therefore, if he is actually the resurrection, it is the eternal and primordial Being that has risen to new life in Lazarus. The underlying pattern is that of the bringing to life of the eternal "Word," the "Word" that is the life to which

Lazarus awakens. There is sickness, but a sickness that does not lead to death but to the glory of God, since it serves to bring about a divine revelation. It is the "eternal Word" that is raised in Lazarus; thus the whole process serves to bring about the manifestation of God in Lazarus.

Through the process Lazarus is completely transformed. Previously the Word, the spirit, was not alive in him. Now it lives in him. The spirit has been born within him. Every birth has an element of sickness, the birth pangs of the mother. It is a sickness, however, that does not lead to death but to new life. That part of Lazarus becomes ill that is to give birth to the "new man"—the one who is united with the eternal "Word."

How are we to understand the "grave" out of which the "Word" is born? We need only recall the expression of Plato, who calls the body the "grave" of the soul. We may remember, too, that Plato speaks of a sort of resurrection, in that the spiritual world stirs to life in the body. The spiritual reality of the "soul," in Plato's terms, corresponds to the *Logos* in the Gospel of John—the "Word" that for him is Christ. Whereas Plato asserts that to become a spiritual being is to raise the divine in human beings from the grave of the body, for John this actually took place through the life of Jesus. It is not surprising that he makes Jesus say, "I am the resurrection."

All this puts it beyond doubt that the events at Bethany constituted a "raising from the dead" in a spiritual sense. Lazarus is transformed from what he formerly was; he rises to a life of which the "eternal Word" can say, "I am the life." What has happened to Lazarus is that the spirit has come to life within him, so that now he participates in "eternal life."

Transposed into the terminology of the Mysteries and initiation, the meaning immediately becomes clear. In Plutarch's formulation of the goal of the Mysteries, they aimed to liberate the soul from corporeal existence and to unite it with the gods. The feelings of an initiate have been characterized in the writings of F.W.J. Schelling: "The initiate receives a consecration, making him a link in the magic chain, himself a Kabeiros, indissolubly bound in relationship, joining the ranks (as an ancient inscription puts it) of the upper gods."[116] As for the revolution in the life of an initiate into the Mysteries, nothing expresses its meaning better than the words of Aedesius to his imperial pupil:

If you were ever to take part in the Mysteries, you would feel ashamed at having been born a mere man.[117]

It is by filling our souls with such feelings that we shall gain a proper attitude to the events at Bethany. John's narrative is indeed extraordinary. We glimpse a reality behind it which no rationalistic exegesis, no amount of critical reconstruction can provide. What stands before us is in the truest sense a mystery.

Into Lazarus the "eternal Word" entered, making him in Mystery terms one of the "initiated." The process described is one of initiation.[118]

Let us survey the entire process from this point of view. Lazarus was "loved" by Jesus. But this cannot mean ordinary personal affection— that would conflict with the perspective of the Gospel of John, according to which Jesus is "the Word." Rather Jesus loved Lazarus because he found him sufficiently ripe that he could awaken "the Word" within him. There were already links between Jesus and the family at Bethany; that simply indicates that Jesus had made everything ready in that family for the final act of the drama, the raising of Lazarus. Lazarus was a pupil of Jesus.

He was a pupil of whom Jesus could be absolutely confident that his "raising from the dead" could be achieved. The final act of the initiatory drama consisted in a symbolic enactment, through which the spirit was revealed. It was not just a matter of grasping the principle expressed in the words "Die and become!"; it had to be consummated through an inward act. The earthly part, of which in the Mysteries the "higher self" learned to feel ashamed, had to be put off. The earthly self had to "die"—that was the reality behind the outer symbol. The body lay for three days in a comatose state. But that was only the outward expression of the immense changes going on within the life of the initiate. It corresponded to a still more radical crisis on the level of the spirit.

This act divides the life of the initiate into two separate parts. Without direct experience of such things it is impossible to understand their deeper meaning. To use a comparison, Shakespeare's *Hamlet* can be summarized in a few words, and anyone who mastered this summary might correctly claim to know "what happens in *Hamlet*." But a very different kind of knowledge would be the outcome of a rich involvement in Shakespeare's treatment of the theme. No mere description could compare with such a living content in the soul, for which the idea of *Hamlet* has become a personal artistic realization. And on a higher level, something similar happens in a person who lives through the magically charged events of the initiatory process. Such a one experiences in symbolic enactments what is achieved in the spirit.

"Symbol" here denotes an outwardly perceptible act, which in itself, however, is only an image—not an unreal image, but one behind which stands a real event.

The earthly body, then, has lain dead for three days. New life rises out of death. Life has overcome death, and there can be henceforth a sense of trust in the new life. Lazarus has experienced this, for Jesus prepared him to be raised from the dead. His illness was quite real, yet at the same time symbolic. His illness was in fact an initiation, and leads after three days to the reality of a new life.[119]

Lazarus had reached a stage of development suited to the fulfillment of these processes. He had put on the vesture of a *mystes*, and lapsed into the condition of lifelessness, the image of death. By the time Jesus came, three days had passed:

> Then they took away the stone from where the dead man was lying.
> And Jesus looked up and said, "Father, I thank you that you have heard me."[120]

The Father had heard Jesus; Lazarus had reached the final act in the great drama of the achievement of knowledge. He had attained the knowledge of resurrection; his initiation into the Mysteries was complete.

Initiation of this kind was understood everywhere in the ancient world. Jesus here plays the role of initiator. The achievement of union with the divine had always been conceived of in this way. The great "miracle" of Lazarus, the transformation of his whole being, places Jesus within the line of traditions from archaic times. Here is the link between Christianity and the Mysteries.

Lazarus was made an initiate by Christ Jesus himself. Hence he could raise himself to higher worlds. But he was also the first Christian initiate, initiated by Christ Jesus: hence he was in a position to recognize that the "Word," which had risen to life in him, had taken on personal existence in Christ Jesus. The figure who stood visibly before him as his awakener was identical with the spiritual power that had manifested itself within him. Thus the further words of Jesus are important:

> I knew that you always hear me; but I spoke for the benefit of the people standing here, that they may believe that you sent me.[121]

That means that Jesus is revealed as the one in whom is present "the Son of the Father." And so when he awakens his own being within another, that person becomes an initiate.

In this way Jesus declares that the meaning of life was concealed in the Mysteries. They led to the knowledge of its meaning. He is the Word of life. What was formerly archaic tradition had become in him an actual person. The evangelist expresses this in the verse where he says that in him "the Word became flesh." For him Jesus is an incarnate Mystery.

For the same reason, the Gospel of John is also itself a Mystery. Read correctly, it tells of events with a totally spiritual meaning. If it had been written by a priest in former ages it would have taken the form of ritual prescriptions. But for John the ritual has taken the form of a person. Hence it is written as a "life of Jesus."

A modern investigator and great expert on the Mysteries pronounced that they "will never be cleared up!"—the words of Jacob Burckhardt.[122] But then, he failed to recognize the path toward understanding them. Let us take the Gospel of John. Let us look upon its drama of the achievement of knowledge. In terms both symbolic and physically real we see it enacting before our gaze what the ancient world performed as the Mystery itself.

The words "Lazarus, come forth" recall the cry with which the initiator in the priestly Mysteries of the Egyptians summoned back to everyday life those who had undergone initiation; they had "died" to the earthly world and become witnesses of eternal life; the events of initiation had transported them for a time from the world. By speaking them, Jesus had revealed the secret of the Mysteries. That is why the Jews felt that they could not allow such an act to go unpunished, as we may now understand. No more could the Greeks have permitted Aeschylus to escape punishment if he had betrayed their Mystery teachings.

Jesus had performed the initiation of Lazarus before all "the people standing by," in a deliberate act revealing the process, that, in the ancient priestly world of the Mysteries, had been enacted only in secret. This initiation prepares us for an understanding of the "Mystery" of Golgotha. Formerly only those who were seers—that is, who were initiated— could know something of the goal of the Mysteries. From now on there could be witnesses to the secrets of a higher reality among those who "have not seen, and yet have believed."

8

THE APOCALYPSE OF JOHN

The Seven Letters

AT THE END of the New Testament sands an extraordinary document. It is the Apocalypse—the secret revelation of Saint John. The esoteric character of the work is apparent from the opening words:

> The revelation of Jesus the Christ, which God granted him in order to show to his servants how the necessary events will shortly run their course. This is communicated in signs sent by God's angel to his servant John.[123]

The revelation is imparted "in signs"; we must not therefore interpret the text literally, but look for a deeper meaning that is signified by the external sense. Nor is this all that points us to a "hidden meaning."

John addresses seven churches in Asia Minor. This cannot mean actually existing communities. Rather, the number seven is a sacred symbol and must have been chosen because of what it represents; there must in reality have been a number of other communities in Asia. Moreover, the way in which John receives the revelation equally suggests an esoteric significance:

> I was in the spirit on the Lord's Day, and I heard behind me a voice like a trumpet saying, "Write what you see in a book and send it to the Seven Communities."[124]

He received the revelation when he was "in the spirit." Also, it is a revelation of Jesus the Christ, presenting in esoteric form the meaning of Christ Jesus' manifestation to the world.

Therefore we are to look for the hidden meaning of the Apocalypse in the teaching of Christ, so that the revelation it contains stands in the same relation to mainstream Christianity as the Mysteries in pre-Christian times stood to the public religion. This would seem to justify us in approaching the Apocalypse as a Mystery.

What then does the Apocalypse mean by addressing the Seven Communities? To understand it, we must take a specific instance from the seven messages, and we may begin with the first one:

> Write to the angel of the community in Ephesus: These are the words of him who holds the seven stars in his right hand, and who walks among the seven golden lights, "I know your deeds, and what you have suffered and also your patient endurance, and that you will not support those who are evil; also, that you have called to account those who call themselves apostles and are not, and that you have recognized them as false. And you are enduring patiently and are building up your work upon my name, and you have not grown weary. But I demand of you that you should attain the highest love: consider from what you have fallen, change your way of thinking, and achieve the highest deeds. Otherwise, I will come to you and remove your light from its place—unless you change your way of thinking.
>
> But this you have, that you despise the ways of the Nicolaitans, which I too despise.
>
> He who has ears to hear what the Spirit says to the Communities, let him hear: "To the victor I will give food from the Tree of Life, which stands in the Paradise of God."[125]

Such is the message to the angel of the first Community. The "angel" is to be understood as the spirit of the community. The angel has entered in the direction indicated by Christianity, and is able to distinguish between the true and false professors of Christian belief. The angel wishes to work in a Christian way, founded upon "the name of Christ."

But the angel is urged not to fall short of the "highest love" through lapsing into any sort of error, and is shown the possibility of going astray through such errors. The way to the divine has been revealed through Christ Jesus: perseverance is needed in order to press forward in the original spirit of the movement. Otherwise it is possible to rest content with one's understanding of Christ too soon, as is the case if one is led a certain way but then abandons this guidance for erroneous fixed ideas about it; one then falls back upon the lower self in human nature. This is the failure to attain to one's "highest love." The knowledge derived from the senses and the intellect is to be exalted, spiritualized and made divine by becoming wisdom, on a higher plane; if it is not, it remains on the level of the transitory.

Christ Jesus has pointed out the path to the Eternal. Knowledge must be tirelessly led along the path which leads to its becoming "divine knowledge." In the spirit of love it must pursue the traces that will lead to its becoming "wisdom."

The Nicolaitans were a sect that did not fully grasp the meaning of Christianity. They say only that Christ is the divine Word, the eternal Wisdom that comes to birth in human beings. They therefore identified human wisdom and divine Word, supposing that the pursuit of human knowledge was the realization of the divine in the world. But Christian wisdom cannot be construed in this way. Knowledge, or human wisdom, is as perishable as everything else if it does not undergo that transformation into "divine wisdom." You, however, says the Spirit to the angel at Ephesus, have not relied in this way upon mere human wisdom. You have persevered in the path of Christianity. Yet to reach the goal you need nothing short of the first and highest love. You need a love greater than all other loves, because only then can it be the "first love." The road to the divine reaches endlessly before you and the first step, once gained, is the starting point for an ascent that leads ever higher.

So must we understand the message to the first of the Communities, and it must serve as an example for the rest.[126]

The Son of Man

John turns round, and he sees "seven golden lights." And:

> Among the lights was one like a Son of Man, dressed in a robe reaching down to his feet and with a golden sash round his chest. His head and his hair were white like wool, as white as snow, and his eyes were like blazing fire.[127]

Subsequently we are told that "the seven lights are the Seven Communities."[128] Hence we must understand them as seven different ways to the divine, each in itself more or less imperfect. But the Son of Man also "had in his right hand seven stars,"[129] and "the seven stars are the angels of the Seven Communities."[130] The guiding spirits or *daimons* of mysteriosophy have here become the guiding angels of the Seven Communities, which are thus presented as the bodies of spiritual entities of which the angels are the soul, on the analogy of the human soul as the guiding power over the body. Each Community represents a way to the divine from a certain limited point of view, and the guides along these ways are the angels. They must therefore come to accept as their own leader the being who in his right hand holds the "seven stars."

> And out of his mouth issued a sharp two-edged sword, and his countenance resembled the shining sun in its glory.[131]

This sword also figures in the Mysteries: the initiand was terrified by a "drawn sword." Such is the situation of John, who wants actual experience of the divine—who wants the countenance of wisdom to shine upon him like the Sun, as does John: it is a testing of his inner strength.

> And when I saw him, I fell at his feet as if dead. He laid his right hand on me and said, "Do not be afraid."[132]

The experiences that must be undergone by the initiand are ones otherwise undergone only when someone dies. The one who guides John through them has to take him into realms where birth and death no longer have any meaning. The initiated one therefore enters on a "new life":

> And I was dead, but see! I am alive throughout all the cycles of time. And I hold the keys of Death and the underworld.[133]

Thus John is brought to the stage of beholding the mysteries of existence.

> And after this I looked, and saw the door of heaven open. And the first voice that was heard was like a Trumpet sounding and it said to me, "Ascend to this place and I will reveal what must take place hereafter."[134]

The messages that were proclaimed to the Seven Churches taught John what had to happen in the physical realm in order to prepare the way for Christianity. What he now sees "in the spirit" leads him to a vision of the spiritual sources of reality.

These are things still hidden behind the physical processes, but after further physical development they will be manifested in a future, spiritualized condition of the world. The initiate experiences spiritually in the present what will be realized in the course of time to come:

> And immediately I was in the spirit. And I saw in heaven a Throne. And there was one sitting upon the Throne, whose appearance was like jasper and carnelian. And there was a rainbow like emerald encircling the Throne.... Also before the Throne was what looked like a sea of glass, clear like crystal.[135]

The images in which the vision is clothed by the seer depict the sources or archetypes of perceptible reality.

> And in the sphere around the Throne were twenty-four thrones, upon which were seated the twenty-four Elders, clad in flowing white robes and with golden crowns upon their heads.[136]

Around the archetypal source of reality we thus find beings who have already advanced far along the path of wisdom, who look upon the Infinite and bear witness to it.

In the center and around the Throne were the Four Living Creatures, full of eyes before and behind. The first Living Creature was like a lion. The second was like a bull. The third looked like a man. The fourth was like a flying eagle. And each of the Four Living Creatures had six wings and was full of eyes around and within. And they cry without ceasing, both day and night, "Holy, Holy, Holy, is God, the Almighty, who was, and is, and is to come."[137]

It is easy to understand the Living Creatures; they represent the supersensible life that underlies the forms of all living beings. Later they raise their voices in response to the sound of the Trumpets—that is, when the life contained in physical forms is transformed and spiritualized.

The Book with Seven Seals

The one who sits enthroned holds in his right hand a book, which marks out the path to the summit of wisdom. Only one person is worthy to open this book:

Look! the Lion of the tribe of Judah, the root of David, has triumphed. He is able to open the book and its seven seals. [138]

The book has seven seals—human wisdom is seven-fold. Once again we encounter the holiness of the number seven.

Seals, in the mystical philosophy of Philo Judaeus, are the eternal cosmic Ideas that come to expression in things.[139] Human wisdom is the quest for these creative Ideas.

Only in the book sealed by them can divine Wisdom be found. The archetypal Ideas behind the created world must be unveiled—the seals opened—and the contents of the book will be revealed. Jesus is the Lion who can break open the seals; He has given a meaning to the Ideas of creation so as to point the way to Wisdom.

The Lamb that was slain, which God has dearly bought with the price of his own blood, is Jesus who, as the bearer of the Christ, has passed in the profoundest sense through the mystery of life and death; it is he who opens the book.[140]

Each time one of the seals is opened, the Living Creatures declare what they know. When the First Seal is broken, John sees a White Horse on which sits a rider with a bow. The first universal power, or embodiment, of the Idea of creation becomes visible. It has a new rider, Christianity, who sets it on the right track. And through the new faith, strife is allayed.

With the opening of the Second Seal, a Red Horse appears. Again it has a rider. He takes away Peace—the second of the universal powers—from the Earth, so that humanity should not neglect through sloth the cultivation of the spiritual life.

When the Third Seal is opened, the universal power of Justice, now led by Christianity, appears; with the opening of the Fourth, it is the power of Religion that appears and that is given a new perspective through Christianity. The significance of the Four Living Creatures emerges clearly: they are the four chief universal powers, which are to be given a new direction by Christianity.[141]

War	Lion
Peaceful work	Bull
Justice	Human countenance
Religious aspiration	Eagle

The meaning of the third Being is made explicit when the Third Seal is opened and the text reads:

A quart of wheat for a day's wages, three quarts of barley for a day's wages.

Thus the rider carries a pair of scales.[142] When the Fourth Seal is opened, the rider who appears is called "Death, and Hell was following close behind him"; the rider stands for righteousness in Religion.

When the Fifth Seal is opened, the souls of those who have already taken up Christianity appear: the creative Idea behind Christianity itself is manifested. But this refers only to the first stage of Christian society, which is no less transitory than the other manifestations of the creative Ideas.

The Sixth Seal is opened. And now it is revealed that the spiritual world of Christianity is something eternal. The people are pervaded by the spiritual reality that actually brought Christianity into existence. They are themselves made holy by what they have created:

> And I heard the number of those who were sealed: one hundred and forty-four thousand out of all the tribes of the children of Israel were sealed.[143]

These are the ones who prepared the way for the Eternal before it took the form of Christianity, and who have been transformed by the impetus given through Christ.

Then comes the opening of the Seventh Seal. This reveals what true Christianity ought really to be for the world. The seven angels "who stand before God" appear. These angels are once again spiritual Beings known in the ancient Mysteries translated into Christian terms. They stand for the true Christian path to the divine vision. The next stage is thus a leading into the presence of God. It is an initiation that John will undergo.

The Seven Trumpets

The proclamations of the angels are accompanied by the necessary features of all initiation. When the first angel blew upon his Trumpet:

> There followed hail and fire mingled with blood, and it was hurled down upon the earth. A third part of the earth was burned up, together with a third part of the trees, and all of the green grass.[144]

Similar portents occur when the other angels blow upon their Trumpets.

However, we also notice that this is not simply an initiation of the kind known in ancient times, but a new form of initiation which is to replace the old. Unlike the ancient Mysteries, Christianity does not exist only for the sake of a chosen few individuals: it is addressed to all humanity, and aspires to the religion of all people. The truth of Christianity is accessible to everyone who "has ears to hear." The *mystai* of the ancient world were singled out from the multitude; but the Christian Trumpets sound for all who are willing to hear them. How to respond is a matter for everyone to decide. That is the reason why the terrors in this "initiation of all humanity" are also so enormously enhanced.

Through his initiation, John sees the condition of the earth and its inhabitants in the far future. The underlying idea behind this is that the seer in the higher worlds already beholds what still lies in the future for the world below, The Seven Letters present the meaning of Christianity for the present age; the Seven Seals show what is being prepared now for the future through Christianity. The future remains as yet veiled, under seal, for the uninitiated. In the process of initiation the seals are opened. At the end of the time covered by the Seven Letters, the earthly age begins to pass over into a more spiritual condition. Life will no longer be limited as it is in its present physical forms, but will appear even externally as an imaging of the supersensible archetypes—represented by the Four Living Creatures and the other pictures connected with the Seals. Still further ahead in the future the earth will take on the form intimated to the initiates by the sounding of the Trumpets.

In this way the initiate has a "prophetic" experience of future conditions. The initiate into the Christian Mystery experiences the impetus given to life on Earth by the entering and onward working of the Christ. Meanwhile everything that remains bound up with the transitory and falls short of true Christianity is shown as meeting death. Then a powerful angel appears, with a little book open in his hand which he gives to John:

> He said to me, "Take it and eat it. It will be bitter in your stomach, but sweet like honey in your mouth."[145]

John is instructed not just to peruse the little book, but to absorb it completely, to make its contents part of himself. Of what value is knowledge if it is not a living power in a person's life. Wisdom must be such a living power. The goal is not mere knowledge of the divine: it is actual divinization. But knowledge of the kind contained in the little book is painful to the transitory nature in human beings, and is "bitter in the stomach." To the same extent however it is bliss to the eternal nature and so "sweet in the mouth like honey."

If Christianity is to become a real force upon earth it can only be in this way—through an initiation of humanity. Thus it strikes dead all that still belongs to the human being's lower nature:

> Their corpses will lie in the street of the great City, which spiritually is called Sodom and Egypt, where their Lord was also crucified. [146]

By these are meant the adherents of Christ, who will be persecuted by the powers of this transitory world. However, it is only in their own transitory nature that they suffer and for their true self it is an inner victory. Their destiny mirrors the archetypal destiny, which was that of Christ Jesus. The "City, which spiritually is called Sodom and Egypt" is the symbol for the life that remains confined to externals and does not take into itself the transforming impetus of the Christ. Christ is crucified everywhere in the lower nature. Where the lower nature triumphs, everything remains dead: the streets of the City are strewn with corpses. But those who overcome their lower nature and awaken the crucified Christ to new life hear the proclamation of the angel with the Seventh Trumpet:

> The kingdoms of the world have become those of the Lord and of his Anointed, who will reign from eternity to eternity. [147]

Upon which, "the Temple of God in heaven was opened, and the ark of his covenant became visible there."[148]

666: The Beast and the Abyss

The initiate's experience brings back in a new form the primaeval struggle between the higher and lower natures. On the Christian path, everything that the initiates in the older Mysteries had to undergo must be recapitulated. As Osiris was threatened by the evil Typhon, so now there is "the great Dragon, the ancient Snake" to be defeated.

From far back the wisdom of the *mystai* had used the snake as its symbol of knowledge. The Snake—knowledge—may be a seductive force, however, unless human beings bring to life within themselves the "Son of God." He it is who crushes the serpent's head:

> The great Dragon was hurled down—that ancient Snake who is called the Devil and Satan and seduces all the world—he was hurled down upon the Earth, together with his angels. [149]

The Mystery-Temple

The Christian Mystery was to replace the many Mysteries of the ancient world with its unique, archetypal Mystery-event. In Jesus the *Logos* had become flesh, and he was to become the teacher of initiation to all humanity. His community of mystai was to be the human race. In place of the old principle of selecting individuals, there was to be the gathering together of all. Hence everyone was enabled to become a *mystes*, insofar as they were sufficiently mature to do so. The Gospel is proclaimed to all, and whoever has an ear to hear is eager to fathom its mysteries; the heart of each has the decisive voice.

Thus it was no longer a case of introducing one person or another into the temples of the Mysteries, but of the word spoken to all and heard now with more, now with less clarity and strength. And it will be left to the *daimon*, the angel in a person's own breast, to decide how far one's initiation can proceed. The Mystery-temple is the entire world.

No longer is blessedness reserved for those who have witnessed within the confines of the Mystery-temples those awe-inspiring enactments that are the types and symbols of eternity. For now, "Blessed are those who have not seen, but who have believed."[150] Even if at first they wander in darkness, the light may yet reach them. There is no secrecy; the way opens out for all.

There is much more in the Apocalypse concerning the threat to Christianity from anti-Christian powers and the eventual triumph of

Christianity. All other gods are taken up into the higher unity of the Christian divinity:

> I did not see a temple in the City, because the Lord, the all-ruling God, and the Lamb are its temple. The City had no need of the Sun nor of the Moon to shine upon it, because the revelation of the divine presence is its light, and its lamp is the Lamb. [151]

The Mystery at the heart of the "Revelation of Saint John" is precisely this: the Mysteries are no longer secret. The angel says to him:

> Do not seal up the prophecies in this book, for the time of God's manifestation is near.[152]

Thus the writer of the Apocalypse expounds, from the standpoint of his own belief, the relationship of his community to those of previous times. His view of the Mysteries has become the content of a Mystery-text. The traditions that have come down about it are appropriate to its Mystery character: the author wrote it down on the island of Patmos, and the revelation is said to have been received in a "cave."

Christianity arose out of the Mysteries. In the Apocalypse, Christian wisdom was a Mystery reborn—but a Mystery which breaks out of the framework of the ancient Mysteries. The Mystery of a unique, single event was to become the Mystery with a significance for all.

There is an apparent contradiction in saying that the secrets of the Mysteries became manifest in Christianity but that in the spiritual visions of the Apocalyptist we nevertheless observe a "Christian Mystery."

To solve the enigma, we must reflect how it was that the secrets of the ancient Mysteries were revealed. It was through the historical events in Palestine, which drew back the veil from what had previously been kept hidden in the Mysteries. Something was introduced into the history of the world through the appearance of Christ, and it is this which constitutes the new Mystery. The initiates of former ages had seen in the spirit how events were leading toward the manifestation of the "hidden" Christ; but with the Christian initiate it is a matter of the "hidden" effects which spring from the Christ who now has been "revealed."

9

JESUS IN HIS HISTORICAL SETTING

T HE FOUNDATION on which Christianity sprang up is to be found in the Mysteries. All that was further required was the conviction that their spirit should be extended into life in general more than had been the case with the Mysteries themselves. Such a conviction was actually widespread, as we can gather from reports about the way of life practiced among the Essenes and the Therapeutae—groups that were in existence well before the time of Christian origins.[153]

The Essenes were one of the sects active in Palestine. They were of a closed nature and with an estimated membership at the time of Christ of around four thousand. They formed a community, whose members were directed to lead a life suited to the development of the higher self within their souls, and so to achieve "rebirth."[154] The aspirant was subjected to stringent tests in order to establish whether or not he was sufficiently mature to make himself ready for the higher life. On being accepted, he had to spend a period as a probationer, and to swear a solemn oath not to reveal to outsiders the secrets of their discipline.

Community life itself was devoted to the crushing of humanity's lower nature, so as to awaken more and more the spirit, which is there slumbering within him. Experience of the spirit permitted members, after a certain stage had been reached, to be admitted into a higher order. This exercised authority, not by compulsion, but as a source of the community's fundamental convictions.[155]

A related group were the Therapeutae, who were to be found in Egypt. All our reliable information about their organization is contained in the work by the philosopher Philo, *On the Contemplative Life*.[156] A few passages from Philo's book will be sufficient to convey an idea of its contents:

> The houses of those thus banded together are quite simple, affording protection against the two things requiring it most, the blazing heat of the sun and the frostiness of the air. They are neither contiguous as in towns, since close proximity is troublesome and displeasing to those assiduously striving for solitude, nor yet far apart, because of the fellowship to which they cleave, and in order to render each other aid in the event of a piratical attack. In each house there is a sacred chamber or *monasterion*, in which in isolation they are initiated into the Mysteries of the holy life....[157]
>
> They have also writings of men of old, who were the founders of their sect, and had left behind many memorials of the type of treatment employed in allegory....[158]
>
> Their interpretations of the Holy Scripture are made in accordance with the deeper meanings conveyed in allegory.[159]

Here we see a democratization of the aims of the Mysteries—though inevitably such a democratization brought a softening of the original character of the cults.

The communities of the Essenes and Therapeutae form a natural transition from the Mysteries to Christianity. But Christianity extended the process further, transforming the aims of such sectarian groups into the wider concerns of humanity as such, though naturally weakening their Mystery-character still further. From the existence of those communities, however, we can appreciate the readiness of the period for an understanding of the "Christ-Mystery." The techniques of the Mysteries prepared people for the dawning of a higher spiritual reality within their souls at the appropriate stage. The communities of the Essenes and Therapeutae translated these into a corresponding way of life that would lead to the awakening of the "higher self."[160]

The next step would be the concept of the reincarnating human individuality, evolving to ever higher stages of perfection.[161] Those who could begin to grasp that idea would be able to recognize in Jesus the presence of a very advanced spiritual individuality. The higher the spirituality, the greater the possibility of achieving something of importance.

The individuality of Jesus would thus be ready to accomplish what the Gospels describe as an overwhelming Mystery, fulfilled through the baptism by John. The personality of Jesus had reached the stage at which it could receive into his soul the Christ-*Logos*. In him the Word became flesh. From that point the ego of Jesus of Nazareth is the Christ-*Logos*, manifesting itself outwardly through his personality. The event which underlies the baptism by John is that the ego of Jesus becomes the Christ.[162]

In the period of the Mysteries, "union with the Spirit" was achieved by the initiates among humankind, by the few. The Essene Community opened the way to this union for all its members. The actions performed by the Christ before the whole of humanity constituted an event through which all of humanity could come to know union—the Christ-Event.

10

THE ESSENCE OF CHRISTIANITY

From the Mysteries to Christianity

N̲O LONGER WAS THE DIVINE—the Word, the eternal *Logos*—to be met with only in the obscure darkness of the Mysteries as a spiritual reality. Henceforth to speak of the *Logos* was at the same time to think of Jesus, an actual historical person. That was the profoundest factor that must have affected the adherents of Christianity. Previously the *Logos* had been expressed within reality simply in the various stages of human perfection; the level of spiritual development in a particular person could be subtly and delicately investigated when someone sought initiation, so as to establish the exact degree to which the *Logos* had been brought to life within such a person. A higher stage of maturation was considered to be a step higher in spiritual development, with its roots in a pre-existing spiritual life. Likewise the present life was seen as the stage of preparation for a spiritual phase of development in the future. Jewish esoteric teaching preserved in the *Zohar* asserts the strict conservation of the soul's spiritual energy, which continues forever:

> Nothing is lost in the world, nothing falls into the void—not even the words and the voice of a man. Everything has its place and its destined part to play.[163]

A particular personality was only one possible manifestation of the soul, which transformed its identity again and again. The life of a person was linked organically in a chain of development reaching into the past and forward into the future. But in Christianity, this manifesting itself in various ways through manifold personalities becomes focused on a unique personality—that of Jesus.

Formerly the *Logos* pervaded the entire world, but now it is concentrated in the single figure of Jesus, who is a "divine man" in a unique way. For the highest human ideal of all future lives, to which one should approach ever closer, was on one occasion actually present in Jesus. The "divinization" of all humanity was what Jesus took upon himself. What had been sought in the depths of one's own soul could henceforth be sought in him. The eternal, divine kernel of the soul was wrested away from the personality; this eternal part was now to be seen in its fullness in Jesus. It was no longer a case of the eternal nature of the soul triumphing over death and awakening to divine life, but rather of the one God who was present in Jesus and who will appear in order to raise up human souls.

The effect of this was to assign a radically new meaning to the personality. It had become detached from humanity's eternal and immortal part, and was left standing in its own right as personality. And so, rather than denying eternal life, it became necessary to ascribe immortality to this very personality. Belief in the cosmic transformation of the soul gave way to belief in personal immortality. Personality took on infinite significance because it was all that humanity could cling to.

From this point onward nothing stands between personality and the infinite God. Its relationship to him is an immediate one. It is no longer a case of various levels, higher and lower, reaching up to the possibility of divinization. A human being is simply human, and stands in a relationship to God that is direct—but at the same time external. This was felt by those who knew the perspective of the Mysteries to be a new note in their attitude to the world. Many individuals found themselves in this situation during the first centuries of Christianity. They were aware of the character of the Mysteries, and if they wished to become Christians they had somehow to come to terms with their former outlook. That could lead to severe psychic struggles. In all sorts of ways they sought to find an accommodation between the two divergent ways of looking at the world. The writings of the first Christian centuries mirror this struggle—not least the writings of those pagans attracted by the exalted nature of Christianity, as well as those of Christians who nevertheless found it hard to relinquish the ways of the Mysteries.

Christianity emerged only slowly out of the Mysteries. Christian convictions might be expressed in the form of Mystery-truths. Christian language might clothe the wisdom belonging to the Mysteries.

One example is Clement of Alexandria (died A.D. 217), a Christian author who had been educated as a pagan. He wrote:

> Thus the Lord did not hinder from doing good on the sabbath, but allowed us to communicate those divine Mysteries and that holy light to those who are able to receive them. He certainly did not disclose to the many what did not belong to the many, but to the few to whom he knew that they belonged, and who were capable of receiving and being molded according to them. But secret things are entrusted to speech, not to writing, as is the case with God.... "God gave to the church some apostles, and some prophets, and some evangelists, and some pastors, and teachers for the perfecting of the saints, for the work of the ministry, for the building up of the Body of Christ."[164]

Individuals sought by the most varied routes to find their way from the ancient ideas to Christian ones.

The Gnostic Crisis

Meanwhile, however, the external organization of the Church was becoming more and more strongly established, and those who thought that they were on the right path called the others "heretics." As more power went to the institution of the Church, the decisions of the Councils increasingly took the place of personal search for recognition of the right way. The concept of "heresy" became increasingly rigid. The Church took it upon herself to decide who had deviated too far from her carefully guarded sacred truths. Yet during the first centuries of

Christianity the search for the way to God was much more individual than in later times.[165] A long road had to be traveled before Augustine could declare:

> I would not believe the message of the Gospel if I were not urged to do so by the authority of the Catholic Church.

It was, however, through the several Gnostic sects and writers that the struggle between the way of the Mysteries and that of Christianity took on its specific coloring.

The term Gnostics is applied to all those writers from the first centuries of Christianity who sought for a deeper, spiritual meaning in its teachings.[166] They are to be understood as thinkers steeped in the ancient mysteriosophy and striving to comprehend Christianity from the viewpoint of the Mysteries. From their perspective Christ is above all a spiritual being, the Logos. In this his primal form he cannot have an external relationship to humanity, but must be awakened to life in the soul. At the same time, there must be a connection between the spiritual Logos and the Jesus of history, and here we come to the crux of the Gnostic controversy. The issue could be resolved in various ways, but the decisive fact remained: the idea of the Christ, for them, could only be grasped on the basis of mysteriosophy and not of ordinary historical traditions.

Some of them appealed to the Neoplatonic philosophy, which also had its roots in the Mysteries. The Gnostics were confident that the "wisdom of man" could give birth to a Christ by whom the historical figure could be measured—in the light of which alone the historical figure could be given his rightful significance.

The Esoteric Tradition

A special interest attaches to the teachings that we find in the books attributed to Dionysus the Areopagite.[167]

It is admittedly the case that these books are never mentioned prior to the sixth century A.D., but the place and date of their composition is not the relevant question here. What interests us is that they present

Christianity, through the medium of ideas of Neoplatonic philosophy, entirely as a spiritual vision of the supersensible world. And this is a form of presentation that actually belongs specifically to the early centuries of Christianity. In the early period this presentation of Christianity was handed down orally—in earlier times it was the most important things that were definitely not entrusted to written form.

We see this Christianity as it were reflected in the mirror of Neoplatonism: the perceptions of the senses darken human vision of the spirit; human beings must raise themselves above the senses. Yet all human thought derives its meaning in the first instance from the observations of the senses. The perceiver calls what is observed "that which is," and what is not observed "that which is not." If, however, someone wishes to gain a real perspective on God, even this distinction between the existent and nonexistent has to be transcended since it belongs to the sphere of sense-observation from which it is drawn. God in this sense neither exists nor does not exist. He transcends existence.

God cannot be approached therefore through the medium of ordinary cognition, which is concerned with things that exist. We have to be raised above ourselves, above our sensory observation, above our rational thinking-processes, and cross over to purely spiritual apprehension. Then we can begin to grasp, in mystical intuition, the perspective of the divine.

However, the superexistent God has brought forth from himself the *Logos*, the wisdom-filled foundation of the universe. And the *Logos* is accessible to the weaker human faculties. He is present in the structure of the world and mediates between God and humanity. The *Logos* may be present in humanity in various degrees, and may be actualized in the world through an institution, whose hierarchy expresses the different levels to which he fills its members. The *Logos* is active in a perceptible way within such a "Church." And the same power that enlivens it had once lived in Christ who became flesh, in Jesus.[168]

Gnosticism had made one thing clear: there was a need to come to terms with Jesus as a personality. Christ and Jesus had somehow to be related. Human personality had been deprived of its share in the divine nature, which had in some manner to be rediscovered. It had to be possible to find it again in Jesus.

The *mystai* had been concerned with levels of divinity within themselves, and with the personality known to the earthly senses. The
Christian was concerned with this, but also with an exalted God, perfect
beyond anything attainable by human beings. If we can grasp this, we
will see how a Christian "mysticism"—the attitude of the soul when it
finds a higher spiritual nature within itself—is possible only when the
inner eye is opened to the light that streams from the Christ in the person of Jesus. Union of the soul with its own inner energy is simultaneously union with the historical Christ. Mysticism is the unmediated feeling or perception of God within one's own soul. Yet a God who transcends utterly everything merely human cannot in the strict sense of the
word be said to indwell the human soul. Gnosticism and the Christian
mysticism which succeeded it represent an effort to participate somehow
in that divinity with one's soul, without any intermediary. Conflict here
was inevitable. For in reality it was possible to find only one's own divine
nature—and that is of course the divine at a certain stage of development, while the God of the Christians is a being complete and perfect
in himself.

It was possible to find the strength to aspire heaven-ward, but nothing was to be found within the soul, at any stage of its development, that
could be declared identical with God. A gulf begins to yawn between the
experience of the soul and the God asserted by Christianity. It is the gulf
between conviction and belief, between knowledge and religious feeling.
For the *mystai* of the ancient world there could be no such divide. They
accepted that God could be known only according to one's own degree,
and understood why this must be so. And they knew that the God
whom they knew in this gradually unfolding way was the true, the living God. They would have found it difficult to speak about a Godhead
perfect and closed in his own nature. The *mystai* were not interested in
knowledge of a perfect God, but in an experience of the divine life. They
wished to "become God," not to establish a relationship to a Godhead
outside of themselves.

It is inherent in Christianity, then, that its mystical striving is not
without presuppositions. The Christian mystic seeks the Godhead
within, but to do so must look to the historical Christ as the physical eye
looks to the Sun. The physical eye tells us that what it can see, it sees by

the light of the Sun, and the Christian initiate tells us that one ascends in one's own inner nature to the vision of God, but the light by which one sees is the light of Christ-made-manifest. It is through him that the mystic ascends to the highest point within. So does the mysticism of medieval Christianity differ from the experiences of the *mystai* in the ancient Mysteries.[169]

11

CHRISTIAN AND PAGAN WISDOM

Philo Judaeus: The Mystery of the Logos

AT THE TIME of Christian origins we also find the development within the ancient pagan culture of certain world conceptions that constitute a continuation of platonic thought, but which also have roots in a mysteriosophy that has been refined, made inward and spiritual. They appear first with Philo of Alexandria (c. 25 B.C.–A.D. 50).

The path to divinization, according to his view, is an entirely inward one taking place in the soul. One might aptly say that for Philo the "Temple of the Mysteries" where he seeks initiation is nothing other than his own inner being and the experiences that it undergoes.[170] He translates the Mystery-rites used in their enactments into processes of a purely psychological and conceptual nature. He does not see any possibility of reaching the divine through the impressions of the senses or through rational understanding. These are concerned only with temporal things. But there is a path of the soul that enables it to transcend these modes of knowledge, and to step outside its ordinary identity, abandoning in ecstatic trance all that it called "I." It is then in a state of spiritual exaltation, or "illumination." It no longer has thought, ideas, or knowledge in the usual sense, but is merged into and united with God. The divine is an experience that cannot be put into the form of thoughts or ideas that express what it is like. It must be experienced. And anyone who has experienced the divine has to admit that it can be conveyed only indirectly, through the living quality of one's words.

The cosmos is an image of this Mystery-Being whose reality is experienced in the deepest strata of the soul. It originated from the invisible and inconceivable God, and the wise ordering of the cosmos directly reflects the divine nature, harmonizing the phenomena of sense perception. In its wisdom and harmony it mirrors spiritually the Godhead, the divine spirit or mind that has been poured out into the world; this is the cosmic Reason or *Logos*, the "offspring" or Son of God. The *Logos* mediates between the perceptible world and the imageless God. Human beings are united with the *Logos* insofar as they really possess knowledge. In them the *Logos* is embodied; a spiritually developed person is a representative of the *Logos*.

Above and beyond the *Logos* is God. Beneath it is the transient world. Our human vocation is to link them in one. The spirit we encounter in our own inner nature is at the same time the spirit of the cosmos.

Much in this way of thinking is reminiscent of the Pythagoreans— that the heart of reality must be looked for in the inner life. At the same time, the inner life includes an awareness of cosmic significance. Augustine speaks in essentially Philonic terms when he says:

> We therefore behold these things which you [God] have created, because they are; but they are, because you see them.

And his further comment on what and how we see them is also striking:

> And we see externally that they are; but inwardly that they are good.[171]

All this has its origins in Plato. Like Plato, Philo interprets the destiny of the human soul as the denouement in a cosmic drama, when the hidden God awakens from the spell.[172]

He describes inner events in which the soul is active by saying that Wisdom follows within human beings the ways of her Father, looking upon the archetypes and shaping forms in accordance with them.[173]

Thus it is not of merely personal significance for someone to give expression to these forms; rather they are the eternal Wisdom—the life of the world. His view accords with the Mystery-attitude toward the familiar myths. The *mystai* looked for the deeper reality behind the myths, and what they did in the case of the pagan mythology, Philo does with the tale of origins contained in the books attributed to Moses. The Old Testament narratives he treats as images of internal, psychic processes. Take the creation of the world recounted in the Bible. To read it as expressing things that happened in an external way is to grasp only one half of its meaning. It does indeed say:

> In the beginning God created the heavens and the Earth. Now the Earth was formless and empty, darkness was over the surface of the deep, and the Spirit of God was hovering over the waters.[174]

But the inner truth that lies behind such words has to be experienced in one's own inner depths.

God must first be found within, and then he will be recognized as "the archetypal essence, sending forth myriads of rays, none of them visible to sense, but all grasped by the mind."[175] That is how Philo describes God. And something almost identical can be recognized in Plato's *Timaeus*:

> When the Father who had begotten it perceived that the universe was alive and in motion, a shrine for the eternal gods [that is, the stars], he was well pleased.[176]

Compare the Bible's "And God saw everything, that it was good." In this platonizing way, Philo assimilates the meaning of the Bible to the experiences of the Mysteries, making the knowledge of the divine arise from the creation-process, which takes place in one's own soul as the working-out of its destiny. The story of creation and that of the soul's divinization are one and the same.

Philo acts on the assumption that the narratives in the Mosaic primordial history can be used to tell the story of the soul in its search for God. Everything in the Bible thus becomes profoundly symbolic, and

Philo is the interpreter of its symbolism, reading the Bible as the story of the soul. It may rightly be said that Philo's method of exegesis corresponds to contemporary techniques pioneered by mysteriosophy. He himself draws attention to the same approach to the ancient scriptures among the Therapeutae:

> They have also writings of men of old, who were the founders of their sect, and had left behind many memorials of the type of treatment employed in allegory.... Their interpretations of the Holy Scriptures are made in accordance with the deeper meanings conveyed in allegory.

Philo's aim was likewise to uncover the deeper meaning hidden in the Old Testament "allegories."

It is worth considering where such exegesis could lead. Reading the creation story, one comes upon something that refers not merely to outer events but furnishes an image for the path of the soul toward divinization. The soul, then, must undertake on the microcosmic level to follow in the footsteps of God; that is the only way of describing its Mystery-striving after wisdom. It is the cosmic drama itself that is played out in every soul. The primal image expressed in the account of the creation finds its fulfillment in the inner life of the Mystery-adept. Moses wrote, not just to recount historical occurrences, but to provide images of the course that will lead the soul to God.

Philo's conception renders everything a spiritual reality within a person's own being. The human experience is a subjective echo of God's cosmic experience. God's Word, the *Logos*, becomes a reality within the soul. God brought the Jews out of Egypt and led them to the Promised Land, subjecting them to trials and privations before giving them the land as their reward—these were outward events. But one has to go through them as an inner experience, departing from the land of Egypt (the perishable world), going through privations (the suppression of the sense-nature) until the promised land of the soul (the Eternal) is attained. Philo turns it all into a sequence of inner happenings.

The Mystery-God who has poured himself out into the world celebrates his return to life in the soul, which has grasped his creative Word, and in which it becomes reality once more. A person then has God within, having inwardly given birth to the divine Spirit, which has taken on human form: the *Logos* (Christ). Philo and those who took up his ideas were able to conceive of spiritual knowledge as the birth of Christ on the level of inner truth.

Plotinus and Neoplatonism

Developing alongside Christianity, the Neoplatonic view of the world also constituted a continuation of the Philonic mode of thought. Let us examine the way Plotinus (A.D. 204–269) describes his inner experience:

> It has happened often.
> Roused into myself from my body—outside everything else and inside myself—my gaze has met a beauty wondrous and great. At such moments I have been certain that mine was the better part, mine the best of lives lived to the fullest, mine identity with the divine. Fixed there firmly, poised above everything in the intellectual that is less than the highest, utter actuality was mine.
> But then there has come the descent, down from intellection to the discourse of reason. And it leaves me puzzled. Why this descent?
> Indeed, why did my soul ever enter my body since even when in the body it remains what it has shown itself to be when by itself?[177]

And elsewhere:

> How is it then that souls forget the divinity that begot them so that—divine by nature, divine by origin—they now know neither divinity nor self?
> This evil has befallen them having its source in willful self-assertion, in being born, in becoming different, in desiring to be independent. Once having tasted the pleasures of independence, they use their freedom to go in a direction that leads away from their origin. And when they have gone a great distance, they even forget

that they came from it. Like children separated from their family since birth and educated away from home, they are ignorant now of their parentage and therefore of their identity.[178]

He continues by describing the way of life and development which the soul should seek:

It must be quiet. Let us assume that quiet too is the body that wraps it round— quiet the Earth, quiet the air and the sea, quiet the high heavens. Then picture The Soul flowing into this tranquil mass from all sides, streaming into it, spreading through it until it is luminous. As the rays of the sun lighten and gild the blackest cloud, so The Soul by entering the body of the universe gives it life and immortality.[179]

The profound affinities between this conception of the world and Christianity are unmistakable. The community of the followers of Jesus proclaimed:

That which was from the beginning, which we have heard, which we have seen with our eyes, which we have looked at and our hands have touched—this we announce concerning the Word of Life.[180]

A Neoplatonic paraphrase might be:

That which was from the beginning, which cannot be perceived with the eyes or ears—this is what must be grasped spiritually as the Word of Life.

Mysticism and Fact

The development of ancient thought thus comes to a head with a sharp polarization. In Neoplatonism and worldviews belonging to the same family, we come to an idea of Christ that is purely spiritual. Elsewhere, we find the identification of this idea of Christ with a historical figure in whom it is manifested, namely Jesus. But one might say that the author of the Gospel of John spans both these views. He says: "In the beginning was the Word." Here he is at one with the Neoplatonic line: The Word is spiritually begotten within the soul as the Neoplatonists hold. And then: The Word became flesh in the person of Jesus. This is the view he holds in common with the whole body of Christians.

The precise sense in which it could be said that the Word became flesh can only be grasped on the basis of ancient thought in the whole sweep of its development. Plato gives us the cosmic side when he describes how God stretched out the *anima mundi* in the form of a cross. This universal soul is the *Logos*, and if the *Logos* is to become flesh it must be through the repetition in fleshly existence of the macrocosmic events, being nailed to the cross and rising to new life. The profoundest idea in Christianity had long before been sketched out, in spiritual terms, by the ancient cosmogonies. The cosmogony was experienced anew by the *mystai* in the rites of initiation. But the one who was "the Word made flesh" had to go through it in historical actuality, so that it should have meaning for all humanity.

The content of the archaic mysteriosophy emerged, through Christianity, to become a historical event; and in this sense Christianity is not only the fulfillment of the hopes expressed by the prophets of Jewish tradition, but also of what had been prefigured in the Mysteries. The cross on Golgotha is the Mystery-cult of antiquity epitomized in a historical fact.

Encountered first in the ancient cosmologies, the cross reappears in the context of a unique historical event, accessible to all humanity. There it forms the point of departure for Christianity. Understood in this way, Christianity has its mystical aspect. As simultaneously mysticism and fact, Christianity is a breakthrough in the historical development of humanity for which the processes of the Mysteries, with the results that they brought about, form a prior evolutionary stage.

12

AUGUSTINE AND THE CHURCH

THE VIOLENCE OF the struggle played out in the souls of those who wrenched themselves free from paganism and made the transition to the new religion of Christian belief can be witnessed in its full force only in the figure of Augustine (A.D. 354–430).[181] To understand the convulsions of his spiritual life is at the same time to participate behind the scenes in those that rocked the souls of an Origen, a Clement of Alexandria, a Gregory of Nazianzus, a Jerome, and the others. And it is in Augustine that their struggles are laid to rest.

Augustine is the sort of person whose spiritual needs arise out of a passionate nature, and so are of the deepest kind. He passed through pagan and semi-Christian ideas, suffered intense doubts when his various ideas seemed impotent in the face of his spiritual crises, was laid low by the feeling of desperation, which asks "Can anything really be known?" When his striving began, he found his ideas bounded by perishable and sense-perceptible things, and was able to conceive of the spirit only in pictorial terms. Getting above this stage was like being set free, as he records in his *Confessions*:

> When I tried to think of my God, I could think of him only as a bodily substance, because I could not conceive of the existence of anything else. This was the principal and almost the only cause of the error from which I could not escape.[182]

Every quest for the spirit must pass through this stage if it is a living search. Despite the fact that many thinkers (and not just a few!) deny the possibility of reaching a thinking utterly purged of sense-perceptible content, they actually confuse their own limitations with what is possible in general. The point is precisely that a thinking purified of all sensory content is the prerequisite of "higher knowledge," whose psychic content does not cease when it is no longer shored up by impressions from the senses. Augustine achieved the ascent to spiritual vision, as he himself relates. He tells how he sought everywhere for "God":

> I put my question to the Earth. It answered, "I am not God," and all things on Earth declared the same. I asked the sea and the chasms of the deep and the living things that creep in them, but they answered, "We are not your God. Seek what is above us." I spoke to the winds that blow, and the whole air and all that lives in it replied to me, "Anaximenes is wrong. I am not your God." I asked the sky, the Sun, the Moon and the stars, but they, too, told me, "Neither are we the God whom you seek."[183]

And Augustine realized that the answer to his question about how to find God could come only from one source—his own soul.

His soul said that the eyes and ears could not tell what lay within it, but that it speaks in an immediate, and moreover in an indubitable fashion:

> Men may doubt whether vital force resides in air or in fire, but who can doubt that he himself lives, remembers, understands, wills, thinks, knows, and judges? If he doubts, it is a proof that he is alive, he remembers why he doubted, he understands that he doubts, he will assure himself of something, he thinks, he knows that he knows nothing, he judges that he must not accept anything hastily.[184]

Unlike external objects, which do not react against attempts to deny their existence, the soul leaps to its own defense. Even the fact that it doubted itself presumes its existence, and in its act of doubt affirms its reality:

We exist; we know that we exist, and we are glad of this existence and this knowledge. In those three things there is no plausible deception to trouble us. For we do not apprehend those truths by the bodily senses by which we are in contact with the world outside us.[185]

A person's experience of God begins when the soul is able to grasp its own inherently spiritual nature, and thence the path into the spiritual world. It was Augustine's achievement that he understood this.

In pagan culture, a similar mood had given rise to the wish among those who sought for knowledge to approach the portals of the Mysteries. In Augustine's time one might instead become a convert to Christianity. The Word that had become man, Jesus, had shown the path by which the soul could come once more to be at peace with itself.

In A.D. 385 Augustine submitted to the instruction of Ambrose in Milan. All his previous reservations about the Old and New Testaments evaporated when his instructor interpreted the major portions not just according to the literal sense but "lifting the veil that concealed their spiritual meaning."[186] The content of what the Mysteries had guarded was thereby incorporated for him into the historical tradition preserved in the Gospels and the Church. He came to accept it as a "reasonable ordinance, that within the bounds of moderation and honesty things for which there was no proof should simply be believed."[187] His conclusion was:

> Who could be so blind as to say that the Church of the apostles deserves to have no faith placed in it, when it is so loyal and is supported by the conformity of so many brethren; when these have handed down their writings to posterity so conscientiously and when the Church has so strictly maintained the succession of teachers down to our present bishops?[188]

Augustine's mode of thought gave him the assurance that since the Event of Christ the conditions for those souls who seek the spirit have changed from what they were. He is certain that in Christ Jesus everything has been revealed, in the external and historical world, which the *mystai* had sought for through the discipline of the Mysteries. Among his profoundest utterances is his declaration:

> What is now called the Christian religion existed already among the ancients, and was not lacking at the very beginnings of the human race. When Christ appeared in the flesh, the true religion already in existence received the name of Christian.[189]

Two courses lie open for one who thinks in such a way. One would be to assume that the soul, by unfolding the powers that lead it to a knowledge of one's true self, could attain, by extension, to a knowledge of Christ and all that it means. That would have been an enriching of Mystery-knowledge through Christ. But it is the other path that Augustine actually took, and which made him the great exemplar to many who came after him.

It amounts to this: at a certain stage of development one arrests the forces of the soul and adopts instead the idea of the Christ-Event contained in the written documents and oral tradition of the Church. The first way Augustine rejected because he felt it sprang from the vanity of the soul, whereas the second was correspondingly full of humility. To those who wished to follow the first course, he said:

> You may find peace in the truth, but for this humility is needed, which does not suit your proud neck.

But it filled him with boundless inner joy to think that since the "appearance of Christ in the flesh" every soul can have an experience of spiritual reality. Every soul must seek to the very limits of its endeavor, and then in order to touch the very heights it must entrust itself to faith in what the texts and traditions of the Christian *ecclesia* have to tell of Christ and his revelation. As he put it:

> What bliss, what abiding enjoyment of supreme and true good is offered to us, what serenity, what a breath of eternity! How shall I describe it? It has been expressed, as far as it could be, by those great incomparable souls who we admit have beheld and still

behold.... We reach a point at which we acknowledge how true is what we have been commanded to believe and how well and beneficently we have been brought up by our mother the Church, and of what benefit was the milk given by the apostle Paul to the little ones.[190]

This is not the place to explore what might be made of the other path of developing a mode of thinking from the knowledge of the Mysteries enriched by the Christ-Event.[191]

In pre-Christian times, the search for the spiritual foundations of life led inevitably to the path represented by the Mysteries. Augustine, however, can direct even those who do not find it within themselves to follow such a path to strive with all their human powers for knowledge, and beyond that faith, belief, will conduct them into those higher regions of spiritual truth.

Note: It was but one step further to assert that by its nature the human soul could only attain to a certain degree of knowledge by its own unaided powers, and that thereafter further progress was dependent upon faith—on belief in the written and oral tradition of Christianity. This direction in spiritual life was taken when "natural knowledge" was assigned a specific domain that the human soul was declared to be unable to transcend. Everything beyond that domain, it was said, was an object of faith and the representatives of this direction of thought demanded a trust in what rested upon the foundations of the written and oral tradition. This is the viewpoint expressed in his writings in the most manifold ways by the greatest teacher known to the Church, Thomas Aquinas (1225–1274). His works express the view that human knowledge is simply unable to progress beyond the point reached by Augustine: knowledge of self and a certainty of the divine. As to the nature of God and his relationship to the world—that is inaccessible to human cognitive powers. It forms the content of revealed religion, and as such is exalted above all knowledge.[192]

We witness these ideas crystallizing in the worldview of John Scotus Erigena, who lived in the ninth century at the court of Charles the Bald. There we find a natural transition from the perspective of primitive

Christianity to that of Aquinas. He derives his conceptual language from Neoplatonic philosophy, and his work *On the Divisions of Nature* constitutes a further extension of the teachings in "Dionysius the Areopagite." Those teachings were based upon the idea of an utterly transcendent God, from whom the sense-perceptible world nevertheless originated. Human beings are caught up in the process of the transmutation of all things back into this God, whose goal is to be what he was from the beginning. Everything is to be reintegrated into God, who has gone forth into the cosmic process and in due course arrives once more at perfection. For this to happen, however, humanity must find the way to the *Logos* that was made flesh. Erigena takes up and extends this idea; for it is in the scriptures that we learn about the *Logos*, and therefore it is belief in what they contain that leads to salvation. Reason and scriptural authority, faith and knowledge, stand side by side. There is no contradiction between them; but faith is necessary to bring what knowledge as such can never attain.

*   *   *

In the interpretation by the Christian tradition, that knowledge of the Eternal that had formed the secret of the Mysteries withheld from the profane multitude, became a matter of faith. It became something intrinsically different from knowledge. In the pre-Christian Mysteries there had been on the one hand the knowledge granted to the mystai, and on the other the faith of the ordinary people in the imagery that expressed it. Now in the Christian Mystery, God had handed over his revelation to all humanity, and human knowledge became an image of that revelation. The Mysteries had been a hothouse plant, and their wisdom was granted to the few who were ripe to receive it. Christian wisdom developed as a Mystery whose content was vouchsafed in the form of knowledge to no one, but to everyone in the form of faith.

Christianity was a continuation of the perspective of the Mysteries. But there were also changes. A share in the truth was no longer to be reserved for the few but was opened to all—in such a way, however, that one had to concede a point at which further knowledge became impossible, and further progress had to be based on faith. The secret of the Mysteries was brought by Christianity from the darkness of the temples into the bright light of day. The revelation of the ancient temples lived on, however, within the inner sanctum of its content of faith.[193]

APPENDIX I

Original Prefaces and Additional Materials

Das Christentum als mystische Tatsache was originally published in Berlin in 1902. It was based on a series of lectures given the previous winter in the "Theosophical Library" of Count Brockdorf there, and was dedicated to the Count and Countess Brockdorf, also to Steiner's friends from his former time in Vienna, Rosa Mayreder and Moritz Zitter. The second, revised edition of 1910 had the title expanded by the reference to the Mysteries of Antiquity (*die Mysterien des Altertums*). The foreword from the first edition was dropped from the second, to which Steiner added a new foreword and a series of appended remarks. Both editions contained a preliminary essay entitled "Points of View," in which Steiner fielded potential objections to the standpoint of his approach to Christian origins from the materialistic science of his day. Although reports of at least some of the original lectures survive, it is impossible to collate them here. Materials from the original and the second edition are translated below, however, for the sake of completeness and their historical value.

— A.J.W.

Foreword to the First Edition (1902)

The Museum in Brussels devoted to the work of the fascinating artist Antoine Wiertz (1806–1865) contains a picture entitled "The Things of the Present before the Man of the Future." It depicts a giant, holding for his wife and his child to see certain tiny things—cannons, scepters, emblems of honor, triumphal arches, the banners belonging to different factions, all such as we know today. These important products of our culture seem tiny to the future world's way of thinking, and to a civilization that is an intellectual "giant" in comparison with ours. We need not dwell on the prophetic intention of this picture; but to an observer of the course of intellectual life who stands before it, it conjures up another idea. For may not our modern philosophies of life and the world seem equally small to the scrutiny of future thought? What an expiation it would then be for the superior tone adopted by certain of our contemporaries toward the "childish" conceptions that our predecessors held about humanity and the universe—notions that we, with our new confession of faith based on the "stupendous progress of the natural sciences" have left "far behind!"

This thought may well occur, even if one does not adhere to any of the established religious teachings, but takes one's stand unequivocally on the ground of natural science itself—indeed, particularly in that instance. There is a profound satisfaction to be gained from viewing the sequence of living beings from microscopic creatures to homo sapiens, and considering the relatedness of all life from the perspective of the evolutionary process. To many of us, Haeckel's *Natural History of Creation* means far more than any "supernatural" account of things. Yet those with deeper natures feel, with painful dissatisfaction, the contradiction between what Rosa Mayreder calls, in illuminating words, "the life of nature according to Darwinian theory, and the goal of the furtherance of human development."

Anyone who looks beneath the surface of modern ideas cannot fail to see the gulf that yawns between two components in contemporary life. The head of modern humanity can only be satisfied by the naturalism of scientific thinking; but the heart is still steeped in the feelings that religious training and a tradition that has remained vital over thousands of years have implanted there. No reconciliation seems possible between intellect and feeling. "Science," says Rosa Mayreder in her essay, "appeals to rational insight; religion sets the goal of committing oneself through faith to the indefinable."

One has to ask whether such a contradiction is inevitable—or is it, perhaps, that the cultured people of today have not yet reached the point where they can affirm in their hearts as progressive and positive what the mind tells them to be true? To this the only possible answer seems to be: we may have learned how to understand our relationship to nature scientifically, but not how to live it.

No, we do not actually live our scientific theories. See how many there are who are delighted when Harnack, for example, says in his *The Essence of Christianity*: "How doubtful would mankind's situation be if the deeper peace for which it longs, and the clarity, conviction and power for which it strives, were dependent upon the degree of its enlightenment and education!" They may admit the truth of natural science with their heads, but with their hearts they long for quite different sources of satisfaction.

For those with eyes to see, it is quite clear that even those who take their stand on the grounds of natural science cannot translate this knowledge into the reality of life. Not even the great scientists can do so. I would not be misunderstood—devout enthusiast for Ernst Haeckel's work as I am—when I say that the polemics Haeckel heaps against Christianity often betray the feelings that have been planted in the heart by distorted versions of Christianity. For how can a protagonist of evolutionary theory look upon Christianity otherwise than as itself the product of an evolution in accord with the laws of nature? Would such a proponent not have to understand that we now live in the presence of a truth that is related to prior conceptions of the world in exactly the same way as, within the order of nature, human beings are related to their animal predecessors? It is one thing for a Christian to lay claim to the unique, the only truth. But it reflects badly upon a representative of "scientific" thinking—it seems too much like "Christian" intolerance—when he will not give to prior forms of thought, which are the stages of development leading to his own truth, proper recognition for their evolutionary role, choosing rather to represent them as worn out, childish systems of belief. One who does not simply accept the truth with the mind but lives with it, lives in it, will see it as part of an ongoing flux of ideas, in continuous evolution like everything else in nature.

If we can learn to know the truth that our minds acknowledge as an evolutionary development from its predecessors, from its ancestral forms of truth—then our hearts will follow where our heads lead. Those who accept the arguments of natural science, however, but in their hearts (without knowing how strongly!) hold to the traditional ideas of religion, are like creatures descended far back from fishes that even now refuse to come out of the water.

Such is the approach I have adopted in tracing one aspect of the emergence of Christianity in this book. There is not a sentence of it that will not jar upon the crude materialism of many of our scientific thinkers; but equally, none that I do not believe could be justified before a natural science that really understands its own nature.

Foreword to the Second Edition (1910)

The title *Christianity As Mystical Fact* was one I gave to this work eight years ago, when I gathered together the content of lectures given in 1902. It was meant to indicate the special approach adopted in the book. Its theme is not just the mystical side of Christianity in a historical presentation. It was meant to show how Christianity came into being, from the standpoint of a mystical awareness. Behind this lay the idea that spiritual happenings were factors in its emergence, which could only be observed from such a point of view. It is for the book itself to demonstrate that by "mystical" I intend nothing in the way of vague intuition rather than strict scientific argument. In many circles mysticism is understood to be just that, and therefore to be distinguished from the concerns of all "genuine science." But in this book I use the term to mean a presentation of spiritual reality—a reality only accessible to a knowledge drawn from the sources of spiritual life itself. Anyone who denies the possibility of such knowledge in principle will find its contents hard to relate to; a reader who accepts that mysticism may coexist with the clarity of the natural sciences, however, may admit that the mystical aspect of Christianity has to be mystically described.

The point of the book was thus not only its subject-matter, but even more the kind of approach to knowledge on which it was based. Hostility toward such an approach, on the grounds that it is inimical to the scientific spirit, is widespread today. And the same must be said of those who come to investigate the nature of Christianity as believers as of those who will hear only of what they call "real scientific knowledge." I have based my work, however, on the idea that the achievements of modern science lead over into a genuine mystical viewpoint. To deny such a possibility, from this point of view, is actually a contradiction of the scientific attitude that underlies those achievements. The epistemological conclusions, claimed by so many to be the only ones grounded in the facts of science, are in reality quite unable to explain the scope of that natural science itself.

This book will not be rejected, then, by those who see that mysticism may properly be combined with an appreciation of our up-to-date understanding of nature. The "mystical knowledge" described here will lead me to show, in this book, how the creative power at work in Christianity was preparing the grounds for its own appearance in the pre-Christian Mystery-cults. The pre-Christian "mysticism" of these cults was the soil in which the seed of Christianity was able to grow and become independent—enabling us to understand Christianity in its own right, while tracing it back to the pre-Christian mystical experience from which it evolved. Any other standpoint will overlook the truth, and all too easily reduce Christianity to a mere development within pre-Christian Mystery-religion. This is a common error nowadays, when the content of Christianity is compared with pre-Christian Mysteries in the belief that Christianity is no more than a continuation of what went before it. In the pages that follow, I emphasize that Christianity presupposes earlier mysticism as a seed presupposes a place to grow. The study of Christian origins will serve to bring out, rather than to obscure, the unique nature of Christianity.

It is a deep source of satisfaction to me that this view of "the essence of Christianity" has been embraced by a writer whose works on the spiritual life of humanity have profoundly enriched our culture: Edouard Schuré, author of *The Great Initiates*. He was so far in agreement as to undertake a translation into French under the title *Le mystère chrétien et les mystères antiques*. As a sign of the longing for the kind of approach to Christianity this book contains, it may be mentioned that the first edition was translated into a number of other European languages besides French.

While preparing this second edition, I have found little to alter in essentials. Some passages from the first edition of eight years ago have been expanded. Sometimes I have been able to add greater detail or to clarify what was then said. It is a source of regret to me that, owing to pressure of work, so long a period has elapsed between the first edition being no longer available and the appearance of this one.

Points of View

The impact of natural science on the way people think today has been pervasive and profound. More and more it has become impossible to discuss the spiritual needs or the soul's inner life without taking into account the scientific context. (True, many people find spiritual satisfaction quite undisturbed by the influence of science. But those who are in touch with the pulse of their time cannot do so.) Our heads are filled, with increasing rapidity, by the ideas stemming from our knowledge of nature and our hearts are drawn unwillingly after, often in despondency and dismay.

What concerns us is not just the numbers of people who succumb to the power that lies in scientific ways of thinking, but the fact itself. That is what convinces the observer that here we have something that cannot be ignored if we are to form a modern conception of the world. Many of the by-products of such thinking admittedly require us to reject its assumptions. Nevertheless, it is clearly not enough just to reject them, given that many people are attracted to them—indeed, drawn to them as by a magic power. Nor is the situation altered simply because some individuals realize that science has actually left behind the shallow stage of seeing everything in terms of force and bits of matter—left it behind long ago. More significant are the voices boldly declaring that it is from science that a new religious system of belief must be constructed. Shallow and superficial as these notions appear to anyone with a grounding in the deeper spiritual concerns of humanity, they must be registered as the real center of contemporary interest and are in all probability destined to become still more prominent in the immediate future.

Then we must consider the other group, whose hearts have not kept pace with their heads. These have accepted the scientific outlook as inevitable; the weight of evidence seems decisive. But the religious needs of their souls remain unsatisfied, and the vista that opens before them appears too dreary. What then? Is the soul of humanity to rise, aspiring to the pinnacles of beauty, truth, and goodness, while in each individual case it turns out to be only a bubble, rising from the material brain and ending in nothingness? Such is the nightmare feeling that affects many people, and the ideas of science seem oppressive to them also because of the huge weight of authority behind them. People contrive to remain blind for as long as possible to the contradiction within their own soul. In fact, they console themselves by saying that such matters are inscrutable. While sense-experience and logical reasoning require it, they think in a scientific way; but they hold on to the religious feelings from their upbringing. They prefer to keep the issue in the darkness of impenetrable obscurity so far as the rational mind is concerned. They lack courage to win through to the light.

The dominant role of science in contemporary culture, then, is past doubt. It must therefore be acknowledged when we come to speak of spiritual matters. Beyond doubt too is the fact that as an immediate solution to spiritual needs, science is shallow and simplistic. Despair would be unavoidable if its way were the right one. Would it not be insupportable if we had to think along the lines of these sentences from a pamphlet by R.G. Ingersoll:

Thought is a form of force. We walk and we think by means of the same form of force. Man's organism transforms certain forces in thought-force, which is sustained by the intake of what we call "food" and turned into what we call "thoughts." What wonderful chemistry that can produce the divine tragedy of *Hamlet* by means of digestion!

Of course, not everyone accepts what is put forward by the proponents of these ideas; but that is not the point, which is that countless people are compelled by the attitude of science to think in this way about the world around them, even if they will not admit it to themselves. The modern prophets of science try to thrust upon us a dreary prospect—dreariest of all for those who have realized that the results of natural science show that in its own terms it is unassailable. They recognize that however much the details may be challenged, however many books are written or researches compiled about the struggle for existence and its random nature, about the decisive character of "natural selection" or its irrelevance, the direction in which science is moving will find (within limits) ever increasing acceptance.

So are the implications of science really what these proponents make them out to be? Their own behavior shows that they are not. For in their own work they do not follow the path shown by the pioneers in other fields. Would Darwin and Haeckel have made their great discoveries in evolution if they had spent their time, not out observing life and the structure of living organisms, but incarcerated in the laboratory experimenting on specimens of tissue? Could Lyell have explained the formation of the Earth's crust if he had examined, not the composition of the various strata as they occur but just the chemical classification of numberless rocks? If we were really to follow in the footsteps of the great figures, the towering geniuses of modern science, we would apply to spiritual life the same approach they brought to bear on nature. That would not bring us to the idea of creating the "divine" tragedy of *Hamlet* by chemical processes of digestion, any more than a natural scientist would claim to have understood the role of heat in the formation of the Earth after having studied a piece of sulfur warmed in a retort, or the structure of the brain after subjecting an extract to the effects of acid rather than investigating how it has evolved out of the organs belonging to lower forms of life.

It is true, then: the investigation of spiritual things can indeed learn from the example of natural science—only it must be a real imitation of scientific discovery, and not be misled by the views of certain proponents of science. There should be research in the spiritual domain as there has been in the physical domain. But that is a different matter from the opinions scientists have formed about the spiritual world, confused by their narrow application to physical phenomena alone. To act in the spirit of natural science would be to study the spiritual evolution of humanity impartially, as the naturalist observes the sense-world. That would lead in the domain of spiritual life to a method of investigation as different from purely natural science as is geology from theoretical physics, or evolutionary theory from advanced chemical research. It would lead to higher methodological principles, which would certainly not be identical with those of natural science, but would be in agreement with all that we really mean by scientific inquiry.

Thus we can modify or correct the one-sided views deriving from scientific research by means of an added perspective. In doing so we are not betraying science, but advancing it. Such advances are necessary if we are to be able to get inside the spiritual processes that shape the inner realities of Christianity or other world religions. To apply these methods may stir up opposition from the scientific establishment, but they are justifiable and in accord with the scientific way of thinking.

This kind of research must go beyond the philological investigation of religious documents. The analogy from natural scientific research still holds: to explain a law of chemistry, it is of no use to characterize the retorts, vessels, or tweezers used in the experiment that led to its discovery! There is just as little point, if we are trying to explain the emergence of Christianity, in pinning down the sources that Luke drew upon for his Gospel, or upon which John based his "Secret Revelation." Their history, in that sense, can only be the outer court to research proper. Tracing how the documents were pieced together will not explain the meaning to be found in the books of the Pentateuch or the Greek Mystery-traditions. Research is concerned with their way of looking at things, of which documents merely provide outer expression. Likewise a scientist working on anthropology does not pursue the origins of the word *man* or its subsequent linguistic history. The subject is interesting, not its name, and in the study of spiritual life we must also hold fast to the spirit and not to its documentary outer forms.

Additional Remarks (1910)

by Rudolf Steiner

Page 3, "spiritual eye"
It is said here that those whose spiritual eyes are open can see in the spiritual world. But that does not mean that they alone can understand the findings of initiates who are able to see for themselves. That may be true for actual research; but everyone can apply rational understanding and evaluate the truth of the results once they have been communicated. And anyone can use them in life and appreciate their value, even if they cannot yet see spiritually.

Page 6, "sink into the mire"
On the meaning of Plato's words, cf. previous remark.

Page 6, "criminal to impart"
Such is no longer the case owing to the conditions of the present day, when spiritual knowledge can be grasped in the form of ideas. Recent humanity has a relationship to ideas that was quite lacking in ancient times. Nowadays it is quite possible for there to be people who experience the spiritual world directly, and people who grasp what they have experienced in ideas. But that would not have been the case in the ancient world. What is said about the impossibility of communicating the teachings of the Mysteries really refers to the kind of experience the initiate has, which certainly cannot be shared by those who have not undergone preparation. But they have always been communicated in a form which the non-initiated could understand— for example, in the myths that made the content of the Mysteries more widely understood in antiquity.

Page 40, "mantic art"
Ancient mystical terminology distinguished between *mantike*, "pertaining to the knowledge gained through spiritual sight," and *telestike*, "pertaining to the path of initiation."

Page 81, "himself a Kabeiros"
The *Kabeiroi* of the ancient Mysteries are beings with a consciousness far transcending that of humanity today. Schelling means that through initiation individuals could gain a consciousness of a higher nature than their own present one.

Page 86, "seven is a sacred symbol"
Its significance is further explained in my *An Outline of Esoteric Science* (Anthroposophic Press, Great Barrington, MA, 1997).

Page 91, "apocalyptic symbols"
The explanations given here are necessarily brief and could naturally be greatly extended; but that lies outside the scope of this book.

Page 129, "Ingersoll"
These assertions from R.G.Ingersoll's *Modern Twilight of the Gods* are not quoted on the assumption that everyone would agree with them. Many would deny them, yet their ideas about the human being and nature would lead to the same conclusion if logically followed through. Theoretical statements of belief are one thing, and the real beliefs implicit in a way of thinking quite another. Someone may despise and ridicule Ingersoll's words, but if they deny a spiritual basis to the manifestations of nature and explain everything in terms of externals, they will logically come to an equally materialistic position.

Page 129, "struggle for existence"
The realities behind the familiar formulae "the struggle for existence," "natural selection," and so on, are clear manifestations of the spirit in nature, for those who are able to discern it. The views that modern science bases on them, however, do not lead in that direction. The spiritual implications of the facts are the reason for science's ever increasing audience; the views based on them by science, however, should not be treated as though they follow from the facts themselves, although the temptation to fall into that mistake is immeasurably great today.

Page 183, "sources that Luke drew upon"
From such remarks it should not be inferred that I undervalue purely historical research, which is not at all the case. Historical research has its rightful place, but it should not be intolerant of the spiritual approach and its perspective. In this book I have not labored to document everything. With good will, however, it will be clear to anyone that established historical truth is nowhere contradicted by what is said here. Any thorough, balanced judgment must admit that. It is quite different in the case of someone for whom the latest fashionable theory is "what we now know"—and for whom the statements in this book are "scientifically untenable" and "without foundation!"

APPENDIX II

Afterword by Michael Debus
Translated by James H. Hindes

With the publication of *Christianity As Mystical Fact* in 1902, Rudolf Steiner, at the age of forty, appears to have taken a radical turn in his work. Until then he was known for philosophical and literary publications in which he stressed the autonomy of human knowledge, rejecting completely any dogmatic worldview, especially the dogmatic Christianity of the Church. Here for the first time he himself is speaking about the substance of Christianity, which until then he had completely rejected in its form as ecclesiastical dogma.

It would be easy to assume that he gave a spiritual-scientific commentary on various aspects of traditional teachings, and supplemented what was already "known" from Christian tradition with profound insights for even deeper knowledge. Rudolf Steiner has been misunderstood again and again in this regard, as, for example, when his lecture cycles are seen simply as anthroposophical commentaries on the Bible. This is precisely what he never intended.

This particular characterization of Nicholas Cusanus contains an autobiographical element; for the path that Cusanus could not take is precisely Rudolf Steiner's own path, on which he clearly rejected any sort of "refuge in a revelation that comes from outside" himself. When Rudolf Steiner speaks concerning Christianity, he does not refer to tradition. Traditional ideas are not his source but rather ideas that he himself has discovered. Only inasmuch as he finds such self-discovered ideas within traditional sources can they have any significance for him and thus be incorporated into his descriptions. To understand the sources he drew upon to speak in such an independent way about Christianity, we must consider Rudolf Steiner's own path.

The starting point for Rudolf Steiner's life work was the question: Is it possible to know reality? Or: Is the "thing-in-itself" (in Kant's sense) inaccessible to the human spirit? Such a conclusion would mean that the human spirit is held captive in its own subjective ideas concerning the world? This is the question of the essence of human knowledge and therefore the question concerning what role the human being should play in the world process. Kant's understanding is, in principle, also extremely common today.

Our understanding of the world takes place, aided by models of thought created by the various sciences according to their specific questions. Such models help us to better master the world, but they are not expected to actually describe reality. It is astonishing to realize that Rudolf Steiner, already on his own path at the age of twenty-one, had philosophically overcome Kant's limiting philosophy. The improbable result of this struggle is a short essay that remained unpublished during his lifetime.[2] The rest of his life is a step-by-step unfolding of an understanding and epistemology of the world that proceeds from the thinking that can comprehend reality. Rudolf Steiner opposed the current view that reality is located somewhere outside our knowing, and that the human thought image that reproduces this reality occurs through knowing, or perhaps specifically not; he held that this reality cannot be found through knowing, because it is only created as reality through the act of our knowing.[3]

Rudolf Steiner's path to knowledge has absolutely no presuppositions. It is grounded in the experience of reality that is possible for every human being. Any assumptions that arise from a particular world view, such as faith in a spiritual world or in reincarnation, would be just as problematic as the materialistic superstition of natural science. For this reason, when Steiner developed a path of knowledge in his basic philosophical writings, the dogmatism of "revealed religion" was rejected just as sharply as the dogmatism of natural science. Such truth can illuminate the path of knowledge only as a goal; it is dogma when placed at the beginning.

Even as a young man Steiner had pointed out that the "*dogma of revelation* ... passes down to people, one way or another, truths about things withheld from their view. People have no insight into the world from which the postulates arise. They must *believe* in such truth, because they have no access to its basis."[4] Steiner objected to such dogmatic faith in the philosophical formulation of his epistemology with increasingly sharp words, and he often mentioned Christianity in this connection. In his autobiography, he described in retrospect what he had in mind:

> Certain things I said and wrote during that time appear to contradict my later descriptions of Christianity. The reason is that, in those days, the doctrine of a world beyond permeated all Christian teachings, and it was these teachings I had in mind when I used the word *Christianity*. All religious experiences pointed to a world of spirit, supposedly unattainable for human intellect. The substance of religion, its precepts for moral life, supposedly stemmed from revelations bestowed upon humanity from a world external to the human being and beyond the reach of human consciousness. For me this was disproved by my direct inner perception of spirit. I had to maintain that both the sense-world and the spiritual world are experienced through what is perceptible in human beings and in nature.[5]

It is indeed surprising when Rudolf Steiner, in looking back at his path, describes so concisely the spiritual experience he had at the turn of the century: "This experience culminated in my standing in the spiritual presence of the Mystery of Golgotha in a most profound and solemn festival of knowledge."[6] The path of knowledge, which began with absolutely no assumptions of any kind, had led him to knowledge of Christ.

How can we imagine this happening? In the little essay already mentioned, the twenty-one-year-old spoke of the "essential being [*Wesen*] of an object." In a similar sense, Steiner says in his epistemology, "In thinking, the ground of being shows itself in its most perfect form." This ultimately leads to: "When thinking therefore makes a connection, forms a judgment, it is the very substance of the ground of the world itself, having flowed into thinking—that is, connected."[7] The "ground of being" is here intended in its philosophical sense, but it can also be thought of in a very concrete way, as the *being* or the *essential existence* of a thing. Thus the sentences quoted here as examples contain a surprising perspective, because the essential being of thinking (that is, the world's essence) has an immediate and direct relationship to the world. The closeness of this essential connection goes so far that Steiner can say, "The 'I' is to be found within thinking."[8]

Following Steiner's descriptions, however, if the mystery of the "I" is so intimately connected with the essential being of thinking—the thinking that is at the same time the essential being of the world—then this points to the hidden role (not yet fully revealed) that Christ plays in the act of knowing. Discussing in his autobiography the time just before the turn of the century, Rudolf Steiner reaches back to a concept from Greek philosophy to describe this hidden aspect of knowledge—that is, the *logos* ("word," or "reason"). Indeed, this is the primary word used in John's Gospel to characterize Christ. "Thus for me this truth became direct inner experience: In the world and all its processes, the *Logos*, the *Wisdom*, the *Word* holds sway."[9]

> We can, of course, understand the three words, *logos, wisdom,* and *word* purely in a philosophical way. But we can also see in them the beginning of the experience of Christ in knowing, the goal toward which Rudolf Steiner forged a path. Those who seek the essential being of the world through thinking will become increasingly aware that they cannot reach the goal alone or merely through their own strength. The essential being of what is known must come to meet them. Rudolf Steiner describes the activity of thinking as twofold. To begin with, through our active and independent efforts to think, we create a *free space*. This first activity of thought "prepares the *appearance* of thinking"—that is, the essential being of the world.[10] Hence, true knowledge is never one's own achievement alone; it always requires, as well, a response from this *essential being*, which appears, as we have seen, only in "relation to the human being" as the *Logos* incarnated. This response is always an act of grace. Knowledge, understood in this way, is an encounter between our own activity and the world's essential being. The deepest form of this knowledge, or encounter, becomes knowledge of Christ.
>
> This path to knowledge of Christ can also be understood as a path of awakening. It begins with the statement: "Hence, the first observation that we make about thinking is that it is the unobserved element in our normal spiritual life."[11] Later, as we have seen, we read, "The 'I' is to be found within thinking." This statement can be seen as the result of a growing ability to observe

thinking—that is, to wake up to one's own being. It is like an awakening within the activity of knowing, which unleashes both knowledge of Christ and knowledge of the true "I" in thinking; it is a step on the path toward the birth of the "I." Rudolf Steiner says of one who experiences such an awakening: "In this moment, one has become a philosopher."[12] He does not say: In this moment one has become a Christian. Later, however, he calls this path of awakening that leads to the birth of the "I" "Pauline thoughts in the realm of epistemology," because, just as Paul awoke on the way to Damascus to the creative reality of Christ, so does anyone who has become a "philosopher" awaken to the creative power that belongs to the essential being of thinking.[13]

In his letter to the Ephesians (5:14), Paul says,

And so it is said:
Awake, you who are sleeping,
Arise from the dead,
The Christ shall be your light!

By mentioning the name of Christ, the Pauline theory of knowledge is also the bridge to actual history. The birth of the "I" is, to begin with, a fact of the inner life of knowledge, timeless, determined alone through biographical factors appropriate to a specific individual. As a historical fact it occurred at a specific date in time. In 1912, when Rudolf Steiner published an anthroposophical "Calendar," he simultaneously produced a surprising way of reckoning years.[14] For the year 1912 it says, "In the 1879th year after the birth of the 'I.'" He is referring to the year 33 and thus to the "Mystery of Golgotha" as the moment when the human "I" was born. The essence of the Pauline theory of knowledge is an awareness that the Mystery of Golgotha is the authentic source of those powers of insight and knowledge that lead the human being to the true birth of the "I."

In the first Goetheanum, for which the foundation stone was laid in 1913, this path of knowledge was expressed architecturally in the double-domed hall from west to east. The path began in the west under the red window of knowledge. In the east, before the background of the stage under the smaller dome, would stand the statue of "The Representative of Humanity," the Christ, who is *striding to meet us* from east to west. Rudolf Steiner's path toward this noble goal of knowledge was an inner path through deserts and abysses, through loneliness of the soul, and through the experience of hell, as described in terms of the Mysteries in *Christianity As Mystical Fact*.[15] He could follow this path only by ignoring consistently all traditional Christianity and all idealistic dogma. He had to follow his own path unperturbed by any external influence. And yet he would not have arrived at his goal had he not gone beyond what appeared in *Intuitive Thinking As a Spiritual Path* as the fruit of the germinal writing of the twenty-one-year-old. He knew the spiritual law: "Knowledge is not gained by asserting only one's own point of view, but through immersion in streams of thought foreign to one's own."[16] Steiner wrote about Nietzsche, and he was considered an absolute "Nietzschean."[17] In Haeckel's work Steiner recognized "the most significant accomplishment of the German spiritual-cultural life of the second half of the nineteenth century," and he was seen as a follower of Haeckel. Steiner wrote, however, "Culture is not served by exposing Haeckel's weaknesses to his contemporaries, but by explaining to them the greatness of his phylogenetic concept."[18] He therefore wrote the two volume work *World and Life Views in the Nineteenth Century* (which later appeared in an expanded version as *The Riddles of Philosophy*), in which he immersed himself in the ways of thinking of many of the philosophers and natural scientists of the nineteenth century.[19] He portrayed them in such a way that he could say of himself, "You have shown your comprehension of current directions of thought by treating them as only someone would who fully supports them."[20] He *understood* his contemporaries.

However, he experienced entirely the opposite from others. On *his* path he remained misunderstood. "Thus at every turn I met the problem: How can I find the way to express in terms understandable to my contemporaries what I inwardly perceive directly as the truth?" And the question became pressing: "Must I remain silent?"[21] His immersion in spiritual streams foreign to himself and his decision not to want his own viewpoint to prevail, led him into a crisis—the loneliness of being misunderstood. But this crisis led to a breakthrough, to the cognitional experience of the Mystery of Golgotha, the "most inward, most earnest

solemnity of knowledge" on the threshold of the century. His thinking was transformed by what finally appeared in written form in his
World and Life Views in the Nineteenth Century; he could then follow
a path he later called "the path of thought" to Christ. On this path the
following holds true:

> The more we develop a social interest in the opinions of other peo-
> ple, even when we consider them false, the more we illuminate our
> thoughts with the opinions of others, the more we place next to our
> own thoughts (which we consider true) those developed by others
> (which we may consider to be in error, but are nevertheless inter-
> ested in), the more we can feel within our soul the words of Christ,
> which must be understood today in the new language of Christ:
> What you find as opinion, as world view in one of the least of your
> fellow human beings, therein seek me myself."[22]

In this way Steiner's method of immersion in spiritual streams foreign to himself became a path of knowledge, a path to Christ through
thinking.

During this time until the turn of the century there was *one* "foreign"
spiritual stream in which it appears he could not immerse himself, and
he differentiated himself from it again and again: the spiritual stream of
the Christian Church and Christian creeds. "I never found the
Christianity I sought in any of the existing denominations."[23] Until the
turn of the century, whenever he spoke of Christianity he was referring
to "the substance of Christianity that lives in the existing confessions."
However, whoever seeks knowledge must reject such content as
Christian faith in revelation.

Apparently, after the turn of the century Rudolf Steiner found himself in an entirely new situation. He had devoted himself with complete
selflessness to the methods of thought of other people. This became for
him a path of thought leading to knowledge of Christ, to Christ himself. Solemnly standing before the Mystery of Golgotha as foundation,
Steiner could now immerse himself also in the ecclesiastical, the
"Church" stream, with understanding. This is an entirely new element
in his biography, and it opens unusual and wonderful perspectives

through which the Church can understand how it was born from pre-Christian Mystery religions. Such an understanding is new and unprecedented in the history of Christianity. Immersion in this stream signified a complete turn-around for Rudolf Steiner.

On this path forged by Steiner, the experience of Christ shows us that the essential being of the world *comes to meet* our human thinking. Anyone who seeks knowledge by beginning the path without the presuppositions of any world-view whatsoever, will sometime at some point on the path, no matter how far-distant, eventually meet Christ.

The direction is reversed in the spiritual stream of the Church, which is not the principle of *encounter* but the principle of *following.* This path is therefore not without presuppositions; it is based instead on a pre-existing relationship to, and experience of, Christ himself, who becomes the leader of whoever follows him. Steiner speaks of this for the first time in *Christianity As Mystical Fact.* It was not yet possible in 1902 to present everything in a fully developed form. The second edition in 1910 is a further development and clarification, and also, in part, a supplement to what was said in 1902.[24]

The new understanding results from the perspective of the pre-Christian Mysteries. They are the ground upon which Christianity has developed. Nevertheless, it cannot simply be derived from the Mysteries; it is the "seed of an independent species." Indeed, we must reverse the causality and say that "the creative power at work in Christianity was preparing the grounds for its own appearance in the pre-Christian Mystery cults."[25] The Mysteries are the dawning light of the rising Sun of Christianity.

What purpose did the Mysteries serve? Expressed in modern terms they were educational establishments for the cultural and political elite, the leaders of that time. In contrast to today, inner development and external professional training were intimately connected. Because of this, the inner training and the experiences associated with the Mysteries were essential. In general, admission into the Mysteries was not open to the public; one could be called to them only when the preconditions had been met. These were people whose personalities and gifts were far too developed for them to be simple, ordinary members of a group—that is, regular folk, and "who sought a deeper religious

life and knowledge than could be found in the popular religions."[26]
They then underwent an intensive training and experienced profound
soul transformations, passing through "death and resurrection." It was
a development that took place in the seclusion of the temple and led
to creative independence. There was a protected space where the air
was prepared for these processes. The initiates were those called to lead
others and, at the same time, to guide cultural life. They were born
ahead of their time, and they brought to birth the I (the ego, or self)
in a particular way that anticipated the development of the general
population. "Initiatory knowledge is thus an actual event in the cosmic process. It is the birth of a divine child—a process just as real as
any natural process."[27]

In this form of the Mysteries, "pre-Christian Christianity" reveals
characteristics that are difficult to recognize in its ecclesiastical form after
Christ, characteristics that nevertheless constitute the essential kernel—
namely the question: Where does the human being belong in the
scheme of creation? Has everything been said when we view the human
being as creature, perhaps as the crown of creation? Or does "image and
likeness of God" perhaps not also mean responsible creativity? What is
the path we must travel in order to be transformed from mere creatures
to increasingly creative beings? What happened in the Mysteries can
convey an impression of this process.

> Yet people are illuminated from within by the power that fashioned
> all things, including themselves. They also feel something urging
> them on to higher creative life. There lies within them something
> that pre-existed their natural being and will outlive it. It brought
> them into existence; nevertheless they can seize hold of it and share
> in its creative force. Such feelings pervaded the life of the ancient
> mystai as a result of their initiation.[28]

Christianity took over from the Mysteries, "when the time was fulfilled" (Galations 4:4). This assumption of the role formerly played by
the Mysteries meant that the Mysteries were now to be proclaimed. The
veil of the temple was torn in two from top to bottom (Matthew
27:51). The cross on Golgotha and the empty grave of the resurrection

are events from the Mystery religions that have become public; from now on people can bear witness to them publicly. "The ritual pattern enacted by the Mystery-cults of the ancient world in the secrecy of their temple precincts was grasped by Christianity in an event of world history."[29] But the publication of the Mysteries had consequences. Previously only the "invited guests" were admitted to the "wedding feast" (Matthew 22). They had been carefully chosen through training and trials. Now all are invited, "both good and evil." Now the pre-requisite for entrance into the wedding hall is no longer one's individual training alone. The extent to which one has developed one's consciousness is no longer the only factor deciding whether or not one can participate in the fruits of initiation.

> Christianity presents itself as the means by which everyone can find the way. Even those who are not inwardly ripe need not forgo the possibility of participating, albeit unconsciously, in the current of the Mysteries.... The fruits of spiritual development could be enjoyed henceforward also by those who had not been able to attain initiation in the Mysteries.[30]

If it is now possible to enjoy the fruits of the Mysteries without preparatory training, then a new access to the Mysteries is indicated. The essential change is the elimination of the sharp separation between the initiate and the folk. "The thought that many were standing outside, uncertain of the way, must have weighed upon the mind of Jesus with nightmare heaviness."[31] For those standing outside, those who were not yet ripe for initiation, a possibility had to be created so they could find a connection to the Mysteries and acquire at least "part of what had formerly been attainable only through the techniques of the Mysteries"[32] but now "to a certain degree unconsciously." This appears to be in direct contradiction to the ancient Mystery religions' principle that spiritual development is based on the development and expansion of consciousness.

How then could an unconscious initiation possibly take place? What would be involved? Two new principles are responsible for making this possible: The role of the *proxy* in initiation and the principle of *community initiation*. The role of a proxy here means that the initiation of *one* is also a living reality for all those who "cling to him."[33] Paul accordingly says that a Christian should suffer with Christ, be crucified, resurrect, live, and be glorified with Christ.[34] This "clinging to Christ" happens through the power of faith, through which community is built in a new way.

> Christ Jesus appeared in his own time as an initiate—but one initiated in a uniquely great way…. Henceforth for the Christian community, mysteriosophy would be indissolubly bound up with the personality of Christ Jesus.[35]

What had previously been the experience of the individual mystic now passes over to the community as a whole.

"In the Mystery-places the spirit had been poured out upon the *mystai* of old. Through the 'Mystery of Golgotha' it was poured out upon the whole Christian community."[36] One man brings the community along with him so that it can receive there the "fruits of the Mysteries."

The consciousness of the angel of the community (Apocalypse 1:20–2:1) carries the consciousness of the individual who is only more or less awakened. This new principle of an "unconscious" initiation belongs to the Christianity of *following Christ*, whose substance we receive through tradition. It is not without presuppositions and requires the traditional images upon which faith is based and through which faith is given direction. But such Christianity also has another side where the principle of consciousness training and expansion is still valid. An intensive immersion in the feelings associated with traditional images leads to Christian mysticism, to the path of *Imitatio Christi*, whose goal is Christian initiation and consciousness of the essence of the Mystery of Golgotha. This *mystical* side of the "following" form of Christianity is mentioned by Steiner in *Christianity as Mystical Fact* very few times. He deals with it in greater detail in later lectures.[37]

Through images that work externally and create community, Christianity as "following Christ" becomes the foundation of the Church and its creed. *Christianity As Mystical Fact* is essentially dedicated to this theme. Christian mysticism as a path for the individual— as well as the Christian Church as the path of community—grew out of the ancient Mysteries. They are ways of following Christ, and therefore they are not without presuppositions, based as they are on what was passed down by tradition.

With this book Rudolf Steiner penetrated with deep understanding (which had not been possible for him before the turn of the century) the substance of traditional Christianity in the clearest way, and thereby illuminated the "following Christ" form of Christianity connected with it. Immersion in foreign spiritual streams was now also possible for Steiner with respect to the "existing confessions" within the stream of the Church. We can say for Rudolf Steiner, in view of *Christianity As Mystical Fact*, the same thing he said about *World and Life Views in the Nineteenth Century*: He displayed an understanding for the ecclesiastical stream of Christianity by treating it only as a total adherent could treat it. For this reason he can point to the moment when the Church lost its connection to the Mysteries. The decisive moment came in the fourth century at the end of the Early Church.

Two paths were thus possible. One path allows that, if the human soul develops inwardly the forces that lead it to true self-cognition, if indeed it goes far enough, it will come to cognition also of the Christ and everything connected with him. This would have been a Mystery knowledge enriched through the Christ event. The other path is the one actually taken by Augustine, through which he became the great example for his successors. It involves cutting off the development of soul-forces at a certain point and the receiving of ideas connected with the Christ event from written accounts and oral traditions.[38]

The ecclesiastical stream of Christianity is united with the "following of Christ," but it has lost its connection with the Mysteries. Christian mysticism, which contains the principle of initiation, is also connected with the stream of the Church. In his later lectures, Steiner describes this form of mysticism as the "Christian-Gnostic path" with its seven steps. This path of esoteric training is based entirely on the *substance* of Christianity, primarily on the Gospel of John. It was not Rudolf Steiner's path to his experience of "standing before the Mystery of Golgotha." His own path was the path of knowledge that did not begin with any presuppositions. Steiner later called it the "Christian-Rosicrucian path." Although it is not based on any presuppositions it is called "Christian," because the knowledge acquired through it can become knowledge of Christ. In his book *How to Know Higher Worlds*, Steiner made this path accessible to anyone who seeks it. It is the appropriate path for modern human consciousness. Beginning with *Christianity As Mystical Fact*, what Rudolf Steiner said after the turn of the century concerning the matter of Christianity shows that the Rosicrucian initiation can produce the substance of Christianity, free of any tradition, and thereby confirm, and even supplement, existing Christian texts.

Access to the substance of Christianity, independent of any documents, is the decisive consequence of Steiner's experience of Christ at the turn of the century. With this event the path of *following* Christ, the path based on the substance of Christianity, begins to merge with the path of *encountering* Christ, which is based on knowledge acquired without presuppositions. Thus a union of the two paths is created, which can be called *anthroposophy*. For this reason, depending on the direction from which one approaches it, anthroposophy is either the working toward knowledge without any presuppositions, or it is comprehensive knowledge of Christ. In *Christianity As Mystical Fact* Rudolf Steiner bore witness to the latter approach for the first time. This book contains anthroposophical Christology in a germinal yet comprehensive form.

Notes

1. See "Cardinal Nicolas of Cusa," in Rudolf Steiner's *Mystics after Modernism: Discovering the Seeds of a new Science in the Renaissance* (CW 7).
2. "Einzig Mögliche Kritik der atomistischen Begriffe" [The only possible critiques of the concept of atomism] in *Beiträge zur Rudolf Steiner Gesamtausgabe*, Nr. 63, Rudolf Steiner Nachlassverwaltung, Dornach, Switzerland, 1978.
3. See Rudolf Steiner's "Notes to the New Edition," 1924, in *The Science of Knowing: Outline of an Epistemology Implicit in the Goethean World View* (CW 2).
4. See "The Ground of Things and Activity of Knowing in *The Science of Knowing*.
5. *Autobiography: Chapters in the Course of My Life, 1861-1907* (CW28). See also regarding Steiner's approach to thinking at that time (1889), *Individualism in Philosophy*, Mercury Press, Spring Valley, 1989.
6. See *Autobiography*.
7. See *The Science of Knowing*.
8. *Intuitive Thinking As a Spiritual Path: A Philosophy of Freedom* (CW 4).

9. See *Autobiography*.

10. *Intuitive Thinking As a Spiritual Path*.

11. Ibid.

12. *Methodische Grundlagen der Anthroposophie, Gesmmelte Aufsätze zur Philosophie, Nauruwissenschaft, Ästhetik und Seelen kunde 1884-1901* (GA 30), Rudolf Steiner Verlag, Dornach, Switzerland, 1989.

13. *The Karma of Materialism* (CW 176).

14. In *Beiträge*, nrs. 37-38.

15. See page 4.

16. Autobiographical sketch by Rudolf Steiner for Edouard Schuré, 1907, in *Correspondence and Documents, 1901-1925* (CW 262).

17. Ibid. Steiner stated that one result of his work in connection with Nietzsche was the publication of a pamphlet against him called "Nietzsche-maniac."

18. Ibid.

19. Originally published in October 1900; *The Riddles of Philosophy* (CW 18).

20. Ibid. Steiner went on to say, "No one will be able to say: this esotericist speaks of the spiritual world because he is ignorant of the philosophical and scientific developments of our time."

21. *Autobiography*.

22. Lecture of February 11, 1919 in *Die innere Aspekt des sozialen Rätsels* (CW 193).

23. *Autobiography*; Steiner continues, "After the severe, inner struggles during that time of testing, I found it necessary to immerse myself in Christianity and, indeed, in the world where spirit itself speaks of it."

24. An excellent study of this is found in Christoph Lindenberg's book, *Individualismus und offenbare Religion, Rudolf Steiner Zugang zum Christentum*, expanded edition, Stuttgart, 1995.

25. See Foreword to the Second Edition, pp 126-127.

26. See page 1.

27. See page 14.

28. See page 10.

29. See page 67.

30. See page 75.

31. See page 75.

32. See page 67.

33. See page 68.

34. Romans 6:6 and 8, 8:17; Galatians 2:19; II Corinthians 7:3; Ephesians 2:6.

35. See page 67.

36. See page 69.

37. See *From Jesus to Christ* (CW 131). In these lectures Rudolf Steiner goes into great detail concerning the various forms and streams of Christianity.

38. See page 117ff.

TRANSLATOR'S NOTES

1. That is, the Mysteries. Rudolf Steiner connects the Mysteries with the
    great cultural developments of the ancient civilizations: India, Iran, Egypt,
    and Babylonia, as well as Greece. They provided the knowledge in practi-
    cal as well as spiritual matters that underlay the myths, religious symbols,
    festival calendars, and so on, by which life was shaped and given meaning.
    But the ordinary people received only the results—they did not know the
    source directly. That was reserved for special leaders: initiate-heroes,
    priests, prophets, or similar persons. Steiner points to the division in
    ancient Greece between the popular or public religion based on the epics
    of "Homer, Hesiod, and learned men" who expounded them, and the
    Mysteries (whose name derives from the term for "initiation"), which led
    back directly to the sources of inspiration. Steiner spoke of new forms of
    Mystery-teaching for our own age and the future. Nowadays, however, the
    Mysteries cannot have the same "exclusive" character they had in ancient
    times, but must keep pace with the evolution of modern humanity's indi-
    vidual self-consciousness. Christianity, Steiner demonstrates, is connected
    both with the archaic Mysteries and with a transformation of the old
    forms whose further elaboration still lies in the future.
2. Historians of religion often restrict the term "Mysteries" to the Greek
    sphere; but it is legitimately used by Steiner wherever we find the combi-
    nation of secret (esoteric) teachings and initiation-rites. Mircea Eliade,
    Rites and Symbols of Initiation: The Mysteries of Birth and Rebirth (Spring,
    Woodstock, CT, 1994) stresses the continuity between the classical
    Mysteries and the initiation-rites of the most archaic societies.
3. See Aristotle, *Nicomachean Ethics* III, I.
4. Plutarch, a fragment preserved in Stobaeus, *Anthology* IV.52.49; it is trans-
    lated in M.W. Meyer's book, *The Ancient Mysteries: A Sourcebook* (Harper
    SanFrancisco, San Francisco, 1987), p. 8.
5. Descent into the underworld figures in many of the Mysteries, whether in
    the legends of their heroes (such as Herakles or Theseus), or in the sym-
    bolic enactments, for example, in the Creation Festival at New Year in
    ancient Babylon. There the initiate-king "died" and entered the dark inte-
    rior of the "world-mountain," but later returned and ascended the ziggu-
    rat, or pyramid with its seven levels, and received cosmic symbols of
    power. He was identified in the rites with the creator-god Marduk, who
    had also died before defeating the powers of chaos and ascending to his
    father, the wisdom-god Ea, in heaven. On the festival, see Henri Frankfort,
    Kingship and the Gods: A Study of Ancient Near Eastern Religion as the

Integration of Society and Nature (University of Chicago, Chicago, 1978), ch. 22. The wonderful "epic" recited on the occasion by the priests is translated in N.K. Sandars, *Poems of Heaven and Hell from Ancient Mesopotamia* (Penguin, New York, 1989). The Mystery significance of the events is further described by Rudolf Steiner, *True and False Paths in Spiritual Investigation* (Rudolf Steiner Press, London, 1985), pp. 33ff. There is an important study of the theme in French: J.E. Ménard, "Le Descensus ad Inferos" in the *Ex Orbe Religionum* II (Supplements to *Numen* series) (Leiden, 1970), where he traces the pattern on into early Christian sources.

6. Lucian of Samosata, *Menippus in Hell*, 6-9. Menippus, known through Lucian's satires, was a historical figure of the third century B.C. The passage describing his descent into hell (Hades) is translated in Marvin Meyer, *The Ancient Mysteries: A Sourcebook*, HarperSan Francisco, 1987, pp. 202-204.

7. Aristides, *Sacred Orations*, B 31.

8. Plato, *Phaedo*, 69 C.

9. Sophocles, fragment 719 (Dindorf). That Sophocles alludes to a formula of the Mysteries is confirmed by an inscription from Eleusis, together with parallels in the Homeric *Hymn to Demeter*, Pindar, and so on.

10. A fragment of Aristotle preserved in Synesius, *Dio* 10 asserts that the *mystai* were "not taught anything, but were put in a certain state of mind."

11. Plutarch, *On the E at Delphi*, 392 A-E.

12. A technical term of the Mysteries—discussed in S. Angus, *The Mystery Religions and Christianity* (Dover, New York, 1975), pp. 106ff. Thus the mystes becomes the god: becomes Attis, Osiris, Bacchus, etc. Some early Christian sources speak of "becoming a Christ." See further now the *Gospel of Philip*, in Meyer, *The Ancient Mysteries*, pp. 235-236: "This one is no longer a Christian but a Christ."

13. Some helpful remarks on the early Greek concept of the *daimon* or "occult self" in: E.R. Dodds, *The Greeks and the Irrational* (University of California Press, Berkeley, London, 1951), p. 153.

14. Plutarch, *On the Cessation of Oracles*, 417 C.

15. Cicero, *On the Nature of the Gods* I, 119.

16. Xenophanes, fragment 14. The main fragments of Xenophanes are translated in Kirk, Raven, and Schofield, *The Presocratic Philosophers* (Cambridge University, Princeton, 1984), pp. 163ff. For a good brief introduction to his thought, see Bruno Snell, *The Discovery of the Mind* (Dover, New York, 1982), pp. 140ff.

17. Xenophanes, fragment 15.

18. On this see the Hermetic "Initiatory Discourse" or *Asclepius*.

19. Xenophanes, fragment 23.

20. The teachings of mysteriosophy remained almost entirely secret—at least until some recent discoveries such as the "Derveni papyrus." Steiner

recognized, however, that the Mystery-teachings could be discerned through their influence on the pre-Socratic philosophers. The new evidence has shown him right. In particular, M.L. West has argued that the Greek Mysteries were part of a diffusion of significant ideas over the ancient Near East concerning "Eternity" (*Aion*) and the origins of the world. These form the basis for the rational development of the views of Parmenides, Empedocles and Pherecydes of Syros as well as Heraclitus and Pythagoras; see West, *Early Greek Philosophy and the Orient* (Oxford University Press, 1971). Steiner also later came to regard Pherecydes as a crucial figure; see *The Riddles of Philosophy* (Anthroposophic Press, Spring Valley, NY, 1973), pp. 16ff.

For Steiner the emergence of rational thought is an evolutionary development—that is to say, it is not to be regarded as sweeping away the "superstition" of more primitive notions, but as rooted in human nature and potential for transformation. The Mysteries accompany this development, and integrate the new sense of independent judgment into the deeper, emotional, and less conscious aspects of human life. The false supposition that the Mysteries should be opposed to rational thought leads, for Steiner, to the tragic dividedness of so much in modern life—and also to a wrong evaluation of ancient myths, and so on, as primitive and irrational, whereas they are in fact a stage on the trajectory that includes philosophical and later scientific thought.

21.   Plato, *Phaedo*, 69 C.
22.   See the epigram in the *Palatine Anthology* IX, 540; also Diogenes Laertius, *Lives of the Philosophers* IX, 5;16. The main fragments of Heraclitus are presented in Kirk, Raven, and Schofield, *The Presocratic Philosophers*, pp. 18lff. In fragment 1 Heraclitus introduces his *Logos* idea—a universal meaning inherent in and sustaining the world; but despite its universality it is accessible only to the few, the "understanders." This is Orphic Mystery-terminology; cf. M.L.West, *The Orphic Poems* (Oxford, 1983), p. 110. According to Steiner, the *Logos-doctrine* had roots in the Mysteries of Artemis in Ephesus, which were concerned with sacred speech (the primary meaning of *logos*) and the origins of the universe; Steiner, *Mystery Knowledge and Mystery Centres* (Rudolf Steiner Press, London, 1973), pp. 81ff. He points out that when the *Logos* appears again, in Christianity, it is in the Gospel of John, and John is associated in legend with Ephesus too. Steiner also referred here to the pioneering work of E. Pfleiderer, *Die Philosophie des Heraklit* (Berlin, 1866).
23.   Plutarch, *On the E at Delphi* 392 B. Cf. Heraclitus, fragments 12 and 91.
24.   Fragment 88.
25.   Fragment 78 A (Bywater).
26.   Fragment 15; and cf. fragment 49 A. Discoveries of Orphic-Dionysiac membership tokens with the formula "Life-Death-Life" again confirm the

Mystery background; Kirk, Raven and Schofield, *The Presocratic Philosophers*, pp. 208, 210.

27. Fragments 110-111.

28. Fragment 61.

29. Fragment 51.

30. Fragment 62.

31. Fragment 52.

32. Philo of Alexandria, living around the beginning of the Christian era, still thinks in the same way. Considering the legal sections of the Bible he writes: "There are those who take a purely symbolic view of the written Law. They inquire diligently after its spiritual meaning, but scorn the actual laws. But I can only blame such people, for they ought to observe both the hidden meaning and the obvious one." (R.St.) See Philo, *On the Migration of Abraham*, 89.

33. *Daimon* is used here in its Greek sense of "spiritual being" (R.St.). Heraclitus, fragment 119.

34. Reincarnation formed an important element in the thought of several pre-Socratic thinkers, notably Empedocles and of course Pythagoras. Rudolf Steiner arrived at an understanding of reincarnation, not through ancient doctrines, but out of evolutionary and developmental ideas, and the factors that shape the life of modern individuals; see "Destiny and the Reincarnation of the Spirit," ch. 2 in *Theosophy* (Anthroposophic Press, Hudson, NY, 1994); *Reincarnation and Karma: Their Significance for Modern Culture* (Anthroposophic Press, Hudson, NY, 1992).

35. Empedocles, fragment 11. The main fragments of Empedocles are included in Kirk, Raven, and Schofield, *The Presocratic Philosophers*, pp. 280ff.

36. Fragment 12.

37. Fragment 15. All three fragments are from Empedocles' lost poem *On Nature*.

38. Cf. fragment 112. For further commentary by Steiner on the character of Empedocles' thought, see *The Riddles of Philosophy*, pp. 30ff.

39. Pindar, fragment 102.

40. See the brilliant study by W. Burkert, *Lore and Science in Ancient Pythagoreanism* (Harvard, 1972). The main fragments are in Kirk, Raven, and Schofield, *The Presocratic Philosophers*, pp. 214ff. See further Steiner, *The Riddles of Philosophy*, pp. 21ff.

41. Aristotle, *Metaphysics* 985, 24-34.

42. Naturally I do not enter here into the astronomical views of the early Pythagoreans. What is said about them here may be applied equally to the ideas of modern Copernicanism. (R.St.)

43. Gregory of Nyssa, *Great Baptismal Address*, 10.

44. Many references are made in the ancient literature to Plato's "unwritten doctrines"; these are evidently connected with ideas closely related to those

of the Pythagoreans just considered. Nevertheless, there has been in general great resistance to considering Plato in the way Steiner recommends. As a result, it might be argued, there has been too much stress on Plato's philosophical doctrines, and no understanding of the kind of thinking, the intellectual process, which he believed brought enlightenment in philosophy. Recently, however, M.L. Morgan, *Platonic Piety: Philosophy and Ritual in Fourth-Century Athens* (Yale University Press, New Haven, CT, 1990) has explored the question from a much more sympathetic angle, in which he sees philosophical dialogue as a transposition into logical, rational terms of "ecstatic" Mystery-ritual. He traces the origins back to Socrates, but sees also a continuing Orphic-Pythagorean influence on Plato (pp. 38ff).

45. Plato, *Seventh Letter* 341 B-D.
46. *Phaedo* 58 E-59 A.
47. *Phaedo* 64 A.
48. *Phaedo* 64 D-65 A.
49. *Phaedo* 65 A-B.
50. *Phaedo* 65 E-66 A.
51. *Phaedo* 67 D-E.
52. *Phaedo* 68 C.
53. Cf. Steiner, *The Riddles of Philosophy*, p. 40.
54. *Phaedo* 79 D-81 A.
55. *Phaedo* 106 B.
56. *Timaeus* 27 C-D.
57. *Timaeus* 48 D.
58. *Timaeus* 22 C-D.
59. *Timaeus* 28 C.
60. *Timaeus* 92 C.
61. Philo, *On the Allegory of the Law* I, 19. See ch. 11 below.
62. Philo, *On the Confusion of Languages*, 63.
63. Philo, *On the Descendants of Cain*, 101-102.
64. Philo, *On the Migration of Abraham*, 34-5.
65. Philo, *That Dreams Are Sent by God* II, 323.
66. Philo, *On the Allegory of the Law* III, 29.
67. Hippolytus, *Refutation of Heresies* V, 8, 9. For further commentary by Steiner on the Mysteries of the Kabeiroi at Samothrace, see *Mystery Knowledge and Mystery Centres*, pp. 167-179. Relevant sources included in M. Meyer, *The Ancient Mysteries*, pp. 38ff.
68. For a similar pattern of ideas in the Eleusinian Mysteries, cf. Steiner, *Wonders of the World, Ordeals of the Soul, Revelations of the Spirit* (Rudolf Steiner Press, London, 1983), pp. 19-20.
69. For more on this, the specifically Orphic version of the myth of Dionysus, see Steiner, *Wonders of the World*, pp. 90ff.

70. Cf. above, ch. 1 and nl 8.

71. On the kinds of explanation developed in the ancient Mysteries, which might be allegorical, "physical" (that is, including cosmic, natural or seasonal events), "mystic," and so on, see W. Burkert, *Ancient Mystery Cults* (Harvard University Press, Cambridge, 1987), pp. 78ff.

72. Sallust, *On the Gods and the World* III, 3-4.

73. Steiner develops such a "structural" approach, for example, in relation to the Adonis Mysteries in *The Easter Festival in the Evolution of the Mysteries* (Anthroposophic Press, 1987), pp.6ff. Thus one might say that for Steiner, as for a modern structural interpreter of myths such as Lévi-Strauss, study must proceed "from the study of conscious content to that of unconscious forms": Claude Lévi-Strauss, *Structural Anthropology* (Harmondsworth, 1972), p. 24. Steiner's interpretation points at once to the origins of the myths on a psychological level in the experience of the initiates, and to their cognitive value for the culture they sustain. The actualization of their unconscious forms (structures) is not opposed to rational thought, as we might think if we merely studied the contents of mythical imagery, but complements and evolves alongside it. Thus Steiner was led to develop an account of the evolution of consciousness from an archaic "clairvoyant" picture-consciousness to the modern sense of personality, in which the transformation processes of the Mysteries played a continuing role; cf. Steiner, *The Evolution of Consciousness* (Rudolf Steiner Press, London, 1991). As individuality evolves, the unconscious creative potential within the members of a culture is unfolded in changing ways. Such a "democratization" is actually inherent in the evolution of the Mysteries.

74. Plotinus, *Enneads* V, 8, 6.

75. Plato, *Phaedrus* 229 D-230 A.

76. This use of myth and parable in Plato can be paralleled in other contexts. For example, in the literature of ancient India there is a parable attributed to Buddha: There was a man who was passionately attached to life, and was on no account willing to die, who found himself pursued by four serpents. He heard a voice warning him to feed and bathe the serpents from time to time, but the man ran away in fear of the serpents. Again he heard a voice, warning him that he was being chased by five murderers; again he ran away. A voice told him of a sixth murderer who was about to cut off his head with a sword; once more he took to flight. He came to a deserted village. He heard a voice telling him that thieves were about to raid the village, and again he took to flight. He came to a great river. Feeling unsafe on this side of it, he made a basket out of straw, twigs, and leaves and in it crossed to the far shore. Now he is safe—now he is a Brahman. The parable is interpreted as follows: an individual must pass through various states on the way to the divine. The four serpents signify the four elements (fire, water, earth, and air); the five murderers are the five senses. The

deserted village stands for a soul that has freed itself from the impressions of the senses, but is not yet secure within itself. If it takes hold inwardly of the lower nature alone, it will inevitably be destroyed. The man must assemble a boat that will take him from the shore of sense-perceptible nature across the river of transience to the other shore, that of eternity and the divine. (R.St.)

77. For more on the background of the mythology of Osiris, see Steiner, *Egyptian Myths and Mysteries* (Anthroposophic Press, Hudson, NY, 1990); also *Mysteries of the East and Christianity* (Rudolf Steiner Press, London, 1972), which relates it to the stages of initiation-experience which are hinted at in the account of his "voluntary death" and new birth by Apuleius, *The Golden Ass or, Metamorphoses* XI. The latter text is translated in Meyer, *The Ancient Mysteries*, pp. 176ff. At the climactic moment he says: "I crossed the threshold of Persephone; I was caught rapt through all the elements; I saw the Sun shining at midnight with a radiant light; I stood before the upper and the lower gods, drew near and adored." (XI, 23)

78. Empedocles, fragment 26.

79. Empedocles, fragment 20.

80. This epistemological doctrine given expression in Goethe's saying:

> *Wär' nicht das Auge sonnenhaft,*
> Wie könnten wir das Licht erblicken?
> Lebt nicht in uns des Gottes eigene Kraft,
> Wie könnt' uns Göttliches entzücken?

> "If the eye were not of the nature of the sun,
> how could we behold the light?
> If God's own power were not at work in us,
> how could divine things delight us?"
> (*Zahme Xenien*). (R.St.)

> Cf. Empedocles, fragment 109.

81. The other labors may, therefore, justifiably be interpreted as corresponding to stages in the soul's development. The conquest of the Nemean lion and his bringing it to Mycenae shows the hero mastering the purely physical power in human nature and taming it. Then his killing of the nine-headed Hydra, conquering it with firebrands and dipping his arrows in its gall, which made them unerring, shows him overcoming the lower, sense-derived knowledge by means of the fire of the spirit: by conquering it he gains the power of seeing lower things in the light of spiritual vision. Heracles captures the hind of Artemis, the divine huntress: he hunts down all that wild nature can offer to the human soul. The other labors may be similarly interpreted—the aim here was only to establish the general principle that they point to a process of inner development. (R.St.)

For Heracles as the type of a certain process of initiation, see further Steiner, *Egyptian Myths and Mysteries*, pp. 36-39. There were no Mysteries of Heracles, but he was regarded as in some sense the archetypal initiate at Eleusis: Burkert, *Ancient Mystery Cults*, p. 76.

82. Steiner considered the Promethean myth to be the expression of an archaic Mystery that had been betrayed—the so-called Vulcan Mysteries: see *An Outline of Esoteric Science* (Anthroposophic Press, Great Barrington, MA, 1997).

83. There is an instructive account of the layout of the sanctuaries in K. Bötticher, *Ergänzungen zu den letzten Untersuchungen auf der Akropolis in Athen*, in Philologus, supplementary volume III, part 3. (R.St.) For a more up-to-date account, see G. Mylonas, *Eleusis and the Eleusinian Mysteries* (Princeton University Press, Princeton, 1961), chs. VI and VII.

84. There are further discussions of the Eleusinian Mysteries by Steiner in *Wonders of the World and Mystery Knowledge and Mystery Centres*. The "official" Eleusinian account of the Demeter-Persephone myth is contained in the "Homeric Hymn to Demeter" from around the seventh century B.C.; it is translated in Meyer, *The Ancient Mysteries*, pp. 20ff. An important survey of the Eleusinian cult is contained in Mircea Eliade, *History of Religious Ideas*, vol. I (University of Chicago Press, Chicago, 1981), pp. 290-301.

85. The spirit of the Eleusinian Mysteries is brilliantly captured by Edouard Schuré in *Sanctuaires d'Orient* (Paris, 1898). (R.St.)

86. It has been called "the greatest coherent literary work that has come down to us from ancient Egypt"; R. Lepsius, *Das Totenbuch der alten Ägypter* (Berlin, 1842), p. 17. (R.St.) A modern English rendering is: R. Faulkner, *The Ancient Egyptian Book of the Dead* (University of Texas, Austin, 1990). The ideas it contains about "astral immortality" are already prefigured in much older Egyptian texts subsequently discovered, for example, the "Coffin Texts" and "Pyramid Texts." On their initiatory significance see M. Eliade, *A History of Religious Ideas*, vol. I, pp. 94ff. The nature, and even the existence, of Egyptian "Mysteries" has been disputed; but see the brilliant remarks by H. Frankfort, *Kingship and the Gods*, ch. 11. Steiner was far ahead of his time in recognizing the initiatory significance of "becoming Osiris." A fine study of the Pharaoh from an anthroposophical point of view is furnished by F. Teichmann, *Die Kultur der Empfindungsseele* (Stuttgart n.d.). The Pharaoh, who "becomes Osiris" and mystically begets his successor from the other world as Horus, the living power of the Sun on Earth, is the prototype of all Egyptian initiates. He is a link between the worlds of life and death; cf. above, pp. 38-41.

87. *Book of the Dead*, ch. 125.

88. Loc. cit.

89. In many of the Mysteries, the sufferings and eventual triumph of the god in the myths provides a model for the struggle of initiation. Cf. F.H.Borsch,

The Son of Man in Myth and History (London, 1967), pp. 92ff. Further comments and reservations in Burkert, *Ancient Mystery Cults*, pp. 77-78.

90. Plato, *Timaeus* 36 B-37 A.; cf. above, pp. 36-37.

91. See the convincing account in Rudolf Seydel, *Buddha und Christus* (Breslau, 1884), esp. pp. 8-14. (R.St.)

92. This will be documented further below. Other versions of the death of Buddha do not concern us here, of profound interest though they may be from other points of view. (R.St.) Rudolf Steiner spoke extensively about the inner connection between Buddhism and Christianity in his lectures on *The Gospel of St. Luke* (Rudolf Steiner Press, London, 1988).

93. Jesus is an "initiate" in the sense that the Christ-Being is present in him. (R.St.) For initiation-stages dramatized in the Gospels, see further Rudolf Steiner, *The Gospel of St. John* (Anthroposophic Press, Hudson, NY, 1962). Jesus provides the prototype for Christian initiation by living the divine pattern: Steiner should not be misunderstood that he was being led through a training in spiritual development; cf. Steiner's comments in *Man in the Light of Occultism, Theosophy and Philosophy* (Spiritual Science Library, Blauvelt, NY, 1989), pp. 155-156.

94. 1 John 1:1, 1:3.

95. Augustine, *Against Mani's So-called Fundamental Epistle*, 6.

96. Matthew 28:20.

97. Otto Schmiedel, *Die Hauptprobleme der Leben Jesu-Forschung* (Tübingen and Leipzig, 1902), p. 15.

98. Adolf Harnack, *The Essence of Christianity.*

99. See above, pp. 152ff.

100. See above, pp. 91ff. For an important study of the relationship, common symbolism, and so on, between Philo and the Gospel of John, see C.H. Dodd, *The Interpretation of the Fourth Gospel* (Harvard University Press, Cambridge, 1968), pp. 55-73. Dodd comments extensively on Philo's use of the language of the Mysteries.

101. On the meaning of this central theme in the preaching of Jesus, and its esoteric dimension, see Steiner, *The Gospel of St. Matthew* (Anthroposophic Press, Hudson, NY, 1985), pp. 132ff.

102. The phrase is attributed to the second century A.D. Neoplatonist, Numenius of Apamea, fragment 10 (Leemans).

103. Cf. G. Scholem, *Major Trends in Jewish Mysticism* (Schocken, New York, 1961), p. 42. To this tradition belong for example the so-called *III Enoch* and the writings of the Merkavah mystics: see I. Gruenwald, *Apocalyptic and Merkavah Mysticism* (Leiden, 1980). For other Mystery groups such as the Essenes and Therapeutae in Judaism at the time of Jesus, see ch. 9 below.

104. *Zohar (Book of Splendor)*, 110 b.

105. Steiner's version is closest to that in the Jerusalem Talmud, *Hagigah* 14 b.

106. John 20:29.

107. Luke 19:10.

108. Luke 17:20-21.

109. Luke 10:20.

110. John 1:1, 1:14.

111. Ernst Renan, *Das Leben Jesu* (Leipzig n.d.), pp. 261-263.

112. John 11:47.

113. Renan, loc.cit.

114. John 11:4.

115. John 11:25.

116. Schelling, *Über die Gottheiten von Samothrake* (Stuttgart and Tübingen, 1815), p. 40.

117. The story is preserved by Eunapius. Earlier editions referred to Constantine, but the allusion is to the Emperor Julian.

118. Steiner's view was remarkably confirmed by the discovery of the "secret Mark" fragment in 1958. For this discovery, and its new version of the Lazarus story in the light of Steiner's approach, see A.Welburn, *The Beginnings of Christianity* (Floris Books, Edinburgh, 1991), pp. 249ff. The "resurrection" of Lazarus culminates in the communication of a *mysterion*, namely "Jesus taught him the mystery of the kingdom of God." The fact that the initiation-experience is presented as central to the Fourth Gospel led Steiner to develop a detailed argument for its authorship and Mystery-character, such as has more recently been urged by such scholars as Floyd Filson; see further Rudolf Steiner, *The Gospel of St. John*, pp. 60ff, and for modern developments, Welburn, *Beginnings of Christianity*, pp. 242ff.

119. All this relates to ancient initiatory practices, which put the candidate into a trance-state resembling sleep for three days. The kind of initiation that belongs to modern times never uses these procedures. It requires on the contrary an intensification of con-sciousness; ordinary consciousness is never suspended during the drama of modern initiation. (R.St.)

120. John 11:41.

121. John 11:42.

122. J.Burckhardt, *Die Zeit Konstantins* (Basel, 1929), p. 163.

123. Apocalypse 1:1. Steiner identified the John who writes under his own name in the Apocalypse with the enigmatic author of the Fourth Gospel; Steiner, *From Jesus to Christ* (Rudolf Steiner Press, London, 1991), pp. 99-100. He rejected, however, the Church's rather belated claim that this John was the same as the apostle John, son of Zebedee. See further, for the whole nature and interpretation of the document, Steiner's lectures *The Apocalypse of St. John* (Anthroposophic Press, Hudson, NY, 1993); also *Reading the Pictures of the Apocalypse* (Anthroposophic Press, Hudson, NY, 1993), and for related themes *The Fall of the Spirits of Darkness* (Rudolf Steiner Press, London, 1993). The Apocalypse is impor-tant to Steiner here because it represents a new form of the ancient

Mystery-teachings and esoteric cosmology, now centered on Christ. However, it is addressed to a number of different representative Communities that preserve certain historical characteristics or reveal already qualities to be developed more widely in the future. It embodies therefore the new principle that Mystery-wisdom cannot just remain a "primordial revelation," but must be modified to meet the changing conditions of evolution in the cosmic rhythms of history. According to Steiner, the defeat of the rebel angels does not refer to a once-and-for-all event, but to the recurring need to renew Mystery-wisdom in its Christian form at the turning-points of new human potential unfolding. The Apocalypse remains our profoundest guide to this form of cultural and spiritual renewal.

124. Apocalypse 1:10-11.
125. Apocalypse 2:1-7.
126. The Communities represent periods defined by the cosmic phenomenon of the precession of the equinox. For the significance of these in cultural evolution, see Steiner, *The Gospel of John*, pp. 128-136. However, the point is not that each should be left behind in history: rather, the quality developed in each can attain a new form, relevant to evolving humanity, through finding a relationship to the divine through Christ—as Steiner describes in an exemplary way for the first Community. The new, Christian Mystery is thereby enriched by all that flows over from the past, and everything in the past spiritual life of humanity is also a key to the future.
127. Apocalypse 1:13-14.
128. Apocalypse 1:20.
129. Apocalypse 1:16.
130. Apocalypse 1:20.
131. Apocalypse 1:16.
132. Apocalypse 1:17.
133. Apocalypse 1:18.
134. Apocalypse 4:1.
135. Apocalypse 4:2, 4:6.
136. Apocalypse 4:4.
137. Apocalypse 4:6-8.
138. Apocalypse 5:5.
139. Philo, *On the Special Laws* I, 47.
140. Apocalypse 5:9-10.
141. The language of "universal," or "catholic," powers is drawn from astrology. "With earthly *genii*, or *daimons* who protected definite spots, were contrasted the celestial gods, who are 'catholic.' This word, which was to have such a great destiny, was at first merely an astrological term: it denoted activities that are not limited to individuals, nor to particular events, but

apply to the whole human race and to the entire earth"; Franz Cumont, *Astrology and Religion among the Greeks and Romans*, (Dover. New York, 1960) p. 63.

142. Apocalypse 6:6. The rider corresponds to the Man-figure among the Living Creatures. He is a prototype therefore of the Son of Man, who only emerges in fully human-divine form in the later Mysteries. He appears in the Apocalypse at the beginning (1:12). See further Rudolf Steiner, *The Apocalypse of St. John*, pp. 54-55. Steiner's lectures expand upon many of the points mentioned in the present chapter.

143. Apocalypse 7:4.

144. Apocalypse 8:7.

145. Apocalypse 10:9.

146. Apocalypse 11:8.

147. Apocalypse 11:15.

148. Apocalypse 11:19.

149. Apocalypse 12:9.

150. Gospel of John 20:29.

151. Apocalypse 21:22-23.

152. Apocalypse 22:10.

153. Since Rudolf Steiner's time, our knowledge of the Essenes in particular has been vastly augmented by the discovery of the "Dead Sea Scrolls"—that is, an Essene library of sacred texts from their ancient center at Qumran. Their enormous relevance to Christian origins is now also firmly established. (In Steiner's day it was usually denied.) See further Rudolf Steiner, *The Gospel of St. Matthew*, pp. 89ff and, for the continuing relevance of Steiner's account to modern developments, Welburn, *The Beginnings of Christianity*, pp. 40ff.

154. See for example I QH III, 3-18—one of the Essene initiation-poems, reproduced with commentary in Welburn, *Gnosis, the Mysteries and Christianity* (Floris Books, Edinburgh, 1994), pp. 70ff. Its principle that "the racking birth-pains come upon all that bear in the womb the seeds of the new life" seems to refer to a personal initiation-experience, but also to the struggles of the community, and a turning-point at which the "man-child long foretold" will be born.

155. The structure of the community and the principle of consent are spelled out in the Essene *Community Rule*—I QS V, 1-3.

156. Any dispute as to the authenticity of this work may now be regarded as settled. Philo undoubtedly describes from experience a community of pre-Christian origin. Cf. G.R.S. Mead, *Fragments of a Faith Forgotten: Gnostics and Mysticism* (Gordon, Newark,1992), pp. 62ff. (R.St.)

157. Philo, *On the Contemplative Life* III, 24-25.

158. Philo, op.cit. III, 29.

159. Philo, op.cit. X, 78.

160. This structuring of Communities was the specifically Jewish contribution to the further development of the Mysteries (above, pp. 76ff). The democratization of their character led consistently to a narrowing and a broadening: a concentrating on the unique individual (in its most intense form, the uniquely initiated one, the Messiah) and looking outward to a wider, ultimately worldwide, sense of collective destiny. On the striking absence of such organization in the older Mysteries, cf. Burkert, *Ancient Mystery Cults*, pp. 45-46. Later, Christianity was to fuse the Mystery-idea with the Jewish inheritance of the "people of God" and extend it to universal community: and the Christ-spirit is active wherever that process is being carried forward. Steiner often referred in this context to the "Christ-Impulse" as a spiritual and evolutionary power, at work in humanity.

161. Cf. Steiner, *The Gospel of St. Matthew*, pp. 79-83; exactly this idea underlies the extraordinary *Apocalypse of Adam*, found in the Gnostic discovery at Nag Hammadi in Egypt, but having Jewish (probably Essene) connections. Cf. Welburn, *Beginnings of Christianity*, pp. 44ff.

162. See further Steiner, *Building Stones for an Understanding of the Mystery of Golgotha* (Rudolf Steiner Press, London, 1985).

163. *Zohar* II, 110 b.

164. Clement of Alexandria, *Miscellanies* I, l (citing Eph. 4:11-12).

165. Steiner here challenges the Church's own highly influential myth about its origins, namely that there had been original agreement and "orthodoxy," only later "degenerating" into conflicting views. Steiner is remarkably emancipated from this perspective. The diversity of early Christianity was first extensively argued by Walter Bauer, *Orthodoxy and Heresy in Earliest Christianity* (London, 1972)—a book still often regarded as controversial.

166. We have already mentioned the brilliant presentation of Gnosticism in its historical development by G.R.S. Mead, in his book, *Fragments of a Faith Forgotten.* (R.St.) More recent discoveries, notably the Nag Hammadi Library of Gnostic writings, have filled in the historical picture more fully. See K. Rudolph, *Gnosticism* (Edinburgh, 1984). There is much to confirm Steiner's basic contention that Gnosticism, based on *gnosis* ("divine knowledge") was a continuation of the ancient Mystery techniques; as such it was prior to Christianity, and distinct from the new esoteric teaching that emerged there. Nevertheless, it was part of the background of ideas taken up and transformed in Christianity, from the earliest phases, for example, in the Gospel of Mark, which Steiner related to an Alexandrian and Gnostic milieu: see Steiner, *The Gospel of St. Mark* (Anthroposophic Press, Hudson, NY, 1986), pp. 187ff. The discovery of the "secret Mark" fragment (cf. note 118) has again strikingly confirmed his insight. Steiner discussed the basic myth of Gnosticism, concerning the divine Sophia and the pre-earthly existence of spiritual worlds ("aeons") in his lectures *Christ and the Spiritual World* (London, n.d.).

167. These include *Mystical Theology, On the Divine Names*, and *On the Celestial Hierarchies*. Dionysius "the Areopagite" was the pupil of Paul in Athens (Acts 17:34) by whom these works claim to be written. Steiner described Dionysius as a teacher of esoteric Christianity in the tradition of Paul (Steiner, *The Gospel of St. John*, New York, 1962, pp. 34-5). His teachings were presumably given written form much later by his pupils. (The present texts use late philosophical language and even include a quotation from the fifth-century A.D. Neoplatonist Proclus.)

168. The theme is dealt with in Dionysius' *Ecclesiastical Hierarchies* (which echo those in heaven). He says explicitly that the incarnate Son of God is "the source and perfection of all hierarchies"—see Andrew Louth, *Denys the Areopagite* (Morehouse, Harrisburg, PA, 1989), p. 42.

169. See further *Mysticism at the Dawn of the Modern Age* (Steinerbooks, Blauvelt, NY, 1980).

170. In a brilliant and controversial study, E.R. Goodenough maintained that Philo interpreted Judaism in the light of a Jewish Mystery cult: see his *By Light, Light: The Mystic Gospel of Hellenistic Judaism* (New Haven, 1935).

171. Augustine, *Confessions* XIII, 38.

172. Cf. above, pp. 89ff.

173. Philo, *On the Confusion of Languages*, 63.

174. Genesis 1:1.

175. Philo, *On the Cherubim and the Flaming Sword* I, 97.

176. Plato, *Timaeus* 37 C-D.

177. Plotinus, *Enneads* IV, 8, 1.

178. Plotinus, *Enneads* V, 1, 1.

179. Plotinus, loc.cit. "The Soul"—the universal soul, *anima mundi*.

180. I John 1:1.

181. Perhaps the single most important figure in the formation of Latin-speaking Christianity in the West. Steiner discussed him in depth, for example, in *The Redemption of Thinking* (Anthroposophic Press, Hudson, NY, 1983), pp. 23ff. (referring also to many of the "Christians and Pagans" just mentioned: Plotinus, Dionysius the Areopagite, as well as Manichaeism).

182. Augustine, *Confessions* V, 10, 19.

183. *Confessions* X, 6, 9. (Anaximenes: the pre-Socratic philosopher who held that air was the First Principle.)

184. Augustine, *On the Trinity* X, 14.

185. Augustine, *City of God* XI, 26.

186. Augustine, *Confessions* VI, 4, 6.

187. Ibid. VI, 5, 7.

188. Augustine, *Against Faustus* XXXIII, 6.

189. Augustine, *Retractions* I, 13, 3.

190. Augustine, *On the Dimension of the Soul* I, 23, 76.

191. See further Rudolf Steiner, *How to Know Higher Worlds: A Modern Path of Initiation*. In a note of 1910, Steiner referred to the account given in *An Outline of Esoteric Science* — see ch. 5.

192. Cf. Steiner, *The Redemption of Thinking*, pp. 76ff.

193. The last sentence is altered in the 1910 edition to: "One line of development within Christianity, as we have seen, came to the conclusion that the Mystery had to be preserved as an object of faith." The other line of development arises out of the evolving human individuality itself. It is, says Steiner, an approach to spiritual knowledge "that can be achieved by individuals themselves, where the Initiator merely gives indications about what ought to be done, and one then gradually learns to find one's own way onward. No considerable progress has yet been made along this path; but little by little there will unfold in humanity a faculty making it possible for a person both to ascend into the macrocosm and to descend into the microcosm without assistance and to pass through these forms of initiation as a free being." (Steiner, *The Gospel of St. Matthew*, p. 125.) The results of that new, and essentially modern path of development would be a new Christ-awareness which Steiner regarded as the fulfillment of the promise of the parousia — not another physical, but a spiritual (etheric) presence of Christ: see Steiner, *The True Nature of the Second Coming* (London, n.d.).

RUDOLF STEINER'S COLLECTED WORKS

The German Edition of Rudolf Steiner's Collected Works (the Gesamtausgabe [GA] published by Rudolf Steiner Verlag, Dornach, Switzerland) presently runs to over 354 titles, organized either by type of work (written or spoken), chronology, audience (public or other), or subject (education, art, etc.). For ease of comparison, the Collected Works in English [CW] follows the German organization exactly. A complete listing of the CWs follows with literal translations of the German titles. Other than in the case of the books published in his lifetime, titles were rarely given by Rudolf Steiner himself, and were often provided by the editors of the German editions. The titles in English are therefore not necessarily the same as the German; and, indeed, over the past seventy-five years have frequently been different, with the same book sometimes appearing under different titles.

For ease of identification and to avoid confusion, we suggest that readers looking for a title should do so by CW number. Because the work of creating the Collected Works of Rudolf Steiner is an ongoing process, with new titles being published every year, we have not indicated in this listing which books are presently available. To find out what titles in the Collected Works are currently in print, please check our website at www.steinerbooks.org, or write to SteinerBooks P.O. Box 749, Great Barrington, MA 01230:

Written Work

CW 1	Goethe: Natural-Scientific Writings, Introduction, with Footnotes and Explanations in the text by Rudolf Steiner
CW 2	Outlines of an Epistemology of the Goethean World View, with Special Consideration of Schiller
CW 3	Truth and Science
CW 4	The Philosophy of Freedom
CW 4a	Documents to "The Philosophy of Freedom"
CW 5	Friedrich Nietzsche, A Fighter against His Own Time
CW 6	Goethe's Worldview
CW 6a	Now in CW 30
CW 7	Mysticism at the Dawn of Modern Spiritual Life and Its Relationship with Modern Worldviews
CW 8	Christianity as Mystical Fact and the Mysteries of Antiquity
CW 9	Theosophy: An Introduction into Supersensible World Knowledge and Human Purpose
CW 10	How Does One Attain Knowledge of Higher Worlds?
CW 11	From the Akasha-Chronicle
CW 12	Levels of Higher Knowledge

Lectures to the Members of the Anthroposophical Society

CW 267   Soul-Exercises: Vol. 1: Exercises with Word and Image Meditations for the Methodological Development of Higher Powers of Knowledge, 1904-1924

CW 268   Soul-Exercises: Vol. 2: Mantric Verses, 1903-1925

CW 269   Ritual Texts for the Celebration of the Free Christian Religious Instruction. The Collected Verses for Teachers and Students of the Waldorf School

CW 270   Esoteric Instructions for the First Class of the School for Spiritual Science at the Goetheanum 1924, 4 Volumes

CW 271   Art and Knowledge of Art. Foundations of a New Aesthetic

CW 272   Spiritual-Scientific Commentary on Goethe's "Faust" in Two Volumes. Vol. 1: Faust, the Striving Human Being

CW 273   Spiritual-Scientific Commentary on Goethe's "Faust" in Two Volumes. Vol. 2: The Faust-Problem

CW 274   Addresses for the Christmas Plays from the Old Folk Traditions

CW 275   Art in the Light of Mystery-Wisdom

CW 276   The Artistic in Its Mission in the World. The Genius of Language. The World of the Self-Revealing Radiant Appearances – Anthroposophy and Art. Anthroposophy and Poetry

CW 277   Eurythmy. The Revelation of the Speaking Soul

CW 277a   The Origin and Development of Eurythmy

CW 278   Eurythmy as Visible Song

CW 279   Eurythmy as Visible Speech

CW 280   The Method and Nature of Speech Formation

CW 281   The Art of Recitation and Declamation

CW 282   Speech Formation and Dramatic Art

CW 283   The Nature of Things Musical and the Experience of Tone in the Human Being

CW284/285 Images of Occult Seals and Pillars. The Munich Congress of Whitsun 1907 and Its Consequences

CW 286   Paths to a New Style of Architecture. "And the Building Becomes Human"

CW 287   The Building at Dornach as a Symbol of Historical Becoming and an Artistic Transformation Impulses

CW 288   Style-Forms in the Living Organic

CW 289   The Building-Idea of the Goetheanum: Lectures with Slides from the Years 1920-1921

CW 290   The Building-Idea of the Goetheanum: Lectures with Slides from the Years 1920-1921

CW 291   The Nature of Colors

SIGNIFICANT EVENTS
IN THE LIFE OF RUDOLF STEINER

1829: June 23: birth of Johann Steiner (1829-1910)—Rudolf Steiner's father—in Geras, Lower Austria.

1834: May 8: birth of Franciska Blie (1834-1918)—Rudolf Steiner's mother—in Horn, Lower Austria. "My father and mother were both children of the glorious Lower Austrian forest district north of the Danube."

1860: May 16: marriage of Johann Steiner and Franciska Blie.

1861: February 25: birth of *Rudolf Joseph Lorenz Steiner* in Kraljevec, Croatia, near the border with Hungary, where Johann Steiner works as a telegrapher for the South Austria Railroad. Rudolf Steiner is baptized two days later, February 27, the date usually given as his birthday.

1862: Summer: the family moves to Mödling, Lower Austria.

1863: The family moves to Pottschach, Lower Austria, near the Styrian border, where Johann Steiner becomes stationmaster. "The view stretched to the mountains...majestic peaks in the distance and the sweet charm of nature in the immediate surroundings."

1864: November 15: birth of Rudolf Steiner's sister, Leopoldine (d. November 1, 1927). She will become a seamstress and live with her parents for the rest of her life.

1866: July 28: birth of Rudolf Steiner's deaf-mute brother, Gustav (d. May 1, 1941).

1867: Rudolf Steiner enters the village school. Following a disagreement between his father and the schoolmaster, whose wife falsely accused the boy of causing a commotion, Rudolf Steiner is taken out of school and taught at home.

1868: A critical experience. Unknown to the family, an aunt dies in a distant town. Sitting in the station waiting room, Rudolf Steiner sees her "form," which speaks to him, asking for help. "Beginning with this experience, a new soul life began in the boy, one in which not only the outer trees and mountains spoke to him, but also the worlds that lay behind them. From this moment on, the boy began to live with the spirits of nature...."

1869: The family moves to the peaceful, rural village of Neudorfl, near Wiener-Neustadt in present-day Hungary. Rudolf Steiner attends the village school. Because of the "unorthodoxy" of his writing and spelling, he has to do "extra lessons."

1870: Through a book lent to him by his tutor, he discovers geometry: "To grasp something purely in the spirit brought me inner happiness. I know that I first learned happiness through geometry." The same tutor allows him to draw, while other students still struggle with their reading and writing. "An artistic element" thus enters his education.

1871: Though his parents are not religious, Rudolf Steiner becomes a "church child," a favorite of the priest, who was "an exceptional character." "Up to the age of ten or eleven, among those I came to know, he was far and away the most significant." Among other things, he introduces Steiner to Copernican, heliocentric cosmology. As an altar boy, Rudolf Steiner serves at Masses, funerals, and Corpus Christi processions. At year's end, after an incident in which he escapes a thrashing, his father forbids him to go to church.

1872: Rudolf Steiner transfers to grammar school in Wiener-Neustadt, a five-mile walk from home, which must be done in all weathers.

1873-75: Through his teachers and on his own, Rudolf Steiner has many wonderful experiences with science and mathematics. Outside school, he teaches himself analytic geometry, trigonometry, differential equations, and calculus.

1876: Rudolf Steiner begins tutoring other students. He learns bookbinding from his father. He also teaches himself stenography.

1877: Rudolf Steiner discovers Kant's *Critique of Pure Reason*, which he reads and rereads. He also discovers and reads von Rotteck's *World History*.

1878: He studies extensively in contemporary psychology and philosophy.

1879: Rudolf Steiner graduates from high school with honors. His father is transferred to Inzersdorf, near Vienna. He uses his first visit to Vienna "to purchase a great number of philosophy books"—Kant, Fichte, Schelling, and Hegel, as well as numerous histories of philosophy. His aim: to find a path from the "I" to nature.

October 1879-1883: Rudolf Steiner attends the Technical College in Vienna—to study mathematics, chemistry, physics, mineralogy, botany, zoology, biology, geology, and mechanics—with a scholarship. He also attends lectures in history and literature, while avidly reading philosophy on his own. His two favorite professors are Karl Julius Schröer (German language and literature) and Edmund Reitlinger (physics). He also audits lectures by Robert Zimmerman on aesthetics and Franz Brentano on philosophy. During this year he begins his friendship with Moritz Zitter (1861-1921), who will help support him financially when he is in Berlin.

1880: Rudolf Steiner attends lectures on Schiller and Goethe by Karl Julius Schröer, who becomes his mentor. Also "through a remarkable combination of circumstances," he meets Felix Koguzki, an "herb gatherer" and healer, who could "see deeply into the secrets of nature." Rudolf Steiner will meet and study with this "emissary of the Master" throughout his time in Vienna.

1881: January: "… I didn't sleep a wink. I was busy with philosophical problems until about 12:30 a.m. Then, finally, I threw myself down on my couch. All my striving during the previous year had been to research whether the following statement by Schelling was true or not: *Within everyone dwells a secret, marvelous capacity to draw back from the stream of time—out of the self clothed in all that comes to us from outside—into our innermost being and there, in the immutable form of the Eternal, to look into ourselves.* I believe, and I am still quite certain of it, that I discovered this capacity in myself; I had long had an inkling of it. Now the whole of idealist philosophy stood before me in modified form. What's a sleepless night compared to that!"

Rudolf Steiner begins communicating with leading thinkers of the day, who send him books in return, which he reads eagerly.

July: "I am not one of those who dives into the day like an animal in human form. I pursue a quite specific goal, an idealistic aim—knowledge of the truth! This cannot be done offhandedly. It requires the greatest striving in the world, free of all egotism, and equally of all resignation."

August: Steiner puts down on paper for the first time thoughts for a "Philosophy of Freedom." "The striving for the absolute: this human yearning is freedom." He also seeks to outline a "peasant philosophy," describing what the worldview of a "peasant"—one who lives close to the earth and the old ways—really is.

1881-1882: Felix Koguzki, the herb gatherer, reveals himself to be the envoy of another, higher initiatory personality, who instructs Rudolf Steiner to penetrate Fichte's philosophy and to master modern scientific thinking as a preparation for right entry into the spirit. This "Master" also teaches him the double (evolutionary and involutionary) nature of time.

1882: Through the offices of Karl Julius Schröer, Rudolf Steiner is asked by Joseph Kurschner to edit Goethe's scientific works for the *Deutschen National-Literatur* edition. He writes "A Possible Critique of Atomistic Concepts" and sends it to Friedrich Theodore Vischer.

1883: Rudolf Steiner completes his college studies and begins work on the Goethe project.

1884: First volume of Goethe's *Scientific Writings* (CW 1) appears (March). He lectures on Goethe and Lessing, and Goethe's approach to science. In July, he enters the household of Ladislaus and Pauline Specht as tutor to the four Specht boys. He will live there until 1890. At this time, he meets Josef Breuer ((1842-1925), the coauthor with Sigmund Freud of *Studies in Hysteria*, who is the Specht family doctor.

1885: While continuing to edit Goethe's writings, Rudolf Steiner reads deeply in contemporary philosophy (Edouard von Hartmann, Johannes Volkelt, and Richard Wahle, among others).

1886: May: Rudolf Steiner sends Kurschner the manuscript of *Outlines of Goethe's Theory of Knowledge* (CW 2), which appears in October, and which he sends out widely. He also meets the poet Marie Eugenie Delle Grazie and writes "Nature and Our Ideals" for her. He attends her salon, where he meets many priests, theologians, and philosophers, who will become his friends. Meanwhile, the director of the Goethe Archive in Weimar requests his collaboration with the *Sophien* edition of Goethe's works, particularly the writings on color.

1887:　At the beginning of the year, Rudolf Steiner is very sick. As the year progresses and his health improves, he becomes increasingly "a man of letters," lecturing, writing essays, and taking part in Austrian cultural life. In August-September, the second volume of Goethe's *Scientific Writings* appears.

1888:　January-July: Rudolf Steiner assumes editorship of the "German Weekly" (*Deutsche Wochenschrift*). He begins lecturing more intensively, giving, for example, a lecture titled "Goethe as Father of a New Aesthetics." He meets and becomes soul friends with Friedrich Eckstein (1861-1939), a vegetarian, philosopher of symbolism, alchemist, and musician, who will introduce him to various spiritual currents (including Theosophy) and with whom he will meditate and interpret esoteric and alchemical texts.

1889:　Rudolf Steiner first reads Nietzsche (*Beyond Good and Evil*). He encounters Theosophy again and learns of Madame Blavatsky in the Theosophical circle around Marie Lang (1858-1934). Here he also meets well-known figures of Austrian life, as well as esoteric figures like the occultist Franz Hartman and Karl Leinigen-Billigen (translator of C.G. Harrison's *The Transcendental Universe*.) During this period, Steiner first reads A.P. Sinnett's *Esoteric Buddhism* and Mabel Collins's *Light on the Path*. He also begins traveling, visiting Budapest, Weimar, and Berlin (where he meets philosopher Edouard von Hartman).

1890:　Rudolf Steiner finishes volume 3 of Goethe's scientific writings. He begins his doctoral dissertation, which will become *Truth and Science* (CW 3). He also meets the poet and feminist Rosa Mayreder (1858-1938), with whom he can exchange his most intimate thoughts. In September, Rudolf Steiner moves to Weimar to work in the Goethe-Schiller Archive.

1891:　Volume 3 of the Kurschner edition of Goethe appears. Meanwhile, Rudolf Steiner edits Goethe's studies in mineralogy and scientific writings for the *Sophien* edition. He meets Ludwig Laistner of the Cotta Publishing Company, who asks for a book on the basic question of metaphysics. From this will result, ultimately, *The Philosophy of Freedom* (CW 4), which will be published not by Cotta but by Emil Felber. In October, Rudolf Steiner takes the oral exam for a doctorate in philosophy, mathematics, and mechanics at Rostock University, receiving his doctorate on the twenty-sixth. In November, he gives his first lecture on Goethe's "Fairy Tale" in Vienna.

1892:　Rudolf Steiner continues work at the Goethe-Schiller Archive and on his *Philosophy of Freedom*. *Truth and Science*, his doctoral dissertation, is published. Steiner undertakes to write introductions to books on Schopenhauer and Jean Paul for Cotta. At year's end, he finds lodging with Anna Eunike, née Schulz (1853-1911), a widow with four daughters and a son. He also develops a friendship with Otto Erich Hartleben (1864-1905) with whom he shares literary interests.

1893:   Rudolf Steiner begins his habit of producing many reviews and articles. In March, he gives a lecture titled "Hypnotism, with Reference to Spiritism." In September, volume 4 of the Kurschner edition is completed. In November, *The Philosophy of Freedom* appears. This year, too, he meets John Henry Mackay (1864-1933), the anarchist, and Max Stirner, a scholar and biographer.

1894:   Rudolf Steiner meets Elisabeth Förster Nietzsche, the philosopher's sister, and begins to read Nietzsche in earnest, beginning with the as yet unpublished *Antichrist*. He also meets Ernst Haeckel (1834-1919). In the fall, he begins to write *Nietzsche, A Fighter against His Time* (CW 5).

1895:   May, *Nietzsche, A Fighter against His Time* appears.

1896:   January 22: Rudolf Steiner sees Friedrich Nietzsche for the first and only time. Moves between the Nietzsche and the Goethe-Schiller Archives, where he completes his work before year's end. He falls out with Elisabeth Förster Nietzsche, thus ending his association with the Nietzsche Archive.

1897:   Rudolf Steiner finishes the manuscript of *Goethe's Worldview* (CW 6). He moves to Berlin with Anna Eunike and begins editorship of the *Magazin fur Literatur*. From now on, Steiner will write countless reviews, literary and philosophical articles, and so on. He begins lecturing at the "Free Literary Society." In September, he attends the Zionist Congress in Basel. He sides with Dreyfus in the Dreyfus affair.

1898:   Rudolf Steiner is very active as an editor in the political, artistic, and theatrical life of Berlin. He becomes friendly with John Henry Mackay and poet Ludwig Jacobowski (1868-1900). He joins Jacobowski's circle of writers, artists, and scientists—"The Coming Ones" (*Die Kommenden*)—and contributes lectures to the group until 1903. He also lectures at the "League for College Pedagogy." He writes an article for Goethe's sesquicentennial, "Goethe's Secret Revelation," on the "Fairy Tale of the Green Snake and the Beautiful Lily."

1888-89: "This was a trying time for my soul as I looked at Christianity. . . . I was able to progress only by contemplating, by means of spiritual perception, the evolution of Christianity . . . . Conscious knowledge of real Christianity began to dawn in me around the turn of the century. This seed continued to develop. My soul trial occurred shortly before the beginning of the twentieth century. It was decisive for my soul's development that I stood spiritually before the Mystery of Golgotha in a deep and solemn celebration of knowledge."

1899:   Rudolf Steiner begins teaching and giving lectures and lecture cycles at the Workers' College, founded by Wilhelm Liebknecht (1826-1900). He will continue to do so until 1904. Writes: *Literature and Spiritual Life in the Nineteenth Century; Individualism in Philosophy; Haeckel and His Opponents; Poetry in the Present;* and begins what will become (fifteen years later). *The Riddles of Philosophy* (CW 18). He also meets many artists and writers, including Käthe Kollwitz, Stefan

Zweig, and Rainer Maria Rilke. On October 31, he marries Anna Eunike.

1900: "I thought that the turn of the century must bring humanity a new light. It seemed to me that the separation of human thinking and willing from the spirit had peaked. A turn or reversal of direction in human evolution seemed to me a necessity." Rudolf Steiner finishes *World and Life Views in the Nineteenth Century* (the second part of what will become *The Riddles of Philosophy*) and dedicates it to Ernst Haeckel. It is published in March. He continues lecturing at *Die Kommenden*, whose leadership he assumes after the death of Jacobowski. Also, he gives the Gutenberg Jubilee lecture before 7,000 typesetters and printers. In September, Rudolf Steiner is invited by Count and Countess Brockdorff to lecture in the Theosophical Library. His first lecture is on Nietzsche. His second lecture is titled "Goethe's Secret Revelation." October 6, he begins a lecture cycle on the mystics that will become *Mystics after Modernism* (CW 7). November-December: "Marie von Sivers appears in the audience...." Also in November, Steiner gives his first lecture at the Giordano Bruno Bund (where he will continue to lecture until May, 1905). He speaks on Bruno and modern Rome, focusing on the importance of the philosophy of Thomas Aquinas as monism.

1901: In continual financial straits, Rudolf Steiner's early friends Moritz Zitter and Rosa Mayreder help support him. In October, he begins the lecture cycle *Christianity as Mystical Fact* (CW 8) at the Theosophical Library. In November, he gives his first "Theosophical lecture" on Goethe's "Fairy Tale" in Hamburg at the invitation of Wilhelm Hubbe-Schleiden. He also attends a tea to celebrate the founding of the Theosophical Society at Count and Countess Brockdorff's. He gives a lecture cycle, "From Buddha to Christ," for the circle of the *Kommenden*. November 17, Marie von Sivers asks Rudolf Steiner if Theosophy does not need a Western-Christian spiritual movement (to complement Theosophy's Eastern emphasis). "The question was posed. Now, following spiritual laws, I could begin to give an answer...." In December, Rudolf Steiner writes his first article for a Theosophical publication. At year's end, the Brockdorffs and possibly Wilhelm Hubbe-Schleiden ask Rudolf Steiner to join the Theosophical Society and undertake the leadership of the German section. Rudolf Steiner agrees, on the condition that Marie von Sivers (then in Italy) work with him.

1902: Beginning in January, Rudolf Steiner attends the opening of the Workers' School in Spandau with Rosa Luxemburg (1870-1919). January 17, Rudolf Steiner joins the Theosophical Society. In April, he is asked to become general secretary of the German Section of the Theosophical Society, and works on preparations for its founding. In July, he visits London for a Theosophical congress. He meets Bertram

Keightly, G.R.S. Mead, A.P. Sinnett, and Annie Besant, among others. In September, *Christianity as Mystical Fact* appears. In October, Rudolf Steiner gives his first public lecture on Theosophy ("Monism and Theosophy") to about three hundred people at the Giordano Bruno Bund. On October 19-21, the German Section of the Theosophical Society has its first meeting; Rudolf Steiner is the general secretary, and Annie Besant attends. Steiner lectures on practical karma studies. On October 23, Annie Besant inducts Rudolf Steiner into the Esoteric School of the Theosophical Society. On October 25, Steiner begins a weekly series of lectures: "The Field of Theosophy." During this year, Rudolf Steiner also first meets Ita Wegman (1876-1943), who will become his close collaborator in his final years.

1903: Rudolf Steiner holds about 300 lectures and seminars. In May, the first issue of the periodical *Luzifer* appears. In June, Rudolf Steiner visits London for the first meeting of the Federation of the European Sections of the Theosophical Society, where he meets Colonel Olcott. He begins to write *Theosophy* (CW 9).

1904: Rudolf Steiner continues lecturing at the Workers' College and elsewhere (about 90 lectures), while lecturing intensively all over Germany among Theosophists (about a 140 lectures). In February, he meets Carl Unger (1878-1929), who will become a member of the board of the Anthroposophical Society (1913). In March, he meets Michael Bauer (1871-1929), a Christian mystic, who will also be on the board. In May, *Theosophy* appears, with the dedication: "To the spirit of Giordano Bruno." Rudolf Steiner and Marie von Sivers visit London for meetings with Annie Besant. June: Rudolf Steiner and Marie von Sivers attend the meeting of the Federation of European Sections of the Theosophical Society in Amsterdam. In July, Steiner begins the articles in *Luzifer-Gnosis* that will become *How to Know Higher Worlds* (CW 10) and *Cosmic Memory* (CW 11). In September, Annie Besant visits Germany. In December, Steiner lectures on Freemasonry. He mentions the High Grade Masonry derived from John Yarker and represented by Theodore Reuss and Karl Kellner as a blank slate "into which a good image could be placed."

1905: This year, Steiner ends his non-Theosophical lecturing activity. Supported by Marie von Sivers, his Theosophical lecturing—both in public and in the Theosophical Society—increases significantly: "The German Theosophical Movement is of exceptional importance." Steiner recommends reading, among others, Fichte, Jacob Boehme, and Angelus Silesius. He begins to introduce Christian themes into Theosophy. He also begins to work with doctors (Felix Peipers and Ludwig Noll). In July, he is in London for the Federation of European Sections, where he attends a lecture by Annie Besant: "I have seldom seen Mrs. Besant speak in so inward and heartfelt a manner...." "Through Mrs. Besant I have found the way to H.P. Blavatsky."

September to October, he gives a course of thirty-one lectures for a small group of esoteric students. In October, the annual meeting of the German Section of the Theosophical Society, which still remains very small, takes place. Rudolf Steiner reports membership has risen from 121 to 377 members. In November, seeking to establish esoteric "continuity," Rudolf Steiner and Marie von Sivers participate in a "Memphis-Misraim" Masonic ceremony. They pay forty-five marks for membership. "Yesterday, you saw how little remains of former esoteric institutions." "We are dealing only with a 'framework'... for the present, nothing lies behind it. The occult powers have completely withdrawn."

1906:   Expansion of Theosophical work. Rudolf Steiner gives about 245 lectures, only 44 of which take place in Berlin. Cycles are given in Paris, Leipzig, Stuttgart, and Munich. Esoteric work also intensifies. Rudolf Steiner begins writing *An Outline of Esoteric Science* (CW 13). In January, Rudolf Steiner receives permission (a patent) from the Great Orient of the Scottish A & A Thirty-Three Degree Rite of the Order of the Ancient Freemasons of the Memphis-Misraim Rite to direct a chapter under the name "Mystica Aeterna." This will become the "Cognitive Cultic Section" (also called "Misraim Service") of the Esoteric School. (See: *From the History and Contents of the Cognitive Cultic Section* (CW 264). During this time, Steiner also meets Albert Schweitzer. In May, he is in Paris, where he visits Edouard Schuré. Many Russians attend his lectures (including Konstantin Balmont, Dimitri Mereszkovski, Zinaida Hippius, and Maximilian Woloshin). He attends the General Meeting of the European Federation of the Theosophical Society, at which Col. Olcott is present for the last time. He spends the year's end in Venice and Rome, where he writes and works on his translation of H.P. Blavatsky's *Key to Theosophy*.

1907:   Further expansion of the German Theosophical Movement according to the Rosicrucian directive to "introduce spirit into the world"—in education, in social questions, in art, and in science. In February, Col. Olcott dies in Adyar. Before he dies, Olcott indicates that "the Masters" wish Annie Besant to succeed him: much politicking ensues. Rudolf Steiner supports Besant's candidacy. April-May: preparations for the Congress of the Federation of European Sections of the Theosophical Society—the great, watershed Whitsun "Munich Congress," attended by Annie Besant and others. Steiner decides to separate Eastern and Western (Christian-Rosicrucian) esoteric schools. He takes his esoteric school out of the Theosophical Society (Besant and Rudolf Steiner are "in harmony" on this). Steiner makes his first lecture tours to Austria and Hungary. That summer, he is in Italy. In September, he visits Edouard Schuré, who will write the introduction to the French edition of *Christianity as Mystical Fact* in Barr, Alsace. Rudolf Steiner writes the autobiographical statement known as the "Barr Document." In *Luzifer-Gnosis*, "The Education of the Child" appears.

1908:   The movement grows (membership: 1150). Lecturing expands. Steiner makes his first extended lecture tour to Holland and Scandinavia, as well as visits to Naples and Sicily. Themes: St. John's Gospel, the Apocalypse, Egypt, science, philosophy, and logic. *Luzifer-Gnosis* ceases publication. In Berlin, Marie von Sivers (with Johanna Mücke (1864-1949) forms the *Philosophisch-Theosophisch* (after 1915 *Philosophisch-Anthroposophisch*) *Verlag* to publish Steiner's work. Steiner gives lecture cycles titled *The Gospel of St. John* (CW 103) and *The Apocalypse* (104).

1909:   *An Outline of Esoteric Science* appears. Lecturing and travel continues. Rudolf Steiner's spiritual research expands to include the polarity of Lucifer and Ahriman; the work of great individualities in history; the Maitreya Buddha and the Bodhisattvas; spiritual economy (CW 109); the work of the spiritual hierarchies in heaven and on Earth (CW 110). He also deepens and intensifies his research into the Gospels, giving lectures on the Gospel of St. Luke (CW 114) with the first mention of two Jesus children. Meets and becomes friends with Christian Morgenstern (1871-1914). In April, he lays the foundation stone for the Malsch model—the building that will lead to the first Goetheanum. In May, the International Congress of the Federation of European Sections of the Theosophical Society takes place in Budapest. Rudolf Steiner receives the Subba Row medal for *How to Know Higher Worlds*. During this time, Charles W. Leadbeater discovers Jiddu Krishnamurti (1895-1986) and proclaims him the future "world teacher," the bearer of the Maitreya Buddha and the "reappearing Christ." In October, Steiner delivers seminal lectures on "anthroposophy," which he will try, unsuccessfully, to rework over the next years into the unfinished work, *Anthroposophy (A Fragment)* (CW 45).

1910:   New themes: *The Reappearance of Christ in the Etheric* (CW 118); *The Fifth Gospel; The Mission of Folk Souls* (CW 121); *Occult History* (CW 126); the evolving development of etheric cognitive capacities. Rudolf Steiner continues his Gospel research with *The Gospel of St. Matthew* (CW 123). In January, his father dies. In April, he takes a month-long trip to Italy, including Rome, Monte Cassino, and Sicily. He also visits Scandinavia again. July-August, he writes the first mystery drama, *The Portal of Initiation* (CW 14). In November, he gives "psychosophy" lectures. In December, he submits "On the Psychological Foundations and Epistemological Framework of Theosophy" to the International Philosophical Congress in Bologna.

1911:   The crisis in the Theosophical Society deepens. In January, "The Order of the Rising Sun," which will soon become "The Order of the Star in the East," is founded for the coming world teacher, Krishnamurti. At the same time, Marie von Sivers, Rudolf Steiner's coworker, falls ill. Fewer lectures are given, but important new ground is broken. In Prague, in March, Steiner meets Franz Kafka (1883-1924) and Hugo Bergmann (1883-1975). In April, he delivers his paper to the

Philosophical Congress. He writes the second mystery drama, *The Soul's Probation* (CW 14). Also, while Marie von Sivers is convalescing, Rudolf Steiner begins work on *Calendar 1912/1913*, which will contain the "Calendar of the Soul" meditations. On March 19, Anna (Eunike) Steiner dies. In September, Rudolf Steiner visits Einsiedeln, birthplace of Paracelsus. In December, Friedrich Rittelmeyer, future founder of the Christian Community, meets Rudolf Steiner. The *Johannes-Bauverein*, the "building committee," which would lead to the first Goetheanum (first planned for Munich), is also founded, and a preliminary committee for the founding of an independent association is created that, in the following year, will become the Anthroposophical Society. Important lecture cycles include *Occult Physiology* (CW 128); *Wonders of the World* (CW 129); *From Jesus to Christ* (CW 131). Other themes: esoteric Christianity; Christian Rosenkreutz; the spiritual guidance of humanity; the sense world and the world of the spirit.

1912: Despite the ongoing, now increasing crisis in the Theosophical Society, much is accomplished: *Calendar 1912/1913* is published; eurythmy is created; both the third mystery drama, *The Guardian of the Threshold* (CW 14) and *A Way of Self-Knowledge* (CW 16) are written. New (or renewed) themes included life between death and rebirth and karma and reincarnation. Other lecture cycles: *Spiritual Beings in the Heavenly Bodies and the Kingdoms of Nature* (CW 136); *The Human Being in the Light of Occultism, Theosophy, and Philosophy* (CW 137); *The Gospel of St. Mark* (CW 139); and *The Bhagavad Gita and the Epistles of Paul* (CW 142). On May 8, Rudolf Steiner celebrates White Lotus Day, H.P. Blavatsky's death day, which he had faithfully observed for the past decade, for the last time. In August, Rudolf Steiner suggests the "independent association" be called the "Anthroposophical Society." In September, the first eurythmy course takes place. In October, Rudolf Steiner declines recognition of a Theosophical Society lodge dedicated to the Star of the East and decides to expel all Theosophical Society members belonging to the order. Also, with Marie von Sivers, he first visits Dornach, near Basel, Switzerland, and they stand on the hill where the Goetheanum will be. In November, a Theosophical Society lodge is opened by direct mandate from Adyar (Annie Besant). In December, a meeting of the German section occurs at which it is decided that belonging to the Order of the Star of the East is incompatible with membership in the Theosophical Society. December 28: informal founding of the Anthroposophical Society in Berlin.

1913: Expulsion of the German section from the Theosophical Society. February 2-3: Foundation meeting of the Anthroposophical Society. Board members include: Marie von Sivers, Michael Bauer, and Carl Unger. September 20: Laying of the foundation stone for the *Johannes Bau* (Goetheanum) in Dornach. Building begins immediately. The third mystery drama, *The Soul's Awakening* (CW 14), is completed.

Also: *The Threshold of the Spiritual World* (CW 147). Lecture cycles include: *The Bhagavad Gita and the Epistles of Paul* and *The Esoteric Meaning of the Bhagavad Gita* (CW 146), which the Russian philosopher Nikolai Berdyaev attends; *The Mysteries of the East and of Christianity* (CW 144); *The Effects of Esoteric Development* (CW 145); and *The Fifth Gospel* (CW 148). In May, Rudolf Steiner is in London and Paris, where anthroposophical work continues.

1914: Building continues on the *Johannes Bau* (Goetheanum) in Dornach, with artists and coworkers from seventeen nations. The general assembly of the Anthroposophical Society takes place. In May, Rudolf Steiner visits Paris, as well as Chartres Cathedral. June 28: assassination in Sarajevo ("Now the catastrophe has happened!"). August 1: War is declared. Rudolf Steiner returns to Germany from Dornach—he will travel back and forth. He writes the last chapter of *The Riddles of Philosophy*. Lecture cycles include: *Human and Cosmic Thought* (CW 151); *Inner Being of Humanity between Death and a New Birth* (CW 153); *Occult Reading and Occult Hearing* (CW 156). December 24: marriage of Rudolf Steiner and Marie von Sivers.

1915: Building continues. Life after death becomes a major theme, also art. Writes: *Thoughts during a Time of War* (CW 24). Lectures include: *The Secret of Death* (CW 159); *The Uniting of Humanity through the Christ Impulse* (CW 165).

1916: Rudolf Steiner begins work with Edith Maryon (1872-1924) on the sculpture "The Representative of Humanity" ("The Group"—Christ, Lucifer, and Ahriman). He also works with the alchemist Alexander von Bernus on the quarterly *Das Reich*. He writes *The Riddle of Humanity* (CW 20). Lectures include: *Necessity and Freedom in World History and Human Action* (CW 166); *Past and Present in the Human Spirit* (CW 167); *The Karma of Vocation* (CW 172); *The Karma of Untruthfulness* (CW 173).

1917: Russian Revolution. The U.S. enters the war. Building continues. Rudolf Steiner delineates the idea of the "threefold nature of the human being" (in a public lecture March 15) and the "threefold nature of the social organism" (hammered out in May-June with the help of Otto von Lerchenfeld and Ludwig Polzer-Hoditz in the form of two documents titled *Memoranda*, which were distributed in high places). August-September: Rudolf Steiner writes *The Riddles of the Soul* (CW 20). Also: commentary on "The Chemical Wedding of Christian Rosenkreutz" for Alexander Bernus (*Das Reich*). Lectures include: *The Karma of Materialism* (CW 176); *The Spiritual Background of the Outer World: The Fall of the Spirits of Darkness* (CW 177).

1918: March 18: peace treaty of Brest-Litovsk—"Now everything will truly enter chaos! What is needed is cultural renewal." June: Rudolf Steiner visits Karlstein (Grail) Castle outside Prague. Lecture cycle: *From Symptom to Reality in Modern History* (CW 185). In mid-November,

Emil Molt, of the Waldorf-Astoria Cigarette Company, has the idea of founding a school for his workers' children.

1919: Focus on the threefold social organism: tireless travel, countless lectures, meetings, and publications. At the same time, a new public stage of Anthroposophy emerges as cultural renewal begins. The coming years will see initiatives in pedagogy, medicine, pharmacology, and agriculture. January 27: threefold meeting: "We must first of all, with the money we have, found free schools that can bring people what they need." February: first public eurythmy performance in Zurich. Also: "Appeal to the German People" (CW 24), circulated March 6 as a newspaper insert. In April, *Toward Social Renewal* (CW 23)—"perhaps the most widely read of all books on politics appearing since the war"—appears. Rudolf Steiner is asked to undertake the "direction and leadership" of the school founded by the Waldorf-Astoria Company. Rudolf Steiner begins to talk about the "renewal" of education. May 30: a building is selected and purchased for the future Waldorf School. August-September, Rudolf Steiner gives a lecture course for Waldorf teachers, *The Foundations of Human Experience (Study of Man)* (CW 293). September 7: Opening of the first Waldorf School. December (into January): first science course, the *Light Course* (CW 320).

1920: The Waldorf School flourishes. New threefold initiatives. Founding of limited companies *Der Kommenden Tag* and *Futurum A.G.* to infuse spiritual values into the economic realm. Rudolf Steiner also focuses on the sciences. Lectures: *Introducing Anthroposophical Medicine* (CW 312); *The Warmth Course* (CW 321); *The Boundaries of Natural Science* (CW 322); *The Redemption of Thinking* (CW 74). February: Johannes Werner Klein—later a cofounder of the Christian Community—asks Rudolf Steiner about the possibility of a "religious renewal," a "Johannine church." In March, Rudolf Steiner gives the first course for doctors and medical students. In April, a divinity student asks Rudolf Steiner a second time about the possibility of religious renewal. September 27-October 16: anthroposophical "university course." December: lectures titled *The Search for the New Isis* (CW 202).

1921: Rudolf Steiner continues his intensive work on cultural renewal, including the uphill battle for the threefold social order. "University" arts, scientific, theological, and medical courses include: *The Astronomy Course* (CW 323); *Observation, Mathematics, and Scientific Experiment* (CW 324); the *Second Medical Course* (CW 313); *Color* (CW 291). In June and September-October, Rudolf Steiner also gives the first two "priests' courses" (CW 342 and 343). The "youth movement" gains momentum. Magazines are founded: *Die Drei* (January), and—under the editorship of Albert Steffen (1884-1963)—the weekly, *Das Goetheanum* (August). In February-March, Rudolf Steiner takes his first trip outside Germany since the war (Holland). On April 7, Steiner receives a letter regarding "religious renewal," and May 22-23, he agrees to address the question in a practical way. In June, the Klinical-Therapeutic Institute opens in Arlesheim under the direction of Dr. Ita Wegman. In August, the Chemical-Pharmaceutical Laboratory opens in Arlesheim (Oskar Schmiedel and Ita Wegman, directors). The Clinical Therapeutic Institute is inaugurated in Stuttgart (Dr. Ludwig Noll, director); also the Research Laboratory in Dornach (Ehrenfried Pfeiffer and Gunther Wachsmuth, directors). In November-December, Rudolf Steiner visits Norway.

1922: The first half of the year involves very active public lecturing (thousands attend); in the second half, Rudolf Steiner begins to withdraw and turn toward the Society—"The Society is asleep." It is "too weak" to do what is asked of it. The businesses—*Die Kommenden Tag* and *Futura A.G.*—fail. In January, with the help of an agent, Steiner undertakes a twelve-city German tour, accompanied by eurythmy performances. In two weeks he speaks to more than 2,000 people. In April, he gives a "university course" in The Hague. He also visits England. In June, he is in Vienna for the East-West Congress. In August-September, he is back in England for the Oxford Conference on Education. Returning to Dornach, he gives the lectures *Philosophy, Cosmology, and Religion* (CW 215), and gives the third priest's course (CW 344). On September 16, The Christian Community is founded. In October-November, Steiner is in Holland and England. He also speaks to the youth: *Becoming Michael's Companions* (CW 217). In December, Steiner gives lectures titled *The Origins of Natural Science* (CW 326), and *Humanity and the World of Stars: The Spiritual Communion of Humanity* (CW 219). December 31: Fire at the Goetheanum, which is destroyed.

1923: Despite the fire, Rudolf Steiner continues his work unabated. A very hard year. Internal dispersion, dissension, and apathy abound. There is conflict—between old and new visions—within the society. A wake-up call is needed, and Rudolf Steiner responds with renewed lecturing vitality. His focus: the spiritual context of human life; initiation science; the course of the year; and community building. As a foundation for an artistic school, he creates a series of pastel sketches. Lecture cycles: *The Anthroposophical Movement; Initiation Science* (CW 227) (in England at the Penmaenmawr Summer School); *The Four Seasons and the Archangels* (CW 229); *Harmony of the Creative Word* (CW 230); *The Supersensible Human* (CW 231), given in Holland for the founding of the Dutch society. On November 10, in response to the failed Hitler-Ludendorf putsch in Munich, Steiner closes his Berlin residence and moves the *Philosophisch-Anthroposophisch Verlag* (Press) to Dornach. On December 9, Steiner begins the serialization of his *Autobiography: The Course of My Life* (CW 28) in *Das Goetheanum*. It will continue to appear weekly, without a break, until his death. Late December-early January: Rudolf Steiner refounds the Anthroposophical Society (about

12,000 members internationally) and takes over its leadership. The new board members are: Marie Steiner, Ita Wegman, Albert Steffen, Elizabeth Vreede, and Guenther Wachsmuth. (See *The Christmas Meeting for the Founding of the General Anthro-posophical Society* (CW 260). Accompanying lectures: *Mystery Knowledge and Mystery Centers* (CW 232); *World History in the Light of Anthroposophy* (CW 233). December 25: the Foundation Stone is laid (in the hearts of members) in the form of the "Foundation Stone Meditation."

1924: January 1: having founded the Anthroposophical Society and taken over its leadership, Rudolf Steiner has the task of "reforming" it. The process begins with a weekly newssheet ("What's Happening in the Anthroposophical Society") in which Rudolf Steiner's "Letters to Members" and "Anthroposophical Leading Thoughts" appear (CW 26). The next step is the creation of a new esoteric class, the "first class" of the "University of Spiritual Science" (which was to have been followed, had Rudolf Steiner lived longer, by two more advanced classes). Then comes a new language for Anthroposophy—practical, phenomenological, and direct; and Rudolf Steiner creates the model for the second Goetheanum. He begins the series of extensive "karma" lectures (CW 235-40); and finally, responding to needs, he creates two new initiatives: biodynamic agriculture and curative education. After the middle of the year, rumors begin to circulate regarding Steiner's health. Lectures: January-February, *Anthroposophy* (CW 234); February: *Tone Eurythmy* (CW 278); June: *The Agriculture Course* (CW 327); June-July: Speech [?] Eurythmy (CW 279); *Curative Education* (CW 317); August: (England, "Second International Summer School"), *Initiation Consciousness: True and False Paths in Spiritual Investigation* (CW 243); September: *Pastoral Medicine* (CW 318). On September 26, for the first time, Rudolf Steiner cancels a lecture. On September 28, he gives his last lecture. On September 29, he withdraws to his studio in the carpenter's shop; now he is definitively ill. Cared for by Ita Wegman, he continues working, however, and writing the weekly installments of his *Autobiography* and *Letters to the Members/Leading Thoughts* (CW 26).

1925: Rudolf Steiner, while continuing to work, continues to weaken. He finishes *Extending Practical Medicine* (CW 27) with Ita Wegman. On March 30, around ten in the morning, Rudolf Steiner dies.

INDEX

abilities, 21, *See also* personality
Adam, as macrocosmic Man, 39
Aedesius, 81
Aeschylus, 2, 85
Agathon, 40
Akiba, Rabbi, 74
allegory
    not associated with myth, 49-50
    in Old Testament, 111
Ambrose, 117
ancient world, *See also* Mysteries
    mysteriosophy of, 6, 43
    spiritual needs of, 1
angels, 89, 93-95
animality, 55, *See also* sensuality
anxiety, 24, *See also* fear
Aphrodite, 49
Apocalypse of John, 86-97. *See also*
    Gospels
    Living Creatures, 91, 92
    Seven Communities, 86-88
    Seven Seals, 91-93
    Seven Trumpets, 93-95
    Son of Man, 89-91
Apsyrtus, 51-52
Aquinas, Thomas, 119
Argonauts, 51-52, 54
Aristides, 5
Aristophanes, 40
Aristotle, 24-25
Artemis, 16
Athene, 56
Augustine, 68, 106-107, 115-119

Beast, 95-96
becoming. *See* birth; life
Being, compared to mortality, 7-8, 17
belief. *See* faith
Bethany, 78-79
Bible, 110, *See also* Gospels
birth, *See also* reincarnation
    and reincarnation, 5-10
    relation of
        soul to, 34, 112

    to death, 34
    to personality, 20-21
    sickness associated with, 80-81
blessedness, 96
body. *See* physical body
Boreas, 46
Buddha, compared to Christ, 63- 69
Burckhardt, Jacob, 84

Calypso, 55
centaur, 53
change, *See also* transitory
    force of in life, 7-8, 16-17
    perception of by human beings, 10
childlike qualities, reclamation of,
    18-19
Chiron, 53-54
Christianity
    communities within, 89-90
    destiny within, 94-95
    esoteric, 104-107
    essence of, 101-107
    faith expressed in, 67-69, 75-76,
        85, 92, 95
    and Gnosticism, 103-104
    heresy within, 103-104
    initiation within, 82-83, 93
    and pagan wisdom, 108-114
    relation to
        Judaism, 73-74
        Mysteries, 83-84, 101-103, 114,
            117, 120-121
        Neoplatonism, 105, 112-113
        paganism, 102-103
    wisdom of, 88, 94-95
Christmas, 68
Church, 68
    in Apocalypse, 86-87
    and Augustine, 115-121
    external organization of, 103
Cicero, 11
Circe, 55
Clement of Alexandria, 103, 115
cleverness, 79, *See also* personality